QuickBooks®
Online

3rd edition

by Elaine Marmel

A Wiley Brand

QuickBooks® Online For Dummies®, 3rd Edition

Published by: **John Wiley & Sons, Inc.**, 111 River Street, Hoboken, NJ 07030-5774, www.wiley.com

Copyright © 2017 by John Wiley & Sons, Inc., Hoboken, New Jersey

Published simultaneously in Canada

No part of this publication may be reproduced, stored in a retrieval system or transmitted in any form or by any means, electronic, mechanical, photocopying, recording, scanning or otherwise, except as permitted under Sections 107 or 108 of the 1976 United States Copyright Act, without the prior written permission of the Publisher. Requests to the Publisher for permission should be addressed to the Permissions Department, John Wiley & Sons, Inc., 111 River Street, Hoboken, NJ 07030, (201) 748-6011, fax (201) 748-6008, or online at http://www.wiley.com/go/permissions.

Trademarks: Wiley, For Dummies, the Dummies Man logo, Dummies.com, Making Everything Easier, and related trade dress are trademarks or registered trademarks of John Wiley & Sons, Inc. and may not be used without written permission. QuickBooks is a registered trademark of Intuit, Inc. All other trademarks are the property of their respective owners. John Wiley & Sons, Inc. is not associated with any product or vendor mentioned in this book.

LIMIT OF LIABILITY/DISCLAIMER OF WARRANTY: THE PUBLISHER AND THE AUTHOR MAKE NO REPRESENTATIONS OR WARRANTIES WITH RESPECT TO THE ACCURACY OR COMPLETENESS OF THE CONTENTS OF THIS WORK AND SPECIFICALLY DISCLAIM ALL WARRANTIES, INCLUDING WITHOUT LIMITATION WARRANTIES OF FITNESS FOR A PARTICULAR PURPOSE. NO WARRANTY MAY BE CREATED OR EXTENDED BY SALES OR PROMOTIONAL MATERIALS. THE ADVICE AND STRATEGIES CONTAINED HEREIN MAY NOT BE SUITABLE FOR EVERY SITUATION. THIS WORK IS SOLD WITH THE UNDERSTANDING THAT THE PUBLISHER IS NOT ENGAGED IN RENDERING LEGAL, ACCOUNTING, OR OTHER PROFESSIONAL SERVICES. IF PROFESSIONAL ASSISTANCE IS REQUIRED, THE SERVICES OF A COMPETENT PROFESSIONAL PERSON SHOULD BE SOUGHT. NEITHER THE PUBLISHER NOR THE AUTHOR SHALL BE LIABLE FOR DAMAGES ARISING HEREFROM. THE FACT THAT AN ORGANIZATION OR WEBSITE IS REFERRED TO IN THIS WORK AS A CITATION AND/OR A POTENTIAL SOURCE OF FURTHER INFORMATION DOES NOT MEAN THAT THE AUTHOR OR THE PUBLISHER ENDORSES THE INFORMATION THE ORGANIZATION OR WEBSITE MAY PROVIDE OR RECOMMENDATIONS IT MAY MAKE. FURTHER, READERS SHOULD BE AWARE THAT INTERNET WEBSITES LISTED IN THIS WORK MAY HAVE CHANGED OR DISAPPEARED BETWEEN WHEN THIS WORK WAS WRITTEN AND WHEN IT IS READ. FULFILLMENT OF EACH COUPON OFFER IS THE SOLE RESPONSIBILITY OF THE OFFEROR.

For general information on our other products and services, please contact our Customer Care Department within the U.S. at 877-762-2974, outside the U.S. at 317-572-3993, or fax 317-572-4002. For technical support, please visit https://hub.wiley.com/community/support/dummies.

Wiley publishes in a variety of print and electronic formats and by print-on-demand. Some material included with standard print versions of this book may not be included in e-books or in print-on-demand. If this book refers to media such as a CD or DVD that is not included in the version you purchased, you may download this material at http://booksupport.wiley.com. For more information about Wiley products, visit www.wiley.com.

Library of Congress Control Number: 2016955190

ISBN: 978-1-119-28380-5

ISBN: 978-1-119-28382-9 (ePDF)

ISBN: 978-1-119-28381-2 (ePub)

Manufactured in the United States of America

10 9 8 7 6 5 4 3 2 1

Contents at a Glance

Table of Contents

Introduction

Have you been thinking about moving your accounting into a web-based product? Are you a QuickBooks desktop user who wants to stick with something you know but wants the flexibility of a web-based product? Are you interested in finding out more about Intuit's web-based product, QuickBooks Online (QBO)? Are you an accountant who is considering beginning to support your QuickBooks clients via QuickBooks Online Accountant (QBOA)? If you answered yes to any of these questions, this book is for you.

QuickBooks Online and QuickBooks Online Accountant are web-based accounting solutions from Intuit. Don't be fooled; they are *not* the desktop product migrated to the web. They've been built from the ground up to function on the Internet.

About This Book

Intuit's web-based accounting product is really almost two products: end users who want to do their accounting on the web use QBO, whereas accountants use QBOA, which enables the accountant to log in to a client's books and make changes and queries as needed. Although much of QBO and QBOA look and behave alike, QBOA incorporates tools that an accountant needs while working on a client's books. And accountants need to manage multiple client companies, whereas end user clients typically do not.

QBO and QBOA are not for everyone. Before you commit to Intuit's web-based solution, you need to explore the available editions and examine the requirements for the products.

Because these products are both similar and different, I've divided this book into three parts. In the first part of the book, I examine what QBO and QBOA are — and what they aren't — and I describe what you need to be able to use QBO and QBOA. I explain the various editions available and the product costs at the time I wrote this book, and I describe the features available. And in Chapter 1, you'll find some information about the available interfaces for QBO and QBOA (you can work with the products using a browser or using an app).

The second part of the book focuses on using QBO and is aimed at the end user; but, the accountant who opens a client's company via QBOA will be able to use the same tools that the end user uses to manage lists, enter transactions, and print reports.

The third part of the book is aimed at the accountant and covers using QBOA.

I don't pretend to cover every detail of every feature in QBO or QBOA. Instead, I focus on covering the tools I think most users will need as they navigate QBO and QBOA.

REMEMBER

As I discuss in Chapter 2, there are different versions of QBO; I used QBO Plus as I wrote this book because it contains the most features. Users of other versions might find references in this book to features they don't have because they aren't using the Plus version.

Before we dive in, let's get a few technical convention details out of the way:

- ≫ Text that you're meant to type as it appears in the book is **bold.** The exception is when you're working through a list of steps: Because each step is bold, the text to type is not bold.

- ≫ Web addresses and programming code appear in monofont. If you're reading a digital version of this book on a device connected to the Internet, note that you can tap or click a web address to visit that website, like this: www.dummies.com.

- ≫ You can use QBO and QBOA from the Windows app for QBO and QBOA or from Chrome, Firefox, Safari, or Internet Explorer; at the time I wrote this book, you could use QBO and QBOA with Microsoft Edge, but you could not use Edge to export to the QuickBooks desktop product. In my experience, QBO and QBOA function best in Chrome. For that reason, I've devoted The Part of Tens chapters in this book to Chrome so that, if you aren't familiar with Chrome, you can get up and running more quickly.

- ≫ When I discuss a command to choose, I'll separate the elements of the sequence with a command arrow that looks like this: ⇨. For example, when you see Chrome Menu ⇨ Settings, that means you should click the Chrome Menu button (on the right side of the Chrome screen — see Chapter 16 for a description of Chrome's screen elements) and, from the drop-down menu that appears, click Settings.

Foolish Assumptions

I had to assume some things about you to write this book. Here are the assumptions I made:

>> You know that you need to manage the accounts for your business, and you might even have some sort of setup in place to record this information. I *don't* assume that you know how to do all that on a computer.

>> You have some interest in managing the accounts for your business using a web-based product.

>> You are probably but not necessarily a QuickBooks desktop edition user.

>> You have a personal computer (that you know how to turn on) running Microsoft Windows Vista, Windows 7, Windows 8.1 or Windows 10. I wrote this book using Windows 10.

>> You might have purchased an edition of QuickBooks Online, but not necessarily.

Icons Used in This Book

TIP

Think of these icons as the fodder of advice columns. They offer (hopefully) wise advice or a bit more information about a topic under discussion.

REMEMBER

This icon points out juicy tidbits that are likely to be repeatedly useful to you — so please don't forget them.

WARNING

Danger, Will Robinson, danger! Well, okay, it's really not life-threatening. In this book, you see this icon when I'm trying to help you avoid mistakes that can cost money.

Beyond the Book

In addition to the content in this book, this product also comes with a free access-anywhere cheat sheet that gives you keyboard shortcuts for QBOL and

QBOL Accountant and some handy tool buttons in QBOL. To get this cheat sheet, simply go to www.dummies.com and search for "QuickBooks Online For Dummies Cheat Sheet" in the Search box.

Where to Go from Here

Simply turn the page. Seriously. You can dive in anywhere you want and come back as often as you like. You don't have to read through this book cover to cover, because each section stands alone and provides step-by-step instructions for common tasks. You should consider this book a reference that you use when you need it.

That said, if you're just getting started with QBO or QBOA, you might want to turn the page and follow, in order, the chapters in Part 1. Then feel free to explore any topic you like, using the table of contents or the index to help you find a topic.

1
Getting Started with QBO and QBOA

Foolish Assumptions

I had to assume some things about you to write this book. Here are the assumptions I made:

>> You know that you need to manage the accounts for your business, and you might even have some sort of setup in place to record this information. I *don't* assume that you know how to do all that on a computer.

>> You have some interest in managing the accounts for your business using a web-based product.

>> You are probably but not necessarily a QuickBooks desktop edition user.

>> You have a personal computer (that you know how to turn on) running Microsoft Windows Vista, Windows 7, Windows 8.1 or Windows 10. I wrote this book using Windows 10.

>> You might have purchased an edition of QuickBooks Online, but not necessarily.

Icons Used in This Book

TIP

Think of these icons as the fodder of advice columns. They offer (hopefully) wise advice or a bit more information about a topic under discussion.

REMEMBER

This icon points out juicy tidbits that are likely to be repeatedly useful to you — so please don't forget them.

WARNING

Danger, Will Robinson, danger! Well, okay, it's really not life-threatening. In this book, you see this icon when I'm trying to help you avoid mistakes that can cost money.

Beyond the Book

In addition to the content in this book, this product also comes with a free access-anywhere cheat sheet that gives you keyboard shortcuts for QBOL and

QBOL Accountant and some handy tool buttons in QBOL. To get this cheat sheet, simply go to www.dummies.com and search for "QuickBooks Online For Dummies Cheat Sheet" in the Search box.

Where to Go from Here

Simply turn the page. Seriously. You can dive in anywhere you want and come back as often as you like. You don't have to read through this book cover to cover, because each section stands alone and provides step-by-step instructions for common tasks. You should consider this book a reference that you use when you need it.

That said, if you're just getting started with QBO or QBOA, you might want to turn the page and follow, in order, the chapters in Part 1. Then feel free to explore any topic you like, using the table of contents or the index to help you find a topic.

Chapter **1**

Introducing QBO and QBOA

Q uickBooks Online (QBO) and QuickBooks Online Accountant (QBOA) are web-based products you can use to manage your business's accounting. This chapter introduces these products and discusses whether you should move into the cloud to manage your accounting. It also examines the system requirements for these products.

QBO for the Client and QBOA for the Accountant

QuickBooks Online offers you the ability to manage your business's accounting in the cloud. The software is divided into two products: one for end users and the other for accountants. Interfaces for both products are available on multiple platforms.

QuickBooks Online (QBO) is the cloud-based product for end users who need to perform typical accounting tasks. QBO is based on the same principles as the QuickBooks desktop product — that is, it uses lists to, for example, manage customers and vendors, and it includes transactions similar to the ones found in the QuickBooks desktop product. But, QBO is *not* simply a "rewrite" of the QuickBooks desktop product for the web.

QuickBooks Online Accountant (QBOA) is the cloud-based portal that accountants use to access client QBO companies, work in them, and communicate with clients. QBOA also comes with one free company that accountants can use to track their own businesses.

Comparing interfaces

QBO and QBOA were initially written and optimized to be used in the major web browsers — Chrome, Firefox, Safari, and Internet Explorer. Later, Intuit added QBO apps that you can use for Windows, Mac, and Android mobile devices. In this section, you explore what QBO and QBOA look like in a browser and in the Windows app.

TIP

In addition to using the QBO mobile apps for iOS and Android, you also can access QBO from your mobile device's browser at https://qbo.intuit.com.

In a browser, an open company in QBO looks similar to the one shown in Figure 1-1. I cover the interface in more detail in Chapter 3, but for the time being, the most important thing to notice is the Navigation bar that runs down the left side of the screen. If you've been a QuickBooks desktop user and you've used the Left Icon bar in that product, you might find the Navigation bar a familiar tool. The Left Icon bar and the Navigation bar work the same way; you click a link in either of them to navigate to a portion of the program.

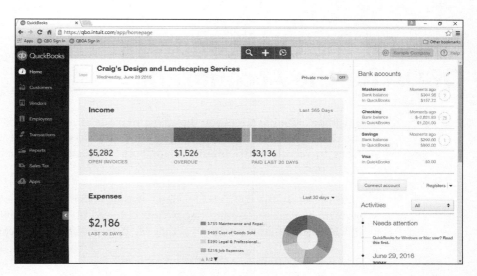

FIGURE 1-1:
An open
company in QBO.

Clicking the arrow in the Navigation bar enables you to collapse the Navigation bar to view just the icons (and clicking it again expands the Navigation bar back to the view in Figure 1-1). When you collapse the Navigation bar (you see an example of it collapsed in Chapter 3), you have more screen real estate to view the right side of the QBO interface.

REMEMBER

At the time I wrote this, the arrow feature was being tested in QuickBooks Labs. I include this feature in some of the figures because I want to give you an idea of things that might make their way into the software. You, too, can turn on features being tested in the lab; see Chapter 3 for details. And, in Chapter 3, I'll show you the new navigation centers being tested for QBO — another feature currently available via QuickBooks Labs.

At the top of the screen, you see tools that help QBO users create transactions, search for existing transactions, and view recent transactions.

Figure 1-2 shows what an accountant sees immediately upon logging in to QBOA. The Navigation bar changes to support an accountant's needs; you can read more about the QBOA interface in Chapter 11.

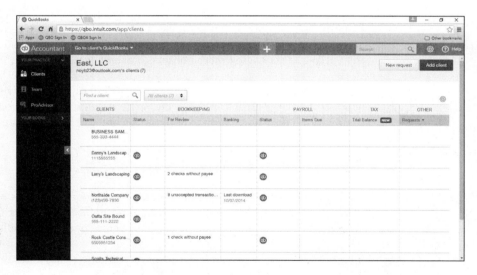

FIGURE 1-2:
The first view an accountant sees when he opens QBOA.

When an accountant opens a client's company from within QBOA (see Figure 1-3), the interface resembles what a client sees, with some minor differences. Compare Figure 1-1 with Figure 1-3. First, you know you're using QBOA because the top of the Navigation pane shows QuickBooks Accountant. Second, the tools used to search for a transaction, go to a report, and view recent transactions are combined into one Search box near the right side of the screen. And third, the Accountant

Tools menu (the briefcase icon) displays tools not found in QBO that help accountants manage client companies.

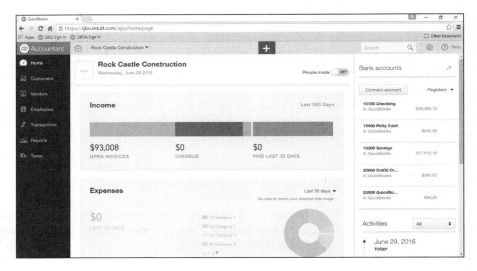

FIGURE 1-3:
An open
company
in QBOA.

Even though an open company looks a bit different depending on whether it is opened using QBO or QBOA, the basic functionality doesn't really change, other than accountants having more options than end users have.

REMEMBER

Because QBOA contains functionality that QBO doesn't have, I've organized this book so that QBO users can focus on Part 2 when using the product, and QBOA users can use the information in both Parts 2 and 3 to work with a company online.

To browse or not to browse . . .

In addition to working in a browser, you also can work in mobile apps. Figure 1-4 shows QBO in the Windows mobile app, and Figure 1-5 shows QBOA just after opening it in the Windows mobile app (but before opening any client company).

TIP

Mobile apps are also available for Macs and iPhone, iPad, and Android devices at no additional cost to you. And, you'll find Pinch and Zoom functionality now in the mobile apps and in browsers on mobile devices.

If you compare Figure 1-4 to Figure 1-1 and Figure 1-5 to Figure 1-2, you'll notice that, once again, QBOA users have the same additional options in the Windows app that they have in a browser. The menus at the top of the screen in the mobile app are the biggest visual difference between QBO and QBOA in the mobile apps and QBO and QBOA in a browser. If you've been a QuickBooks desktop product user, you know that you can use the menus to navigate. Under the hood, the Windows app offers some options that you won't find readily available in a browser, such as the ability to work in multiple windows.

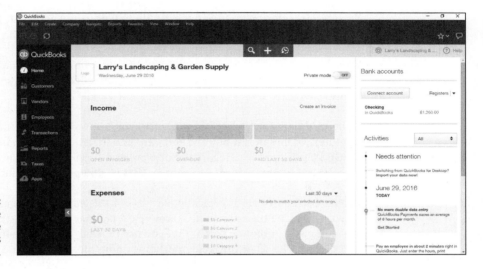

FIGURE 1-4:
QBO while working in the Windows mobile app.

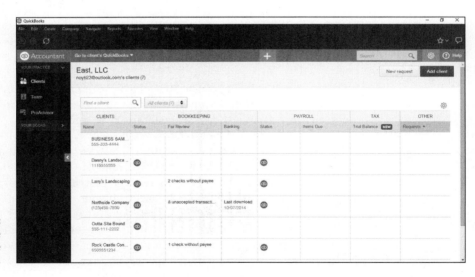

FIGURE 1-5:
QBOA while working in the Windows app.

So take your choice: Work in a browser, work in a mobile app, or work in both, depending on your needs at the moment! You're not limited; you don't have to choose between an app and a browser. Work in one or the other, as suits your needs at the moment.

Understanding the Cloud

Just to make sure we're on the same page here, I'm defining the *cloud* as software and data housed securely in remote data centers (not on your office premises) and accessed securely using the Internet. Working in the cloud can increase your efficiency by offering you the opportunity to work anywhere, communicate easily with others, and collaborate in real time.

REMEMBER

Regardless of whether you use QBO or QBOA in a browser or in an app, both the software and the data are housed on servers controlled by Intuit and accessible via the Internet.

In the traditional model of software use, you buy software and install it on your computer. Or you might buy the software and install it on a vendor's server. QBO and QBOA fall into the category of Software as a Service (SaaS). You typically don't buy SaaS software; instead, you rent it (that is, you purchase a subscription).

Because SaaS software is typically web-based software, you typically access SaaS software over the Internet using a browser. A *browser* is software installed on your local computer or mobile device that you use to, well, browse the Internet, looking up cool stuff like what the stock market is doing today, what kind of weather can you expect on Friday when your vacation starts, how to get to your boss's house for the party he's having, and — oh, yes — to work with web-based software such as QBO and QBOA. In the case of QBO and QBOA, you can work with these web-based SaaS products using either a browser or an app you download to your computer.

Using web-based software can be attractive for a number of reasons. For example, using web-based software, you have access to that software's information anywhere, anytime, from any device — stationary or mobile.

REMEMBER

Some folks see the "anywhere, anytime" feature as a potential disadvantage because it makes information too readily available — and therefore a target for hackers. Intuit stores your data on servers that use bank-level security and encryption, and Intuit automatically backs up your data for you. Other folks see the "anywhere, anytime" feature as a disadvantage for exactly the reason that they have access to the software's information anywhere, anytime, and from any device, offering the opportunity to work more than they'd like. You are in charge of your life, so . . . no comment on this "disadvantage."

In addition, web-based software like QBO and QBOA promotes collaboration and can help you save time. Using QBO and QBOA, accountants, bookkeepers, and clients can communicate about issues that arise, as described in Chapter 14.

Then there's the issue of keeping software up to date. Desktop software such as QuickBooks is updated typically once each year. Unlike their desktop cousin, QBO and QBOA are updated every two to four weeks.

REMEMBER

Because updating occurs so frequently to QBO and QBOA, by the time this book is published, things (and screens) might have changed. Actually, make that "probably have changed."

Should You Move to the Cloud?

Before you make the move to the cloud, you should consider the needs of your business in the following areas:

>> Invoicing, point of sale, electronic payment, and customer relationship management

>> Financial and tax reporting

>> Budgeting

>> Time-tracking and payroll

>> Inventory, job costing, and job scheduling

>> Managing company expenses and vendor bills

Beyond the advantages described in the preceding section, the particular needs of a business might dictate whether you can use QBO. For example, QBO *won't* work for you if your business has industry-specific needs or is mid-sized and needs to use ODBC-compliant applications. In addition, QBO won't work for you if you need to

>> Track your balance sheet by class

>> Process more than 350,000 transactions annually

>> Track labor costs

>> Manage a robust inventory

>> Prepare and track progress invoices

REMEMBER

Robust inventory means that you make and sell goods instead of selling finished goods. If you sell finished goods, QBO will work for you.

In any of these cases, you would probably be better off with one of Intuit's desktop products.

TIP

When QBO and QBOA were first released, the US version didn't support multiple currencies. That feature has been added to both products. And, you can set a "home currency" without enabling multicurrency support. See Chapter 3 for more information.

System Requirements

Using a web-based software product typically doesn't require a lot of hardware and software; in fact, the demands of QBO and QBOA aren't extensive. In particular, you need

>> An Internet connection — Intuit recommends a high-speed connection

>> One of the four supported Internet browsers:

- Chrome

- Firefox

- Internet Explorer 10 or higher

- Safari 6.1 if your operating system is iOS 7 or higher

REMEMBER

At the time I wrote this, you could use Microsoft Edge but not to export to the QuickBooks desktop.

Although QBO and QBOA work in all the major browsers, they work best, in my experience, in Chrome, with Firefox coming in a close second. Therefore, I use Chrome throughout this book, and the Part of Tens chapters cover using Chrome so that you can get comfortable with that browser. If you're a Firefox user, give QBO and QBOA a try in Firefox.

You also can use the QuickBooks Online mobile app, which works with Windows phones and tablets, the iPhone and the iPad, and Android phones and tablets. The requirements for the QuickBooks Online mobile app are the same as those outlined for the non-mobile versions: You need a browser on your device and an Internet connection. Be aware that mobile devices do not support all features of QBO and QBOA.

REMEMBER

In this book, I use a Windows 10 desktop computer and the Chrome browser.

Whether you work on a desktop computer or on a mobile device, the computer or device should meet the basic requirements of the operating system you use on that computer or device. For example, if you're using a Windows desktop computer, you need the amount of RAM (random access memory) specified by Microsoft to load Windows on the computer before you ever launch your browser. If you don't have sufficient RAM to run the operating system, you certainly won't be happy with the behavior of QBO and QBOA. You won't be happy with the behavior of the computer, either.

Basic requirements (and I stress the word *basic*) for a Windows 7, 8.1, and 10 computer, as specified by Microsoft, are

>> 1-gigahertz (GHz) or faster 32-bit (x86) or 64-bit (x64) processor

>> 1 gigabyte (GB) of RAM (32 bit) or 2GB of RAM (64 bit)

>> 16GB of available hard disk space (32 bit) or 20GB (64 bit)

>> A display that supports at least 800 x 600 dpi

>> DirectX 9 graphics device with WDDM 1.0 or higher driver

These versions of Windows work with multi-core processors, and all 32-bit versions of Windows can support up to 32 processor cores, whereas 64-bit versions can support up to 256 processor cores.

And a word on the word *basic*. You'll be a whole lot happier if your desktop computer components have higher numbers than the ones listed above. If you have a computer that's fairly new — say, three to four years old — you might need only to add some RAM or possibly hard disk space. If your computer is older than three or four years, you should consider purchasing new equipment, simply because you'll be unbelievably happier with the computer's performance. Technology continues to improve dramatically in short spurts of time.

If you buy a new computer, you don't need to worry about much to meet more than the basic requirements. I'm pretty sure you can't buy a new computer containing a 1-gigahertz processor; most computers today come with at least 2.5-gigahertz processors and they support better graphics than the DirectX 9 graphics listed in the basic requirements. And most monitors available for purchase today don't support low resolutions such as 800 x 600; you most likely own a monitor that supports higher resolution. In my opinion, 1GB of RAM is insufficient; your desktop computer should have at least 4GB of RAM, and you'll be much happier if it has 8GB of RAM. On the hard drive requirement, if you don't have the 16GB or 20GB of available space specified, you probably should be considering a hard drive replacement for your computer.

TECHNICAL STUFF

The amount of RAM your computer can successfully use depends on the computer's architecture — in particular, if your computer uses a 32-bit processor, as older computers often do, your computer might not be able to "see" more than 4GB of RAM. So, you could put 16GB of RAM in the computer and only be able to use 4GB. And part of that 4GB goes to other stuff, like your video card; so, with most 32-bit processors (there are a few exceptions), your computer can use only 3GB of RAM. Bottom line here: Newer computers use 64-bit processors and can take advantage of much more RAM, which makes them much faster.

Chapter **2**

Embracing the QBO/QBOA Format

QBO and QBOA are not traditional software that you buy and install on your local computer. In this chapter, we explore the QBO/QBOA software format, and I assume that you've read Chapter 1 and evaluated whether QBO can meet your needs.

It's All about Subscriptions

QBO and QBOA fall into the category of Software as a Service (SaaS). As such, you don't buy the software. Instead, you rent it; that is, you buy a subscription to use the software for a time period specified by the seller.

REMEMBER

Traditionally, you buy a *license* to use software that you install on your computer, and typically, that license permits you to install the software on only one computer.

And, of course, a QBO user can pay varying amounts for a subscription, depending on the subscription level purchased.

QBO is available at four different subscription levels, and each subsequent subscription level costs more and contains more functionality. The QBO subscriptions available at this writing are

>> Self-Employed

>> Simple Start

>> Essentials

>> Plus

REMEMBER

All versions of QBO share three attributes in common. First, you can use a tablet, smartphone, or desktop computer to access your data. Second, your data is automatically backed up online. And third, all versions of QBO use 128-bit Secure Sockets Layer (SSL), the same security and encryption used by banks to secure data sent over the Internet.

After you assess your needs as described in Chapter 1, use the following information to identify the lowest subscription level that will meet your requirements. At this point in time, you can upgrade to a higher level, but you cannot downgrade to a lower level.

Accounting professionals signing up clients for QBO and creating client companies originally couldn't switch client companies from one version of QBO to another if the accounting professional created the client as part of the Intuit Wholesale Pricing program. However, that's no longer true. So, you no longer need to anticipate your client's requirements for more advanced features like the ability to track inventory or prepare 1099s.

The Self-Employed version

This version of QBO is aimed at freelancers and self-employed individuals, basically, those who receive Federal Form 1099 to account for the money they've been paid and pay their taxes using Schedule C of IRS Form 1040. Using the Self-Employed version, you can

>> Separate business from personal spending

>> Calculate and pay estimated quarterly taxes

>> Track mileage and IRS Form 1040 Schedule C (the IRS form that most self-employed people must complete to determine business net income or loss) information

>> Track income and expenses

>> Download transactions from your bank and credit card accounts

Like the other versions of QBO, you can use a tablet, smartphone, or desktop computer to access your data. In addition, the Self-Employed version uses the same security and encryption as banks, and your data is automatically backed up online. As you might expect, this version has the fewest reports available — only three — and only one person can access QBO.

REMEMBER

Be aware that, when I wrote this, the Self-Employed version of QBO didn't link with QBOA.

If you opt to include TurboTax in your subscription, you also can pay your estimated quarterly taxes online and export Schedule C information from QBO to Turbo Tax so that you can prepare your tax return more easily. With TurboTax as part of your subscription, you receive one federal and one state electronic tax return filing at no extra cost.

The Simple Start version

The Simple Start version of QBO is great for a new business with basic bookkeeping needs. With Simple Start, you can

>> Track your income and expenses

>> Download transactions from your bank and credit card accounts

>> Create an unlimited number of customers

>> Send unlimited estimates and invoices

>> Print checks and record transactions to track expenses

>> Import data from Microsoft Excel or QuickBooks desktop

>> Invite up to two accountants to access your data

>> Integrate with available apps

Although the Simple Start version supports Accounts Receivable functions, you can't track bills due in the future in the Simple Start version because it doesn't include any Accounts Payable functions. And, one other important consideration: The Simple Start version also has no general ledger.

Although the Simple Start version allows two accountants to work in the client's company, Simple Start is still designed for a single user. Therefore, the accountant cannot create the client's company for the client. At the time the company is created in QBO, whoever creates the company becomes, in QBO parlance, the Master Administrator.

In addition to the single-user restriction, the Simple Start version offers more than 20 reports. And Simple Start users can memorize report settings and produce memorized reports.

REMEMBER

For subscription levels that support multiple users, the accountant can create the company for the client and then assign the Master Administrator role to the client. And, if the accountant doesn't make the client the Master Administrator when creating the company, the accountant can, later on, transfer the Master Administrator role to the client.

The Essentials version

The Essentials version of QBO includes all the features found in Simple Start. In addition, with the Essentials version, you can

» Set up invoices to automatically bill on a recurring schedule

» Take advantage of Accounts Payable functions, including entering vendor bills and scheduling their payment for later

» Compare your sales and profitability with industry trends

» Compare your sales and profitably with industry trends

» Create and post recurring transactions

» Control what your users can access

The Essentials version permits three simultaneous users and two accountant users. In addition, the Essentials version contains the reports found in Simple Start and 20 additional reports.

The Plus version

The Plus version of QBO is the most full-featured version of QBO. It contains all the features found in the Essentials version. In addition, you can

» Create, send, and track purchase orders.

» Track inventory using the first in, first out (FIFO) inventory valuation method. QBO supports light inventory needs: If you sell finished goods, QBO should be able to manage your needs. But if you need to assemble finished goods to sell, QBO won't meet your needs on its own. You can look for an app to supplement your inventory needs; I talk about apps at the end of this chapter.

>> Track, create, and send 1099-Misc forms.

>> Categorize income and expenses using class tracking.

>> Track sales and profitability by business location. You can assign only one location to a transaction, but you can assign multiple classes to a transaction.

>> Give employees and subcontractors limited access to the QBO company to enter time worked.

>> Track billable hours by customer.

QBO supports light job-costing needs, but it does not allow you to automatically cost labor.

REMEMBER

>> Create budgets to estimate future income and expenses, and create multiple budgets per year, location, class, or customer.

REMEMBER

I used QBO Plus as I wrote this book because it contains the most features, therefore users of other versions might find references in this book to features they don't have. Accounting professionals: The company that comes with QBOA is a Plus company.

The Plus version supports five simultaneous users and two accountant users and can be scaled up to support 20 users. The Plus version also contains more than 65 reports: all the reports found in both the Simple Start and the Essentials versions, and some additional reports.

Essentials and Plus with Payroll

If an end user signs up for QBO Essentials or Plus on his own and creates his own company, he can create the company using the Plus Payroll option, or later he can sign up for QBO Payroll (QBOP) separately. An accountant also can create the company that uses QBOP for a client. For details, see the section "Addressing Payroll Needs" later in this chapter.

What Does It Cost?

The big question: What's it cost? The price is dependent primarily on the QBO version you choose.

If you are an end user who signs up on your own for a QBO subscription, the price per month as of the date this book was written appears in Table 2-1.

REMEMBER

The prices shown in Table 2-1 are monthly subscription prices, and, at the time I wrote this, the sale price was good for six months. In some cases, when you sign up, you'll be offered the option to pay for an entire year. And, paying for a full year might turn out to be less expensive than paying on a monthly basis.

TABLE 2-1

QBO Subscription Pricing

QBO Version	Regular Price	Sale Price
Self-Employed	$10/month	$5/month
Simple Start	$13/month	$10/month
Essentials	$27/month	$18/month
Plus	$40/month	$24/month

REMEMBER

At the time I wrote this, Intuit offered a bundle for the Self-Employed version — QBO and TurboTax for $12/month instead of the regular price of $17/month.

You'll receive a bill on a regular basis from Intuit. Intuit gives you a free 30-day trial that includes payroll processing along with the rest of the subscription's features. If you opt to continue QBO Payroll after the 30-day trial, your subscription fee increases. The free trial also includes the Payments app, which gives you the ability to process online and mobile payments with rates per use as low as 1.75 percent + 25 cents per swipe and 50 cents per bank payment/ACH.

REMEMBER

If you opt for a 30-day free trial, you won't get the sale price for the subscription. But, if you "buy now," Intuit gives you a 60 day, money-back guarantee on your purchase.

If you are an accounting professional, you can sign up for the Wholesale Pricing program and use QBOA for free. If you create a client's company as part of the Wholesale Pricing program and you manage the client's subscription, Intuit sends you the bill for the client's subscription. It is your responsibility to bill the client for the QBO subscription. The bill you receive from Intuit is a single consolidated bill for all the QBO subscriptions you manage. For a little more information on the Wholesale Pricing program, see Chapter 11. But, for the complete skinny on the Wholesale Pricing program, contact Intuit. Note that accounting professionals might be able to get QBO for their clients at a reduced price.

REMEMBER

If an accounting professional creates a company through QBOA, the company does not come with a 30-day free trial. Instead, at the time the accounting professional creates the company, he must provide a payment method to ensure uninterrupted service.

If your client initially sets up QBO with his or her own subscription, you can move that existing QBO subscription to your consolidated bill at the discounted rate. And, if your arrangement with your client doesn't work out, you can remove the client from your consolidated bill, and the client can begin paying for his own subscription.

Addressing Payroll Needs

QBO can handle payroll regardless of whether an end user or an accountant creates the QBO company.

If an end user signs up for QBO Essentials or Plus on his own, he can create his own company using the appropriate "with Payroll" option — Enhanced or Full Service Payroll — or, after the fact, he can sign up for QBO Payroll from the Employees screen (see Figure 2-1).

REMEMBER

The distinction between the two options, besides price, is that you choose Enhanced Payroll if you want to prepare payroll on your own; for details on preparing payroll in QBO, see Chapter 9. Alternatively, you can subscribe to QBO Full Service Payroll, which integrates with QBO, where Intuit prepares payroll for you.

REMEMBER

It's easy to get confused here . . . I know I was. Intuit also offers another payroll product, Intuit Full Service Payroll, which is a standalone product that doesn't integrate with QBO.

Click here to turn on payroll.

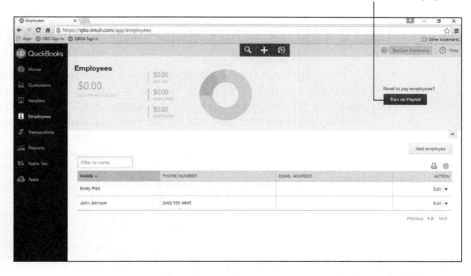

FIGURE 2-1:
If you sign up for QBO on your own, you can turn on payroll from the Employees screen.

Both Enhanced and Full Service QBO Payroll sport the following features:

>> Paying employees with printed checks or by directly depositing paychecks

>> Automatically calculating tax payments and paying them electronically

>> Processing Federal and State quarterly and annual reports and preparing W-2 forms

>> Processing payroll for employees in multiple states

>> Keeping payroll tax tables up to date without having to install updates like you do with the QuickBooks desktop product

>> Using the QBO Payroll mobile app to pay employees, view past paychecks, electronically pay taxes, and electronically file tax forms

If an accountant who is not enrolled in the Intuit Wholesale Pricing program creates a QBO Essentials or Plus company for a client, the client company can turn on QBO payroll (QBOP) from the Employees screen in the client's company (refer to Figure 2-1). Clients can prepare payroll for themselves or accounting professionals can manage all payroll functions for clients.

If the accountant is enrolled in the Intuit Wholesale Pricing program and creates a QBO Essential or Plus company for a client as part of the program, the accountant can set up the QBO company to use QBO Payroll (QBOP).

Last, an accountant can add an Intuit Full Service Payroll subscription to a client company subscription through QBOA, regardless of whether he or she is enrolled in the Wholesale Pricing Program.

Switching from QuickBooks Desktop

At this point (or maybe earlier than now), you might have been wondering if you can easily switch to QBO if you have been a QuickBooks desktop program user. And, the answer is yes. Chapter 12 provides details on importing QuickBooks desktop data into QBO. And, the import process doesn't affect your original desktop company; it's still available via the desktop product. After you import your data into QBO, you should run the Profit & Loss report and the Balance Sheet using the Accrual method for all dates from both QBO and QuickBooks desktop to ensure both versions show the same information.

And, if you want some reassurance that you'll get the same accurate information from QBO that you got from QuickBooks desktop, you can "run in parallel" for a time period you specify. For example, you might decide to enter all your transactions in both versions of the software for one month; at the end of that time, you can run reports from both products and make sure you see the same information.

WARNING

Although you can continue to use the QuickBooks desktop, once you make the switch to QuickBooks Online, be aware that no synchronization occurs between QuickBooks desktop and QBO. So, changes you make in one are not reflected in the other. Unless you're temporarily running in parallel, continuing to use both products could really mess up your books, because you might accidentally enter transactions into one product and not the other.

Where Add-On Apps Fit In

QBO doesn't operate as a complete, standalone accounting solution. It has functional limitations. The section "Addressing payroll needs" highlights one such limitation — and shows how you can use Intuit add-ons to achieve more functionality in QBO. And, earlier in this chapter I briefly mention Intuit's Payments app, which supports electronic customer payment processing and integrates with QBO.

But those aren't the only apps available for QBO; third-party developers have been creating apps to enhance the functionality of QBO. And, over time, you can expect more apps to be developed.

You can click the Apps link in the Navigation bar that runs down the left side of QBO to visit the App Center and explore available apps (see Figure 2-2).

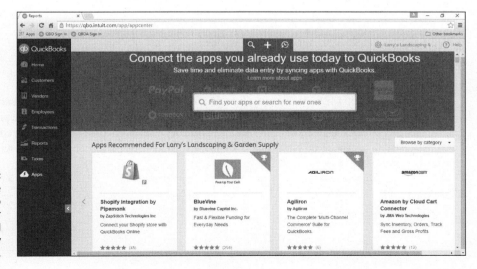

FIGURE 2-2: Take a trip to the App Center to search for additional functionality for QBO.

Click any app to navigate to a page that describes the app, provides pricing information, and often provides a video about the app (see Figure 2-3).

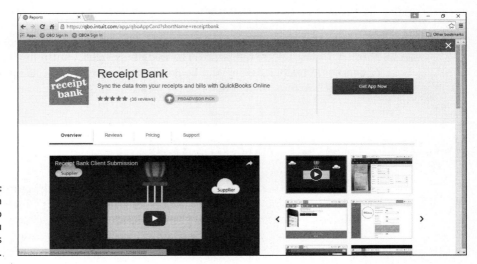

FIGURE 2-3:
When you click an app in the App Center, you see details for the app.

Although add-on apps can provide additional functionality in QBO, some functionality is still missing; no doubt, that functionality will appear over time. For example, using QBO, you can't

» Track your balance sheet by class

» Process more than 350,000 transactions annually

» Track labor costs

» Manage a robust inventory

» Prepare and track progress invoices

But apps are making inroads to eliminating these limitations. For example, Lettuce, an app that provided advanced inventory management features for QBO, did such a fine job of handling inventory functions that Intuit acquired Lettuce for the purpose of integrating it into QBO.

2

Managing the Books for the End User

IN THIS PART . . .

Become familiar with the QBO interface.

Manage list information needed to use QBO.

Enter transactions in QBO to update your company's books.

Use reports to examine the condition of your company.

IN THIS CHAPTER

» Signing up for a QBO account

» Setting up a new QBO company

» Understanding the interface

» Working with company settings

» Updating the Chart of Accounts

» Working with multiple currencies

» Examining QuickBooks Labs

Chapter **3**

Creating a Client Company in QBO

After you sign up for QBO, you log in. QBO then prompts you to set up your company. With certain limitations, you can import a company if you've been using a QuickBooks desktop product. Or, you can use the QBO Setup wizard, as shown in this chapter.

For details on importing a company, see Chapter 12 (or ask your accountant to help you with the import). And, don't worry, if you don't import your entire desktop company; you can import just the list information from that company, as described in Chapter 4. Importing lists will still save you a lot of time and setup work.

Signing Up for QBO

After you complete the sign-up process for a QBO account, Intuit, by default, logs you in to your account and walks you through the process of setting up your QBO company. The process is short — much shorter than the one you go through when setting up a QB desktop product company — and you need the following information:

>> Your company's name and address

>> The industry in which your company operates

>> Your company's legal organization (such as S-Corp or Limited Liability Partnership)

>> Whether you want to import company information from a QuickBooks desktop product

>> The types of payments you accept from your customers (that is, cash, checks, and credit cards)

>> The way you want to handle payroll

To sign up for a QBO account, follow these steps:

1. **Visit quickbooks.intuit.com/online.**

2. **Scroll down the page until you find the three boxes describing each version of QBO.**

3. **In the version of QBO that you want to try, click the Free 30-Day Trial link.**

The Free 30-Day Trial link appears below the Buy Now button.

REMEMBER

Be aware that the price you pay for QBO depends on whether you choose the Buy Now option or the Free 30-Day Trial. If you opt to "buy now," you pay less for your subscription because discounts don't apply to the Free 30-Day Trial.

4. **Fill in your name, email address, and a password (see Figure 3-1).**

If you already have an Intuit user ID, supply that user ID and password.

Your password must be between 6 and 32 characters and consist of a mix of letters and numbers. The password can also contain some special characters; I included an exclamation point (!) in my password and it was accepted. The user ID and password you supply are the ones you use each time you log in to QBO.

5. **Click the Sign Up button below the boxes you completed in Step 4.**

At the time that I wrote this, a window appeared that offered the option to skip the free trial and buy the product at a discounted rate. You can buy, but I opted to click the Continue to Trial button.

QBO sets up your free trial, logs you in to QBO, and displays the Set Up wizard . . . read on.

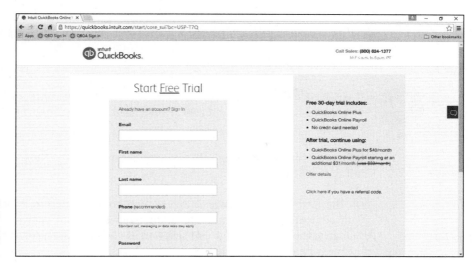

FIGURE 3-1:
Fill in the
information
needed to start
the free trial.

Setting Up a New Company

When you first sign up for a QBO account, Intuit logs you in to your QBO account and, by default, displays the set up wizard. The first screen of the wizard, shown in Figure 3-2, asks for basic company information.

FIGURE 3-2:
Provide basic
company
information.

As you supply address information, QBO automatically prepares an invoice form that contains the information; you'll use this form (or a variant of it) to prepare the invoices you send to customers.

TIP

If you have a basically square company logo in JPG, GIF, BMP, or PNG format, you can upload it to include it on your invoice. Just click the Logo button to navigate to your logo.

When you finish providing address information, click the Next button in the lower left corner of the screen.

On the next screen, shown in Figure 3-3, you provide more information about your company so that Intuit can customize QBO to suit your needs: Supply your industry, the type of things you sell, and, if you have the information handy, your business type and age. Then click Next.

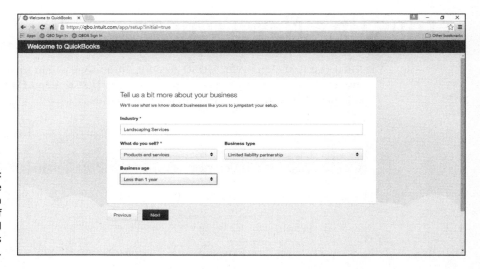

FIGURE 3-3:
Provide
information
about the stuff
you sell and
your company's
industry.

REMEMBER

Only your industry and the type of stuff you sell are required. Supplying your business type helps QBO set up your Chart of Accounts more accurately.

If you're keeping track of your business information now, supply the method you currently use on the next screen. You can choose from the following:

» Excel

» Google

- » Pen and paper
- » QuickBooks Desktop
- » Online banking
- » Other software

The answer you provide determines the screen you see next. For example, if you select QuickBooks Desktop, you then answer questions about importing information from the QuickBooks desktop product. For this book, I chose "pen and paper," which assumes you have nothing in electronic form to import.

TIP

If you opt not to import desktop information, you can change your mind later, as long as you do so within 60 days of starting your QBO subscription. If you decide that you want to import data after 60 days, you must cancel your subscription and start a new one.

When you click Next, the wizard then asks you to select the elements that matter to you most; you can choose all of the following that apply to you:

- » Invoicing
- » Expense tracking
- » My accountant
- » Mobile
- » Point of sale
- » E-commerce
- » Sales tax
- » My employees

For my trial company, I chose invoicing, expense tracking, sales tax, and my employees. If something matters to you later (like working with an accountant), you can set that up in your company when it suits you. So, don't worry if you don't select something that you later determine you should have selected.

Click Next, and QBO searches online for businesses similar to yours and establishes appropriate options and settings; when QBO finishes the search, you see a message that your QuickBooks is ready and you click the Let's Dive In button to get started.

When you click Next, QBO displays your company's Home page and displays links to options you might want to set up to get started. In my case, I see boxes containing options to use Bill.com to easily pay bills online, along with options to set up sales tax and payroll (see Figure 3-4).

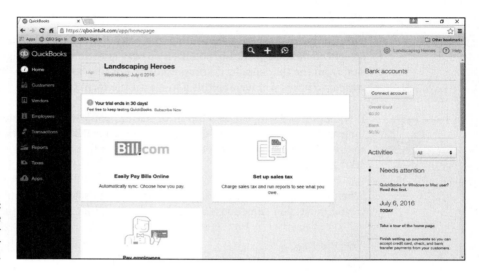

FIGURE 3-4:
Your QBO Home
page just after
creating your
company.

We'll examine the Home page in the next section, but essentially you've just completed most of the initial setup work; I'll cover other program settings later in this chapter.

Understanding the Home Page

When you first see your QBO company, your Home page contains boxes with links to options you can use to set up features in QBO that are important to you (refer back to Figure 3-4). You can use those links and set up those options now, or, you can wait until later. To hide the options, slide your mouse over any item, and an X appears in the upper right corner of the box (see Figure 3-5).

When you click the X, QBO offers you the option to permanently dismiss the box or to see it later (see Figure 3-6). Click your choice. If you choose to see the option later, the box will reappear the next time you log in to your QBO company.

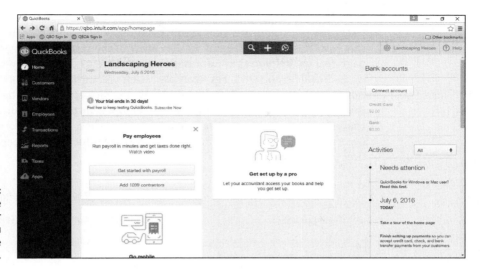

FIGURE 3-5:
You can close the
boxes that offer
to help you
perform some
QBO set-up work.

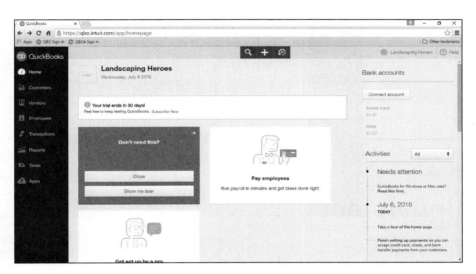

FIGURE 3-6:
The QBO Home
page after closing
the boxes.

Don't worry; you can still set up the options associated with any of these boxes. And, be aware that each box you dismiss is replaced by another associated with the list of options that matter to you that appear at the end of the preceding section.

Once you close the boxes, your Home page displays information specific to your company.

You can click the Take a Tour of the Home Page link in the Activities section to let QBO show you, interactively, the things I'm about to show you.

In Figure 3-7, I'm using a company that already has some data in it to try to make things a bit more meaningful. In the center of the screen, using most of the Home page real estate, you find information that changes depending on what you have clicked while using QBO. For example, when you initially open QBO, the information is overview company information. If you click an entry in the Navigation bar (on the left side of the screen), the information in the center of the Home page changes to information related to the entry you click. If you select a setting on the Gear menu (discussed later in this section), the information is related to the setting you select.

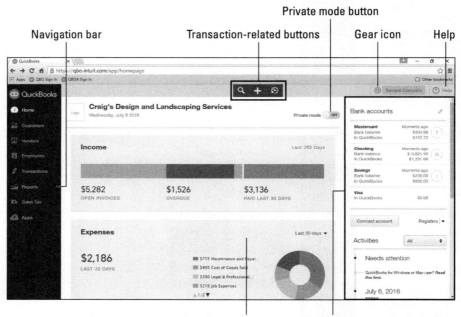

FIGURE 3-7:
Examining Home
screen elements.

TIP

You might have noticed the Private Mode button in Figure 3-7. This button appears after you have entered at least one transaction, and you can use it to temporarily hide financial information on your Home page. For example, you might want to turn Private Mode on if you're using QuickBooks in a public place or even in your office when you're not alone. Once you turn Private Mode on, it remains on until you turn it off again.

As I just mentioned, the Navigation bar runs down the left side of the screen. You use the Navigation bar the same way you'd use a menu; click an item in the Navigation bar to, well, navigate to that part of QBO. For example, you can click Transactions in the Navigation bar to see the available transactions in QBO and then click one to use that type of transaction.

REMEMBER
The highlighted entry in the Navigation bar does not always change to match the information shown in the main portion of the Home page. You use the Navigation bar to navigate to a portion of the program, not to determine the portion of the program you are viewing. In other words, don't depend on the Navigation bar to "tell you" how you got to what you're viewing.

On the right side of the screen, you find a list of the bank accounts you've set up as well the Activities list — a list of things that QBO thinks need your attention. The list is interactive, so you can click items in the list to take various actions.

When you click the Help button, you see a menu of common topics related to the area of QBO you are currently viewing, and you can type in the search box to find help on a particular topic (see Figure 3-8).

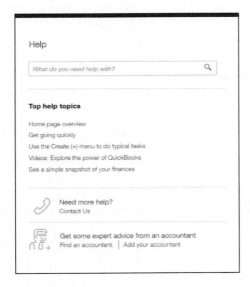

FIGURE 3-8:
The Help menu.

For example, when you click the Home page overview link, QBO displays the QBO Welcome Guide, which provides a brief overview of the Home page along with a list of topics you can use to help you further configure QBO (see Figure 3-9).

In the center of the top of the screen, you see three transaction-related buttons that display lists you can use to work with transactions. Figure 3-10 shows what you see when you click the leftmost transaction button, the Search button.

Figure 3-11 shows the Create menu that appears when you click the center transaction button.

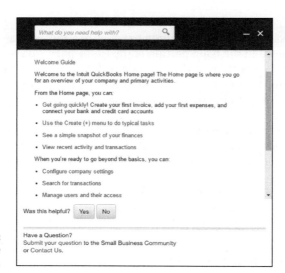

FIGURE 3-9:
A sample
Help topic.

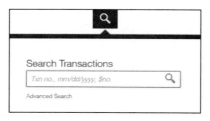

FIGURE 3-10:
Click the leftmost
button to
search for past
transactions.

FIGURE 3-11:
Click the center
button to create a
new transaction.

REMEMBER

The Create button appears as a plus sign (+) when the menu is closed and an X when the menu is open; compare Figures 3-7 and 3-11.

When you click the third transaction button — the one that looks like a clock — you see a list of recently entered transactions; you can click any transaction in the list to open that transaction (see Figure 3-12).

Recent Transactions

Credit Card Expense	07/05/2016	$34.00	
Credit Card Expense	06/16/2016	$42.40	Hicks Hardware
Credit Card Expense	06/22/2016	$19.99	Squeaky Kleen Car Wash
Credit Card Expense	06/15/2016	$19.99	Squeaky Kleen Car Wash
Credit Card Expense	06/15/2016	$18.97	Bob's Burger Joint
Credit Card Credit	06/24/2016	$900.00	
Check No.Debit	06/08/2016	$19.99	Squeaky Kleen Car Wash
Cash Expense	06/06/2016	$3.86	Bob's Burger Joint
Cash Expense	06/01/2016	$19.99	Squeaky Kleen Car Wash
Cash Expense	06/01/2016	$5.66	Bob's Burger Joint

More...

FIGURE 3-12: Click the right button to display a list of recently entered transactions.

To the right of the three transaction-related buttons, you see the Gear button followed by your company's name. If you click the Gear button, you see the menu shown in Figure 3-13, which you use to look at and change QBO company settings; view lists; work with tools such as import and export, reconciliation, and budgeting tools; and view information about your QBO account. Note that the Gear menu is divided into four columns that organize related commands.

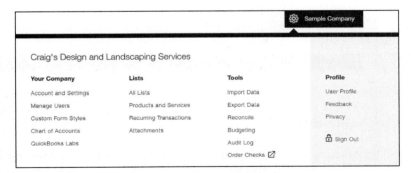

⚙ Sample Company

Craig's Design and Landscaping Services

Your Company	Lists	Tools	Profile
Account and Settings	All Lists	Import Data	User Profile
Manage Users	Products and Services	Export Data	Feedback
Custom Form Styles	Recurring Transactions	Reconcile	Privacy
Chart of Accounts	Attachments	Budgeting	
QuickBooks Labs		Audit Log	🔒 Sign Out
		Order Checks 🔗	

FIGURE 3-13: Use this menu to work with settings, lists, tools, and your QBO account.

Establishing Company Settings

After you set up your company, you should review the default settings Intuit established and make changes as appropriate. To examine and make changes to payroll settings, see Chapter 9.

Examining company preferences

Choose Gear ⇨ Account and Settings to display the Company tab of the Account and Settings dialog box (see Figure 3-14).

TECHNICAL STUFF

At the time I wrote this, QBOA users working in client companies were still seeing older Gear menu options — and so would see Gear ⇨ Company settings instead of Gear ⇨ Account and Settings. I use the newer interface options throughout Part II of the book, so, QBOA users, be aware: When I say choose Gear ⇨ Account and Settings, you'll be choosing Gear ⇨ Company settings.

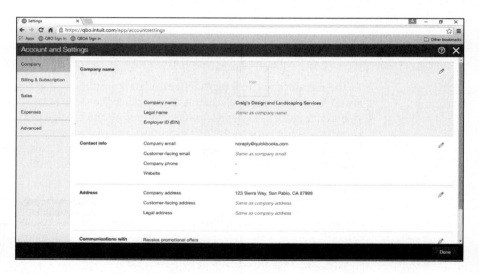

FIGURE 3-14: Review company settings.

On this tab, you can make changes to your company name, address, and contact information.

To change any setting, click anywhere in the group where the setting appears. When you finish making changes, click the Save button that appears in the group of settings. You can then move on to other settings on the page.

If you make changes, click Done in the lower right corner of the screen to save them.

Examining billing and subscription settings

To review the settings related to your QBO billing and subscription, choose Gear ⇨ Account and Settings to display the Account and Settings dialog box. Then click Billing & Subscription in the pane on the left.

TECHNICAL STUFF

QBOA users choose Gear ⇨ Your Account.

This page, shown in Figure 3-15, shows you the status of your QBO, Payroll, and Payments subscriptions. From this page, you can convert your trial version of QBO and of the QBO Payroll product to a regular subscription; converting cancels your trial. You also can use this page to order checks and supplies, should you need them.

REMEMBER

The subscription Payments product that Intuit offers enables you to receive online payments from your customers. If you already have a subscription to the Payments product, you can connect to it from the Billing & Subscription page of the Account and Settings dialog box. If you don't have a subscription, you can (naturally) subscribe from the Billing & Subscription page.

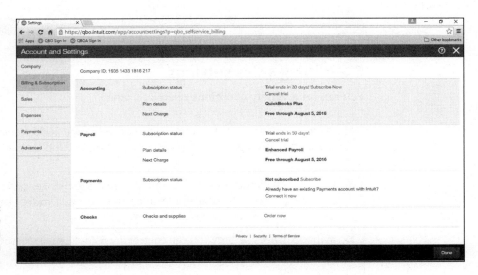

FIGURE 3-15: Review QBO billing and subscription settings.

Setting sales preferences

To review the Sales preferences of your QBO company, choose Gear ⇨ Account and Settings to display the Account and Settings dialog box. Then click Sales in the pane on the left.

At the top of the page that appears (see Figure 3-16), you can click the Customize Look and Feel button to customize the appearance of the invoice you send to customers. We'll return to the customization process at the end of this section; first, let's examine the settings available to you.

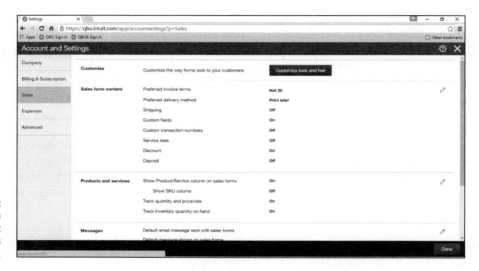

FIGURE 3-16:
The Sales page of the Account and Settings dialog box.

Examining sales settings

You can set a variety of options related to sales:

>> In the Sales Form Content section, you can define the fields that appear on the form you complete to prepare invoices, sales receipts, and other sales forms.

>> In the Products and Services section, you can make changes to the product- and service-related fields that appear on sales forms. If you're using QBO Plus, this is where you turn on inventory tracking.

>> In the Messages section, you can control the default email message sent to customers with sales forms and the default message that appears on those sales forms.

>> If you scroll down the Sales page, you can set, in the Online Delivery section, email delivery options for sales forms such as attaching the sales form as a PDF, showing a summary or details of the sales form in the email, and email formatting options for invoices.

>> In the Statements section, you can specify whether to show the aging table at the bottom of the statement.

Customizing form appearance

To customize forms that your customers receive, click Customize Look and Feel at the top of the Sales page in the Account and Settings dialog box to display the Custom Form Styles page shown in Figure 3-17.

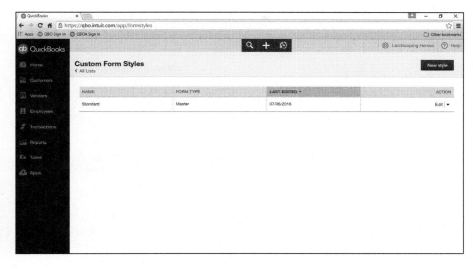

FIGURE 3-17: Use this page to edit an existing form style or set up a new form style.

The Custom Form Styles page lists any form styles you have already created. By default, QBO creates one form style for you when you sign up; that form style is named Standard and is used by default for invoices, estimates, and sales receipts.

If you are satisfied with the appearance of the majority of the form style, you can edit it instead of creating a form style. Alternatively, you can create separate customized forms for invoices, estimates, and sales receipts. To do so, click New Style in the upper-right corner of the Custom Form Styles page. Whether you edit or a create a new form style, QBO displays the Customize Form Style dialog box, whose appearance varies only slightly, depending on whether you are editing or creating a new form style. In particular, if you opt to create a form style, the dialog box gives you the option to select the type of form style (see Figure 3-18).

You use the tabs that run down the left side of the dialog box to establish form style settings:

>> From the Style tab, shown in Figure 3-18, you can select a style for the form: Airy, Modern, Fresh, Friendly, or Bold. The preview shown in Figure 3-18 is the Fresh form style.

Use this list to select the type of form style you want to create.

FIGURE 3-18:
The dialog box
you use to
customize sales
forms.

>> From the Appearance tab, you can modify the appearance and placement of your logo; set the form's font, line height, and page margins; and specify whether to print your form to fit in a standard window envelope. You also can opt to show an account summary table, which shows your customers how much past due they are in paying you.

>> From the Header tab, you can define the names used for each form and the fields that appear in the header area of the form — such as your company name, address, contact information, payment terms, due date, and form number. You also can opt to show your customer's terms, due date, shipping and payment methods, as well as set up custom fields.

>> From the Activity Table tab, you can control the appearance of the body of the invoice, determining whether to display, in columns, information such as the quantity, rate, and description for each item — and the order in which the elements appear. For each row of information, you also can specify whether to display billable time and markup on billable expenses (most people don't display markup on billable expenses), and you can choose whether to show the employee's name and the hours and rate. You also can choose the way you want to group activity (by day, week, month, or type), and, if you group activity, you can choose to subtotal by group. You also can combine rows that show the same rate and description and omit the dates for those rows.

TIP

Chapter 6 contains an example of customizing the Activity Table so that you can include subtotals on an invoice.

>> From the Footer tab, you can control the information that appears in the footer portion of the form, along with messages to your customer.

You can click the Preview or Print button to preview your invoice in a browser window but in PDF format.

Click the Save button to save changes you make to the appearance of your forms.

Importing form styles

REMEMBER

At the time I wrote this, importing form styles was a feature "under construction" in QBO and is therefore not available unless you enable it using QuickBooks Labs. For details on using QuickBooks Labs, see "Working with QuickBooks Labs," later in this chapter. For purposes of this discussion, I have enabled the feature.

If the form templates supplied with QBO don't meet your needs, you can use Microsoft Word 2010 or later to create a form style and then upload it into QBO. As part of the import process, you map fields you've identified on your Word document form style to QBO fields.

The tricky part of this process is getting the form correctly designed in Word. But, luckily, Intuit anticipated the challenge and provides sample forms and instructions to simplify the process. To download the samples and instructions, you need to pretend you've already created your form style in Word. If this feels like I'm putting the cart in front of the horse, well . . . I am, sort of.

To get the sample information and instructions, enable the Import Form Styles feature through QuickBooks Labs. Then click Gear ➪ Custom Form Styles. On the Custom Form Styles page, click the down arrow beside New Style, and choose Import Style. QBO displays the page shown in Figure 3-19.

To download the sample information, click the Download a Sample Invoice link. A Zip file downloads, containing two sample forms you can use as starting points.

REMEMBER

The Zip file also contains detailed instructions that describe what to do and what not to do when creating a form style. For example, the instructions list the fonts QBO will recognize and also describe the best way to use Word tables. Suffice it to say, use these instructions and save yourself some pain.

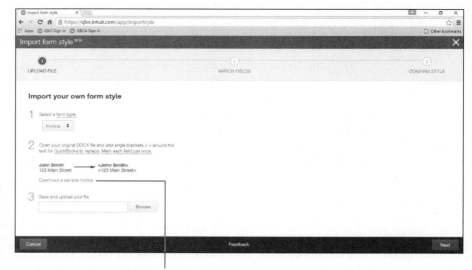

FIGURE 3-19:
Use the Import
Form Style page
to download
sample forms
and instructions
to create your
own form style.

Click here to download sample files and instructions.

Open either of the sample files to see how a customized form style should look in Word (see Figure 3-20). Note, for example, that you simply type information that won't change, but you place less than and greater than brackets around fields you want to replace with QBO data, such as your customer's billing and shipping addresses and item information.

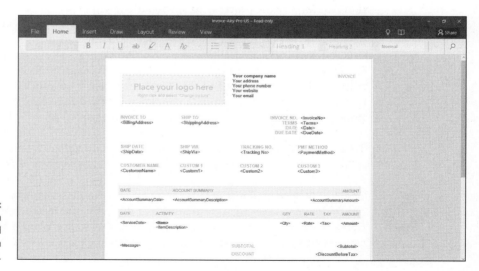

FIGURE 3-20:
Place information
that QBO should
replace in
brackets.

When you're ready to upload your form style, follow these steps:

1. **Choose Gear ⇨ Custom Form Styles to display the Custom Form Style page.**

2. **Click the arrow beside the New Style button and choose Import Style to redisplay the page shown earlier in Figure 3-19.**

3. **Click the Browse button and navigate to the Word document you created for your form style.**

4. **Click Next.**

   QBO uploads the document and scans it for fields you placed in brackets. If you successfully upload the Word document, you'll see a message telling you that you succeeded in uploading. If this process is not successful you will see errors; review the instruction document included with the sample files for details on errors and how to correct them.

   Assuming your document uploads successfully, a page appears where you can map the fields on your form style to fields in QBO.

5. **Match the fields on your form style to QBO fields; when you finish, click Next.**

   A preview of the new form style appears on the Confirm Style page.

6. **If you're happy with what you see, click Save and supply a name for your form style. It's now ready to use.**

   If you're not happy, click Back and correct any problems.

Taking a look at expense preferences

From the Expenses tab of the Account and Settings dialog box, you can control expenses related to purchase orders, bills, and payments you make to vendors (see Figure 3-21). Choose Gear ⇨ Account and Settings ⇨ Expenses.

In the Bills and Expenses group of settings, you can opt to display a table on expense and purchase forms so that you can itemize and categorize the products and services you buy. If you purchase goods and services for your customers, you can

>> Add a column to the table so that you can identify the customer for whom you made the purchase.

>> Add a column where you identify expenses and items for which you want to bill customers.

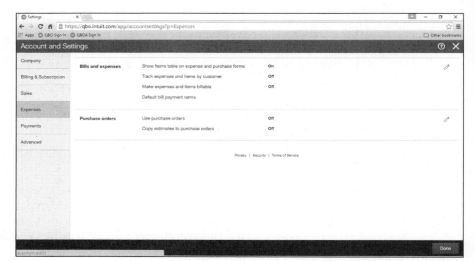

FIGURE 3-21:
Expense
preferences you
can control.

You also can set default bill payment terms.

In the Purchase Orders group, you can opt to use purchase orders and you can opt to copy estimates to purchase orders. For more information about converting an estimate to a purchase order, see Chapter 6.

Examining options to receive customer payments

The Payments tab of the Account and Settings dialog box offers you a way to connect with Intuit Merchant Services via a QuickBooks Payments account. If you don't have a QuickBooks Payments account with Intuit and you want one, click the Learn More button. If you already have a QuickBooks Payments account, you can click the Connect button to connect your QBO account with your QuickBooks Payments account.

TIP

QuickBooks Payments is the name Intuit uses to describe the service it offers that enables you to accept credit cards or bank transfers from your customers and email invoices that contain a Pay Now button so that your customers can pay you online. You might also know this service as GoPayment or Merchant Services.

Reviewing advanced preferences

The Advanced tab of the Account and Settings dialog box enables you to make changes to a variety of QBO settings (see Figure 3-22). Choose Gear⇨ Account and Settings⇨ Advanced to view and update these settings:

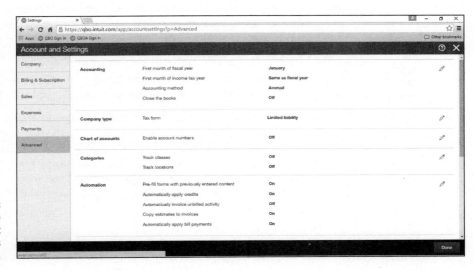

FIGURE 3-22:
The Advanced tab of the Account and Settings dialog box.

>> In the Accounting group, you can control fiscal year settings and the accounting method your company uses (cash or accrual).

>> Use the Company Type group to establish the legal organization of your company.

>> In the Chart of Accounts group, you can turn on account numbers — something most accountants prefer you do.

>> Depending on the version of QBO you use, you can use the Categories section to opt to track information using classes, locations, or both. You also can opt to have QBO warn you if you don't assign a class to a transaction, and you can opt to assign classes individually to each line of a transaction or assign one class to the entire transaction. For locations, you can choose from seven different labels; one of these choices might better describe your intended use of the Location category.

>> In the Automation group, you can control some of QBO's automated behavior. For example, if you don't want QBO to prefill new forms with information from forms you entered previously, feel free to turn that setting off.

>> In the Time Tracking section, you can control the appearance of timesheets. For example, you can opt to add a service field to timesheets so that you can

select services performed for each time entry. By default, QBO includes a customer field on timesheets so that you can optionally charge work performed to a customer.

>> Use the Currency section to turn on multicurrency tracking and to set your company's Home Currency. If you change the home currency symbol, QBO changes the symbol for future transactions; existing transactions will still be calculated at the original currency value. For more information about Multicurrency and Home Currency, see the section "Working with Multiple Currencies" later in this chapter.

WARNING

Turning on multicurrency eliminates your ability to change your home currency. Further, you can't turn multicurrency off after you turn it on.

>> In the Other Preferences group, you can make changes to a variety of settings, such as date and number formats, whether QBO warns you if you reuse a check number or bill number you used previously, and how long QBO should wait before signing you out because you haven't done any work. And, if you prefer to call your customers something other than Customer (such as Client, Patron, or Shopper), you can change the label you use to refer to those who buy stuff from you.

CATEGORIES, CLASSES, AND LOCATIONS . . . OH, MY!

Don't confuse the options you see in the Categories section of the Account and Settings dialog box (QBO classes and locations) with QBO categories. The QBO Category feature is entirely separate from the class and location features shown in the Categories section of the Account and Settings dialog box.

If you turn on the Class and Location options shown here in the Account and Settings dialog box, you can then assign classes and locations to transactions to help you further break down financial data beyond the account level. To create classes and locations, first enable them in the Account and Settings dialog box. Then choose Gear ⇨ All Lists. Then click Classes to create new classes and click Locations to create new locations.

QBO categories, NOT shown in the Account and Settings dialog box (and no need to turn them on), replace sub-items and are available to users of QBO Plus to help organize item information for reporting purposes; see Chapter 4 for details.

Working with Multiple Currencies

The Plus version of QBO supports using multiple currencies. Typically, you use the Multicurrency feature when you sell products and services to customers or buy products and services from vendors whose base currency is different from your home currency. If you don't need to record transactions in multiple currencies, don't turn on this feature because you can't turn it off again.

Also be aware that the multicurrency feature in QBO doesn't support customer- or currency-specific pricing. If you need either of those features, you need to use QuickBooks desktop.

Because you can assign only one currency to each account, customer, or vendor, you need to add new asset and liability accounts, customers, and vendors for each different currency that you will use in transactions; as you create these new elements in QBO, you assign to them the currency you want to use. Be aware that, once you've posted a transaction to an account, a vendor, or a customer, you cannot change the currency of the account, vendor, or customer.

REMEMBER

Income and expense accounts continue to use your home currency — the currency of the country where your business is physically located.

So, if you've decided to use the Multicurrency feature, do these things in the order listed:

1. Turn on the Multicurrency feature.

2. Set up the currencies you intend to use.

3. Add customers, vendors, and necessary asset and liability accounts for each currency you expect to use. Note that QBO automatically creates Accounts Receivable and Accounts Payable accounts in the foreign currency after you create one foreign sales and one foreign purchasing transaction, so you don't need to set up those accounts.

4. Enter transactions.

WARNING

DO I NEED THE MULTICURRENCY FEATURE?

You need the Multicurrency feature *only if* you work with customers or vendors whose base currency is different from your own base currency. Suppose that your home country does not work in U.S. dollars but you only buy and sell using your home country's currency. In this case, you work in a single currency and you don't need the Multicurrency feature. Instead, you need to use the International version of QBO and set your home currency to the proper denomination — and you'll find steps to set your home currency in the section "Turning on the Multicurrency feature."

If you turn on the Multicurrency feature, you cannot change your home currency.

How the Multicurrency feature changes QBO

After you turn on the Multicurrency feature, you will see new fields in QBO. Specifically, you'll see changes on these screens:

>> When you open the Gear menu, you'll see the Currencies option at the bottom of the Lists column. You use the Currencies list to establish the foreign currency you want to use, along with the exchange rate. I'll describe using this option after I show you how to turn on the Multicurrency feature.

>> When you view the Chart of Accounts, you'll find a Currency column that shows the currency assigned to each account. You'll also find a new account — an Other Expense account called Exchange Gain or Loss.

>> When you view Bank and Credit Card registers, the currency of each transaction appears in brackets in the Payment, Deposit, Sales Tax, and Balance Due columns.

>> Sales and purchase forms use both your home currency and the foreign currency; QBO does all the conversions for you on the screen.

>> On QuickBooks reports, you find that QBO converts all foreign currency amounts to home currency amounts, automatically reflecting exchange rate changes.

Turning On the Multicurrency feature

You can change your home currency from the same place that you enable the Multicurrency feature. Follow these steps:

WARNING

Once you turn on the Multicurrency feature, you cannot change your home currency.

1. **Click Gear ⇨ Account and Settings.**

   QBO displays the Account and Settings dialog box.

2. **Click Advanced.**

3. **Scroll down to the Currency section.**

4. **Set your home currency by clicking the Home Currency list box.**

   Choose the currency of your country. If you're not in the United States, don't set the United States as your home currency.

5. **Select Multicurrency (see Figure 3-23).**

   QBO warns you that, once you turn on the Multicurrency feature:

   a) You can't turn it off, and

   b) You can't change your home currency.

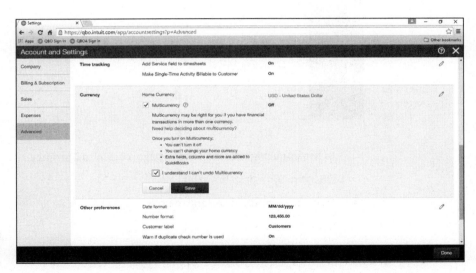

FIGURE 3-23:
Turning on Multicurrency.

6. **Select I Understand I Can't Undo Multicurrency.**

7. **Click Save.**

8. **Click Done.**

REMEMBER

You can't turn off the Multicurrency feature because it affects many accounts and balances in QBO.

Setting up currencies

After enabling the multicurrency option, you'll find an option to display the Currencies list if you click the Gear button; the Currencies option appears at the bottom of the Lists section on the Gear menu. Follow these steps to set up the currencies you need to use:

1. **Click Gear ⇨ Currencies.**

QBO displays the Currencies page (see Figure 3-24).

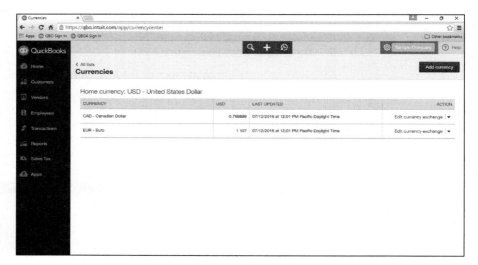

FIGURE 3-24:
The Currencies
page.

2. **In the upper right corner of the page, click Add Currency.**

QBO displays a drop-down list.

3. **Select a currency you want to use.**

4. **Click Add.**

QBO redisplays the Currencies page with the new currency added.

QBO always records exchange rates, shown on the Currencies page, as the number of home currency units needed to equal one foreign currency unit. QBO downloads exchange rates every four hours from Wall Street On Demand, but you can, if you want, provide your own exchange rate. Click the Edit Currency Exchange link beside the rate you want to edit and supply the rate you want to use.

Using multiple currencies

Let's examine, briefly, the effects of creating an invoice that uses multiple currencies; creating a purchase transaction for a foreign vendor works in a similar fashion.

Suppose that you have a customer whose base currency is the Canadian dollar and your home currency is the U.S. dollar. So, in this example, when I refer to the "foreign currency," I mean the Canadian dollar.

REMEMBER

At this time, QBO doesn't support letting either your employees or contractors record time entries (using either the Weekly Timesheet or the Single Time Activity) associated with a foreign currency customer.

First, create the customer: Click Customers ⇨ New Customer. Fill in the window as you usually would with the following addition: Click the Payment and Billing tab. Then open the This Customer Pays Me With list and select the customer's currency. In Figure 3-25, my customer, uninspiringly named Foreign Currency, uses the Canadian Dollar.

FIGURE 3-25:
Assigning a foreign currency to a new customer.

REMEMBER

You'll find a similar setting available when you create a new vendor.

Once you save the customer, if you look at the Customer list page, you'll see the customer listed, and, in the Currency column, you'll see the foreign currency. Your home currency customers display your home currency.

Next, in the Invoice window, select your "foreign transaction" customer. QBO automatically displays, below the customer's name, the two currencies (first the foreign currency and then your home currency) associated with the transaction (see Figure 3-26).

Foreign currency followed by domestic currency

FIGURE 3-26:
Creating an invoice for a customer who uses a foreign currency.

Once you add products or services to the invoice, as shown in Figure 3-27, the amounts for each line appear in the foreign currency, and totals appear in both currencies. The Balance Due on the transaction appears in the foreign (customer's) currency so that your customer knows how much to pay.

REMEMBER

Saving your first sales or purchase document for a customer or vendor using a foreign currency makes QBO automatically establish a foreign currency–related Accounts Receivable and Accounts Payable account.

Reports in QBO show values in your home currency. Figure 3-28 shows the A/R Aging Summary; the customer who uses a foreign currency is the third customer on the list.

FIGURE 3-27:
An invoice for a foreign currency customer shows values in both the home and foreign currency.

Totals appear in both currencies.

The Balance Due appears in the customer's currency.

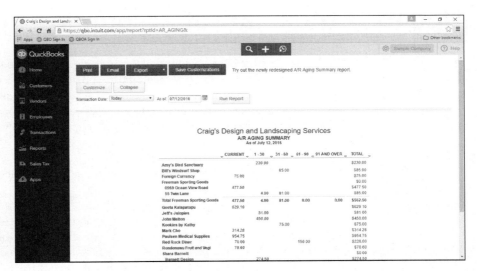

FIGURE 3-28:
Values on reports appear in your home currency.

Figure 3-29, the Balance Sheet, shows the multiple Accounts Receivable accounts QBO uses when you've enabled the Multicurrency feature and created a sales transaction using a foreign currency; the values on the report appear in the home currency.

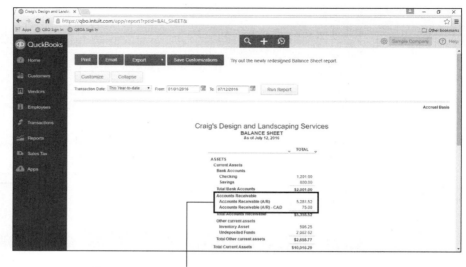

FIGURE 3-29:
QBO establishes
separate
Accounts
Receivable
accounts for
transactions
involving foreign
currency
customers.

Multiple Accounts Receivable accounts
when you use the Multicurrency feature

Updating the Chart of Accounts

On the Advanced tab of the Account and Settings dialog box, you see that you can turn on account numbers for the accounts in your Chart of Accounts. To make changes to those accounts, choose Gear ➪ Chart of Accounts or Transactions ➪ Chart of Accounts. On the page that appears (see Figure 3-30), you can perform a variety of functions. For example, you can print a list of your accounts if you click the Run Report button, which is at the top of the page.

REMEMBER

If you've enabled the Multicurrency feature, you'll see a Currency column on the Chart of Accounts page.

For individual accounts, you can perform a few actions. Balance Sheet accounts have registers; you can view the transactions in the account by clicking View Register in the Action column. You can identify Balance Sheet accounts by looking in the Type column. Balance Sheet accounts display one of the following account types:

>> Bank

>> Accounts Receivable

>> Other Current Assets

>> Fixed Assets

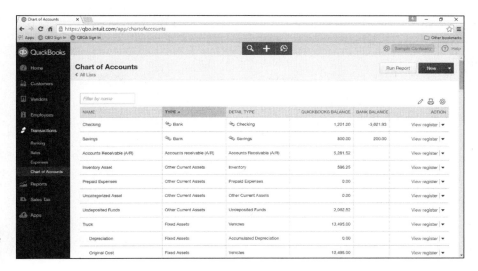

FIGURE 3-30:
The Chart of
Accounts page.

» Other Assets

» Credit Card

» Other Current Liabilities

» Long Term Liabilities

» Accounts Payable

» Equity

For other accounts — the ones without registers — you can run reports for the account by clicking Run Report in the Action column.

You also can edit any account and you can delete an account you have not yet used. Click the down arrow in the Action column (at the right edge of the account's row) to display a short menu of the actions you can take for the account.

WARNING

If you edit an account, don't change its type unless you're sure you know what you're doing. Consider consulting your accountant before you make a change to an account's category or detail type. You also can identify if the account is actually a sub-account of another account.

If you decide to turn on account numbers, you can click the Batch Edit icon (it looks like a pencil and appears just above the Action column). The appearance of the Chart of Accounts page changes to enable you to quickly assign account numbers (see Figure 3-31).

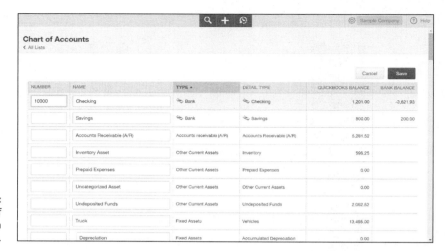

FIGURE 3-31:
The Chart of Accounts page in Batch Edit mode.

A FEW NOTES ON PAYING OWNERS

Many small business owners wonder about the accounts they should use to pay themselves. Owners and partners typically are not considered employees and therefore are not paid through payroll. To pay an owner or partner, use the Chart of Accounts page to set up a Draw account (Owner's Draw, Partner's Draw, whatever is appropriate; if you have multiple partners, set up draw accounts for each partner) and use it to pay owners. The Draw account is an equity account. Similarly, owners and partners sometimes put their own money into the business; to account for these contributions, set up equity accounts (again, one for each owner or partner) called Owner's Contribution, Partner's Contribution — again, whatever is appropriate.

Note that you use the Draw account not only to pay the owner but also to account for personal items an owner might buy using the business's money. You record the withdrawals using the appropriate bank account and the appropriate Draw account. Note that these transactions don't show up on your Profit and Loss report because they are *not* business expenses. To find out the total amount paid to an owner, run a report for the Draw account.

And, finally, housekeeping about the Draw and Contribution accounts: At the end of your fiscal year, you need to enter a journal entry, dated on the last day of your fiscal year, that moves the dollar amounts from the appropriate Draw or Contribution account to Retained Earnings — another equity account. If I just lost you, talk to your accountant about how to handle closing the year.

REMEMBER

If you've enabled the Multicurrency feature, the Chart of Accounts page in Batch Edit mode also contains a Currency column.

Type a number for each account; when you finish entering all the numbers, click the Save button at the top of the page. QBO displays the account number as part of the account name on the Chart of Accounts screen.

TIP

You also can establish budgets for accounts; see Appendix A for details.

The screens you use to add or edit an account look almost exactly alike. Because you'll need a Bank account for your company, we'll examine the screens as you create your Bank account. If you plan to connect your QBO Bank account to its corresponding account at a financial institution, don't follow these steps; instead, see Chapter 8 for details on creating the account. And, if you decide now that you don't want to connect and later you decide that you *do* want to connect, all isn't lost. Once again, see Chapter 8 for details on merging the Bank account you create here with an online version.

To ensure an accurate bank balance in QBO, reconcile your bank account before you set up the account in QBO. Follow these steps to create an account in QBO:

1. **Click the New button on the Chart of Accounts page to open the Account dialog box (see Figure 3-32).**

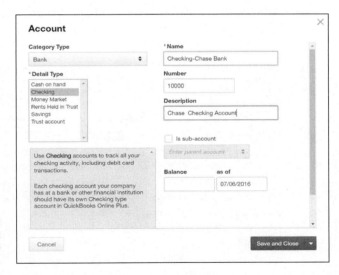

FIGURE 3-32:
The dialog box you use to create an account.

2. **Open the Category Type list and choose Bank.**

3. **Click the entry in the Detail Type list that most closely matches the type of account you want to add.**

   QBO uses the choice you make in the Detail Type list as the account's name, but you can change the name to something else. For my example, I chose Checking, changed the account name to Checking-Chase Bank, and supplied Chase Checking account as the description.

4. **If you're using account numbers, supply a number for the new account.**

   You can, optionally, supply a description for the account.

REMEMBER

   If you've enabled the Multicurrency feature, the dialog box you use to create a bank account — or any type of asset or liability account except an Accounts Receivable (A/R) or Accounts Payable (A/P) account — also contains a list box from which you select the currency for the account. QBO automatically creates currency-related A/R and A/P accounts when you create transactions for foreign customers and vendors.

5. **You can enter your account's balance as it appears on the last statement you received from your bank.**

   My example company is just starting out and has no opening balance yet, so I'm not entering an opening balance. See the sidebar, "Proper account balances," for details on what to do here.

6. **Click Save.**

   QBO redisplays the Chart of Accounts page and your new account appears in the list.

PROPER ACCOUNT BALANCES

If you've been in business for a while, transactions have occurred. To ensure accurate account balances, you need to account for these transactions in QBO.

To make sure that you start your work in QBO with correct account balances, begin by deciding on the first date you intend to use QBO. This date determines the "as of" date of historical information you need to collect. Try to start using QBO on the first day of an accounting period — either on the first day of your company's fiscal year or on the first day of a month. If you start using QBO Payroll (QBOP) on January 1, you do not need to enter any historical payroll information.

Although it might seem like more work, I suggest that the easiest way for you to ensure proper account balances is to enter $0 as your Bank account's opening balance in Step 5 in the preceding steps for creating a Bank account. Then enter all transactions that have occurred so far this year.

If you've been in business since before the beginning of the year, enter $0 for your Bank account's balance and ask your accountant for opening amounts for your Balance Sheet accounts as of December 31 of last year. Enter these amounts by entering a journal entry: Click the plus sign (+) icon at the top of QBO and choose Journal Entry from the Other column in the list.

The transactions you enter for the current year will ultimately affect your bank balance (for example, a customer eventually pays an invoice), and, when you finish entering the transactions, your QBO Bank account balance should agree with the one your financial institution has. So, I suggest that you enter transactions for *all* customer invoices (and corresponding payments customers made) and *all* vendor bills (and corresponding payments you made) during the current year.

If you choose to ignore my suggestion and enter an opening amount for your bank balance in Step 5, you need to then enter all transactions that have affected your bank account *since the last statement*.

QBO posts balances you enter while creating an account to the Opening Balance Equity (Equity) account, an account created by QuickBooks. Most accountants don't like this account and will want to create journal entries to move the balances to proper accounts.

That second approach sounds like a lot less work and, if you don't use payroll, or you make payroll payments from a separate bank account, you can safely ignore my suggestion and enter an opening amount for your bank balance in Step 5 and then enter outstanding customer invoices and unpaid vendor bills.

But, if your company does prepare payroll, has prepared one or more payrolls so far this year, and you use only one bank account, I strongly urge you to take my suggestion because you need accurate *annual* information to successfully manage payroll. The easiest way to ensure that you have accurate annual payroll information is to enter all payrolls you've completed this year so far — and these payrolls will affect your Bank account, so, entering a Bank account balance in Step 5 will lead you into trouble. Yes, you can try to do a mix of both approaches and subtract payroll amounts from the bank balance you previously entered in Step 5, but that approach is seriously error-prone.

If you use one bank account for everything and you feel that entering all transactions that have occurred so far this year is just too much work, I suggest that you enter your bank account's balance as of your last bank statement, enter outstanding invoices and unpaid vendor bills, and then contact Intuit technical support for help entering historical payroll information.

Taking Advantage of QuickBooks Labs

You might be wondering about the QuickBooks Labs option on the Gear menu (you can see it if you refer back to Figure 3-13). Intuit calls QuickBooks Labs its "high-tech playground." If you're adventurous, check out the lab and turn on experimental features to see how they work.

REMEMBER

In most cases, features you find in QuickBooks Labs eventually become part of QBO.

For example, when I wrote this, the Import Style feature discussed earlier in this chapter was a QuickBooks Labs feature and therefore didn't appear by default. Here's how you turn on a QuickBooks Lab feature:

1. **Log in to your company.**

2. **Click Gear ➪ QuickBooks Labs.**

   The QuickBooks Labs window appears (see Figure 3-33).

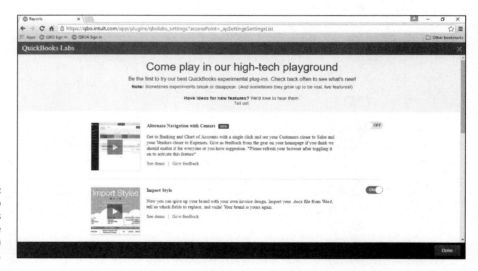

FIGURE 3-33:
Use this page to turn on features not yet available by default in QuickBooks.

TIP

Note that you can provide feedback on QuickBooks Labs features. The more positive feedback a feature receives, the more likely that feature will become a standard part of QBO.

3. **Check out the features available and, for any you want to try, click the Off button.**

   The Off button changes to the On button.

4. **When you finish turning on features, click Done.**

   Your QBO company reappears, with the features you selected enabled.

REMEMBER

You might need to refresh the browser page to see the new features you choose to make available. Click your browser's Refresh button or press F5 on your keyboard.

Signing In to and Out of QBO

If you followed the process in this chapter to sign up for QBO, you're currently signed in to QBO. But, obviously, you don't sign up for QBO every time you want to use it. And then, of course, there's the question of how you sign out of QBO each time you finish using it.

To sign out of QBO, click the Gear button and, from the menu shown earlier in Figure 3-13, click Sign Out (at the bottom of the list of commands under Your Company).

To sign in to QBO in the future, visit qbo.intuit.com (you get redirected to a long web address you don't need to type) and supply your username and password (see Figure 3-34). I suggest you bookmark this page to make signing in easy.

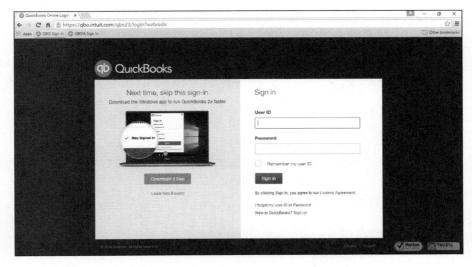

FIGURE 3-34: Use this page to sign in to your QBO company.

Chapter **4**

Managing List Information

L ike its cousin the QuickBooks desktop product, QBO relies on lists to help you store background information that you'll use again and again. For the most part, you enter information about the people with whom you do business — customers, vendors, and employees — and the stuff you sell or buy. But you also store other background information in lists, such as the accounts your company uses and the payment methods your company accepts. In this chapter, you'll find information that all QBO users need about setting up customers and vendors. And, QBO users will be interested in the portions of this chapter that focus on setting up items you sell or buy. Finally, at the end of the chapter, you learn where to find other lists you might need.

Importing People into a List

If you've been running your business for a while, you probably have lists of customers and vendors. If they're stored electronically, you might be able to save yourself some setup time in QBO if you import them. And, because most people tend to worry about accounting "later," after they've been running the business for a bit, I'll start this chapter by assuming you do have lists stored in some electronic form. In the Adding New People to a List section of this chapter, I'll show you how to manually set up a customer or vendor. That will be important to those of you who don't have anything already in electronic form, and to all of you as your business grows and you add new customers and vendors.

If you've been using the QuickBooks desktop product, you can import your list information from it into your free trial of QBO, which can help you become accustomed to QBO using list information you already recognize.

REMEMBER

Importing list information is not the same as importing a QuickBooks desktop company. For details on importing a company, see Chapter 12 in Part 3.

Even if you haven't been using QuickBooks desktop, be aware that you can import list information from an Excel file or a CSV file. CSV stands for *comma-separated values*; most programs, including QuickBooks desktop, enable you to export information to a CSV format. Coincidentally, Excel can open and save CSV files. So you can open a CSV file, edit it in Excel as needed, and then resave it as a CSV file. Or, after editing, you can save the file as an Excel 97-2003 workbook.

TIP

You can create a CSV file by saving an Excel file in CSV format. With the Excel file open, choose File⇨Save As. In the Save As dialog box, change the Save As Type list below the filename from Excel Workbook to CSV (Comma Delimited).

You use the same process to import customers or vendors from a QuickBooks desktop product. QBO is more obvious about encouraging you to import customers, as you can see from Figure 4-1, which appears when you click Customers in the Navigation bar before you've added any customers. Because the screens for importing customers or vendors are the same *after* the first screen, I'll show you how to import vendors (QBO is less obvious in its encouragement to import vendors).

Follow these steps:

To successfully import information into QBO from a CSV file or an Excel workbook, the information must conform to a specific format. And, luckily, QBO gives you the option to download a sample file in Excel format so that you can view the required format for importing list information; you can use this sample as a guideline for setting up the data in your own file.

TECHNICAL STUFF

The steps that follow assume you have installed Excel on your computer. If you don't own a copy of Excel, you can use Excel Mobile, the free app from Microsoft. To make editing changes to your files in Excel Mobile, you need to sign in to Excel Mobile with your Microsoft account email and password.

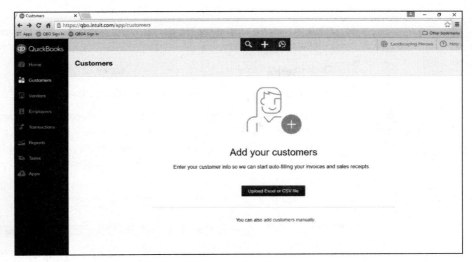

FIGURE 4-1:
QBO is very
encouraging
when it comes to
importing
customers.

To download and view the sample file for vendors, follow these steps:

1. **Click Vendors in the Navigation bar to display the Vendors page (see Figure 4-2).**

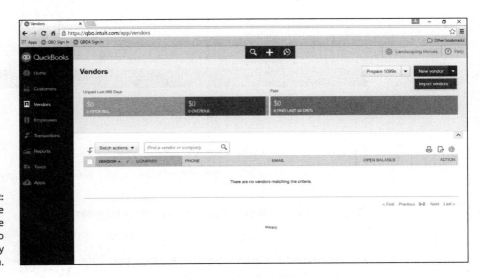

FIGURE 4-2:
Start from the
appropriate page
when you want to
create a list entry
for a new person.

2. **Click the down arrow beside the New Vendor button in the upper-right corner of the screen.**

3. **Click Import Vendors.**

   QBO displays the Import Vendors page (see Figure 4-3).

REMEMBER

   If you're working on importing customers, skip Steps 1 to 3 and instead, click Customers in the Navigation bar and then click the Upload Excel or CSV File button to have QBO display the Import Customers page. From this point on, the steps to import customers and vendors are identical.

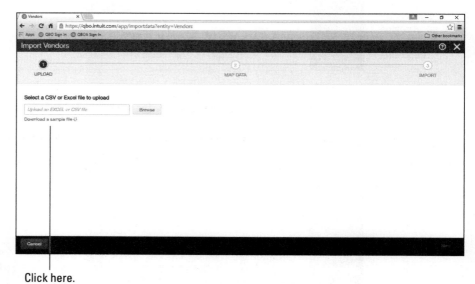

FIGURE 4-3:
The Import
Vendors page.

Click here.

4. **Click the Download a sample file link.**

   Once you click the link, QBO downloads the sample file and displays a button in the Windows taskbar for it.

5. **Click the sample file's button in the Windows taskbar.**

   The sample file opens in Excel (see Figure 4-4).

6. **Examine the file's content by scrolling to the right to see the information stored in each column.**

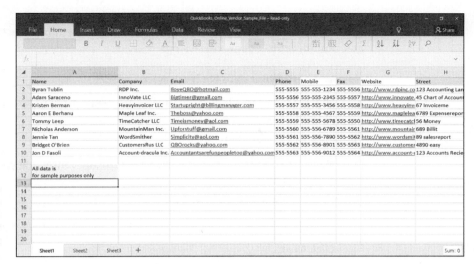

FIGURE 4-4:
A file showing the
format you need
to successfully
import list
information.

7. **Create your own file, modeling it on the sample file.**

   If you've been using QuickBooks desktop, you can export lists to CSV or Excel files; see QuickBooks desktop Help for details.

REMEMBER

   You'll find that importing your data works best if you can match the headings in your data file to the ones found in the sample data file. Also, your data file cannot contain more than 1,000 rows or exceed 2MB in size. Don't forget to save your data file as either an Excel 97-2003 workbook or as a CSV (comma-delimited) file.

THE DATA FILE'S LAYOUT IN EXCEL

Excel stores the information in the sample file (and you'll need to store the information in your data file) in a table format, where each row in the Excel file contains all the information about a single vendor or customer (each row is referred to as a *record*), and each column contains the same piece of information for all customers and vendors (each column is referred to as one *field* in a record). For example, in Figure 4-4, all the information about Adam Saraceno appears in Row 3, and all vendor email addresses appear in Column C. Also note that Row 1 contains a label that identifies the type of information found in each column; don't forget to include identifying labels in your data file.

After you have created an Excel file or a CSV file containing your list information, you can import it. Follow these steps:

1. **Make sure your data file is not open.**

2. **Follow Steps 1 to 3 to display the Import Vendors page shown previously in Figure 4-4.**

3. **Click the Browse button.**

4. **Navigate to the folder where you saved the file containing your list information.**

5. **Select the file and choose Open.**

   QBO updates the Import Vendors page with the name of the file you selected.

6. **Click Next.**

   QBO uploads your file and displays the Map Data screen shown in Figure 4-5.

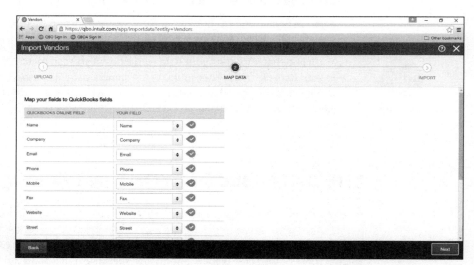

FIGURE 4-5:
Match the fields
in your data file
to QBO fields.

7. **Make sure that the fields in your data file correctly match fields in QBO.**

   As needed, open the list box beside each QBO field name and match it to the labels in your data file.

8. **Click Next.**

   QBO displays the records it has identified (see Figure 4-6).

FIGURE 4-6:
The records QBO
will import from
your data file.

9. **Review the records QBO proposes to import to make sure the information is correct.**

You can make changes to the information in any field by clicking that field and typing. You also can uncheck any row to avoid importing the information in that row to QBO.

10. **When you are satisfied that the information is correct, click the Import button in the lower right corner of the screen.**

QBO imports the information and displays a message that identifies the number of records imported. The list you imported appears on the appropriate page (see Figure 4-7).

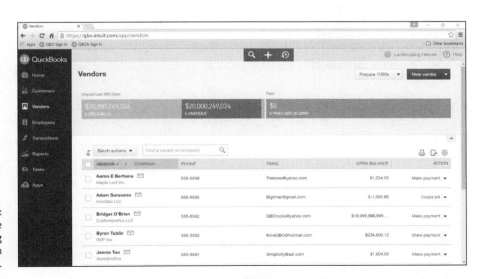

FIGURE 4-7:
The Vendors page
after importing
vendors using an
Excel file.

Adding New People to a List

You use the Customers, Vendors, and Employees links in the Navigation bar to work with, well, your customers, vendors, and employees. In this section, I'll show you how to set up a new customer. The steps are the same to set up a new vendor or a new employee; you just start by clicking the appropriate link in the Navigation bar. Follow these steps to set up a new customer in QBO:

REMEMBER

If you have determined that your company needs to use the Multicurrency feature, turn it on before you start creating people so that you have available the fields you need to establish each person's currency. See Chapter 3 for details on the Multi-currency feature.

1. **Click Customers in the Navigation bar to display the Customers page shown in Figure 4-8.**

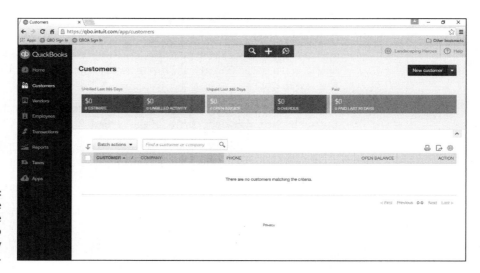

FIGURE 4-8:
Start from the appropriate page when you want to create a list entry for a new person.

TIP

If you see the page shown earlier in Figure 4-1, you can, for Step 2, click the You Can Also Add Customers Manually link at the bottom of the page.

2. **Click the New Customer button in the upper right corner of the page.**

QBO displays the Customer Information dialog box shown in Figure 4-9.

3. **Type the requested information.**

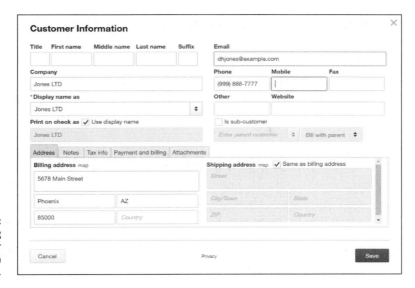

FIGURE 4-9:
Use this dialog
box to enter
information for a
new customer.

4. **Click Save.**

   QBO saves the customer and displays a page showing information specific to that customer, such as the customer's transactions. If you click Customers in the Navigation bar, the Customers list page reappears, and the new customer now appears in the list.

You can make any list entry inactive. Click that entry in the appropriate list, and then click the Action down arrow at the right edge of the list. In the list that opens, click Make Inactive.

TIP

WHAT'S A SUB-CUSTOMER?

Sub-customers are a way for you to create a hierarchy for customers, and you can use sub-customers pretty much any way you want. For example, if you're an architect, sub-customers might represent jobs or projects. If you're an attorney, sub-customers could represent cases.

If you set up sub-customers, you can choose to bill either the parent or the sub-customer. Sub-customers' balances are included in the parent customer's balance. Transactions for sub-customers appear in the sub-customer's register as well as the parent customer's register.

You can create as many sub-customers as you want, but, for any given customer, you can assign sub-customers up to five levels deep, including the parent customer.

Searching Lists for People

You can use the Customers, Vendors, and Employees pages in a variety of ways. From the Customers, Vendors, or Employees pages that list all the people in those categories, you can sort the people in the list, export the list to Excel, and perform actions on a selected group of people on the list.

Working with a particular person

You can select a particular customer, vendor, or employee and view the transactions associated with that person as well as the person's details, and you can attach files to the person. For this section, I'll work with customers.

To search for a particular person, type some characters that match the person or company name in the search box that appears above the list of people (see Figure 4-10).

Type here.

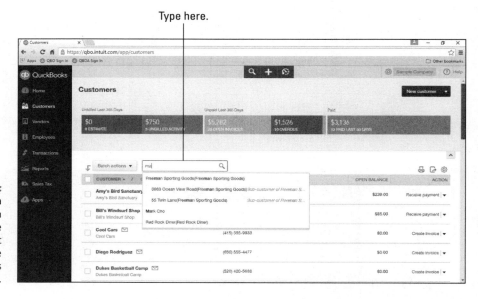

FIGURE 4-10:
To find a particular person on a list, use the search box that appears above the names on the list.

When you select any person from the list, QBO displays the page specifically associated with that person. The page has two tabs; in Figure 4-11, you see the Transaction List tab, and in Figure 4-12, you see the Customer Details tab.

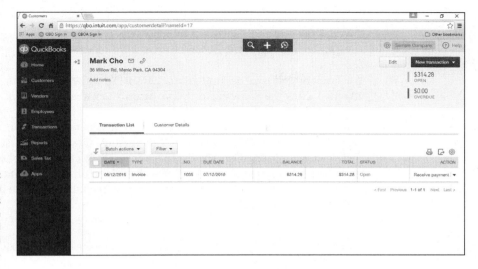

FIGURE 4-11:
The Transaction
List tab shows
transactions in
QBO associated
with the selected
person.

From either tab, you click the Edit button to edit information on the page; you also can click the New Transaction button to add a transaction associated with that person.

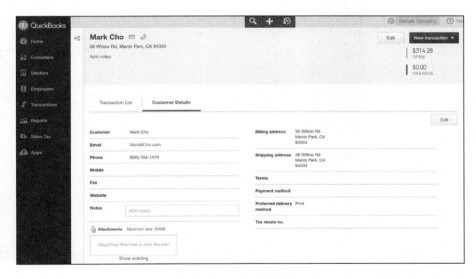

FIGURE 4-12:
The Customer
Details; all detail
tabs show, well,
details for that
person.

From the details page of a person, you can attach files to keep track of important financial information. For example, you can attach a vendor's 1099 document, a customer's contract, or an employee's receipts. You're not limited to text documents; you also can attach photos. Simply drag and drop the item into the Attachments box at the bottom left side of the appropriate details page; if you prefer, you can click the box and a standard Windows Open dialog box appears so that you can navigate to and select the document you want to attach.

The attachment size is limited to 25MB. To view documents you've already attached, click the Show existing link below the Attachments box.

While viewing the Transaction list of a particular person, you can add the Attachments column to the table. Display the person's Transaction List page and then click the Gear button. From the list that appears, click Show More (see Figure 4-13). Show More changes to Show Less and a check box for Attachments appears; click it and the Attachments column appears as part of the table grid. You can identify it as the column heading with a paper clip.

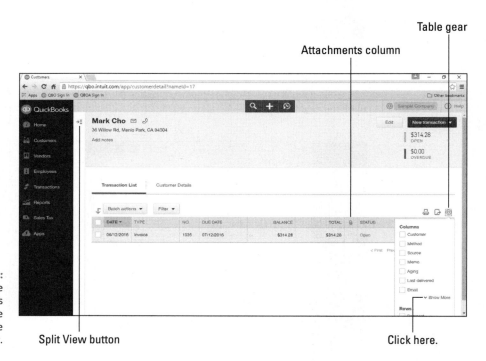

FIGURE 4-13:
Adding the Attachments column to the table on the Transaction List.

Split View button   Click here.

TIP

Displaying the Attachments column for one person displays it in the Transaction List table for all persons in that category.

When you finish working with one person, you can easily switch to another in that list using the list's Split View. You can click the Split View icon, shown earlier in Figure 4-13, to display the people stored in the list (see Figure 4-14).

Close Split View button

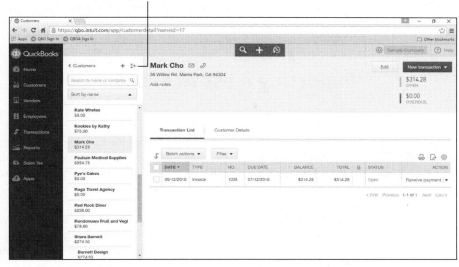

FIGURE 4-14:
Displaying a list's
Split View.

From the Split View, you can scroll down to find a person, or you can type a few letters of the person's name or company name in the search box at the top of the list to find that person in the list. Or, you can sort the list by name or by open balance. Click a person to switch to that person's page.

To add a new person to the list, click the plus (+) symbol at the top of the list to see the dialog box shown earlier in Figure 4-9. To display the Customers page shown earlier in Figure 4-7, click Customers at the top of the Split View list or click Customers in the Navigation bar.

To close Split View, click the Close Split View button (refer to Figure 4-14).

Sorting a list

In addition to sorting in Split View, you can sort the lists on the Customers and Vendors page by name or open balance. By default, QBO sorts the entries on these pages alphabetically by name in ascending order.

To change the sort order for either of these lists, click the Customers or Vendors link in the Navigation bar to display the appropriate page; for this example, I use the Customers page.

Next, click the heading for the column by which you want to sort. If you click the Customer/Company column heading, QBO displays the customers in descending alphabetical order. If you click the Open Balance column heading, QBO sorts the list in Open Balance order, from lowest to highest.

Once you turn on payroll, you can sort the employees that appear in the payroll list alphabetically in ascending or descending order by clicking the Name column heading.

Exporting a list to Excel

You can export a list of your customers or vendors to Excel.

TECHNICAL STUFF

In this section, I assume you have a copy of Excel on your computer; otherwise, downloading your list to an Excel file wouldn't make much sense. If you don't have a copy of Excel on your computer, you can download and use the free mobile version of Excel.

Click the appropriate link in the Navigation bar to display either the Customers page or the Vendors page; I use the Vendors page in this example. At the right edge of the page, just above the list, three buttons appear. Click the middle button, and QBO exports the list to an Excel file; a button for the file appears at the bottom of the screen (see Figure 4-15).

Click here to export the list.

![Vendors page screenshot showing export buttons]

FIGURE 4-15:
Exporting a
vendor list to
Excel.

Click here to open the Excel file.

Click the button at the bottom of the screen, and Excel opens the file. You can edit the file if you click the Enable Editing button in the yellow bar at the top of the window.

REMEMBER

If you're using Excel mobile, you need to sign in using your Microsoft account to edit the file.

Working with a batch of people

When you work with customers or vendors, you can take certain actions simultaneously for a group of people. For example, you can select specific vendors by clicking the check box beside each name and then send the same email to those vendors.

For customers, in addition to sending email, you can send statements to them.

To use one of these actions for a group of people, click the appropriate link in the Navigation bar to display the associated page. For this example, I used the Customers page.

Next, click the check box beside the names you want to include in your action and then click the Batch actions button (see Figure 4-16). Select the action you want to take, and then follow the prompts onscreen to complete the action.

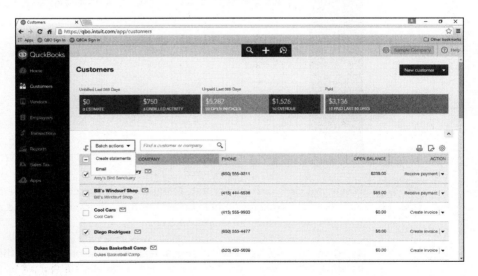

FIGURE 4-16:
Performing an action for several customers.

Changing Settings for People Lists

You can, to some extent, control the appearance of the lists on the Customers page, the Vendors page, and the Employees page. For example, you can opt to show or hide street address, email, and phone number information, and you can opt to include or exclude inactive entries in the list. You also can control the number of entries displayed on each page, as well as adjust those entries' column widths.

Click the appropriate link in the Navigation bar to display the associated page; for this section, I worked on the Vendors page.

To control the information displayed in the list, click the Gear button at the right edge of the page just above the list's labels (see Figure 4-17). Then select or deselect check boxes to display or hide information. Click outside the list when you finish.

Click this gear.

FIGURE 4-17:
Controlling
the information
that appears
in the list.

TIP

When you click outside the list, I suggest that you click in the empty area at the bottom of the Navigation bar (below the Apps link) so that you don't accidentally navigate away from the current page.

To adjust the width of any column, slide the mouse pointer into the row of column heading labels above the list and place it over the right edge of the column you want to adjust. Drag the mouse when the mouse pointer changes to a pair of vertical lines and a pair of horizontal arrows pointing outward, (see Figure 4-18). A vertical bar appears to guide you in resizing the column. Release the mouse button when you're satisfied with the column width.

TIP

QBO remembers column width adjustments you make in registers and on pages like the Customers and Vendors pages, even after you sign out of QBO and then sign back in again.

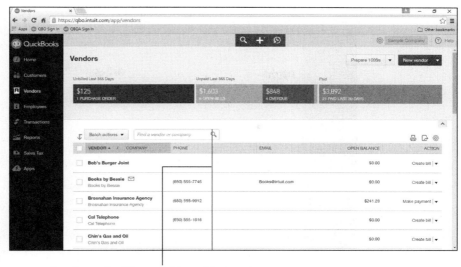

FIGURE 4-18:
Adjusting the
width allotted to
the vendor's
name on the
Vendors page.

Use the vertical line to guide resizing a column.

Working with Products and Services Items

Inventory tracking is available in the QBO Plus edition, and you need to turn on the feature. Click Gear ➪ Account and Settings. In the Account and Settings dialog box, click Sales and, in the Products and Services section, click Track Inventory Quantity On Hand.

REMEMBER

QBO Plus can support inventory tracking capabilities, but, if you're looking for inventory capabilities to support manufacturing, you'll be happier in QuickBooks desktop.

The Products and Services list, shown in Figure 4-19, is the QBO equivalent to the QuickBooks desktop product's Items list.

TAKING ADVANTAGE OF SKUs

You can control whether SKU information appears on the Products and Services list and on transaction forms from the Account and Settings dialog box. Click Gear ➪ Account and Settings ➪ Sales. Click in the Products and Services section and check or uncheck the Show SKU column. Click Save and then click Done. Using a custom form style (see Chapter 3 for information on creating custom forms), you can add the SKU to your invoice form.

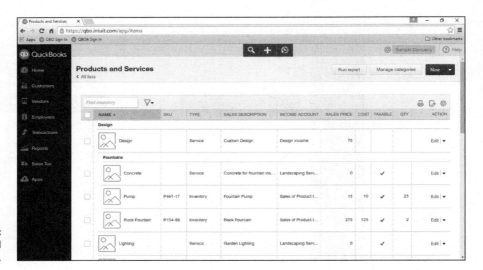

FIGURE 4-19:
The Products and
Services list.

You use the Products and Services list pretty much the same way you use the Customer and Vendor lists; for example, you can search for an item by its name, SKU, or sales description. You can identify the columns you can use to sort the list if you slide your mouse over the column heading; if the mouse pointer changes to a hand, you can click that column to sort the list using the information in that column.

REMEMBER

Enabling the Multicurrency feature, described in Chapter 3, has no effect on inventory item valuations; QBO assesses and reports inventory item values in home currency units, regardless of the currency used by the vendor who sold you the items. For that reason, the Products and Services list shows no distinctions related to currency.

You can import and export items using an Excel or CSV file, the same way you import and export people information. See the sections "Importing People into a List" and "Exporting a list to Excel" earlier in this chapter.

REMEMBER

The importing and exporting processes include the information about the item's taxability.

You also can print a basic report by clicking the Print button on any list page; the Print button appears just above the Action column. And, you can print a more detailed report for a list entry by selecting it and then clicking the Report button.

Establishing categories

Categories replace sub-items for QBO Plus users in all regions except France. You can use categories to organize what you sell and, using various Products and

Services reports, hopefully help you better understand what people are buying from you. Categories do not affect your accounting or your financial reports and you cannot assign categories to transactions.

TIP

Use classes and/or locations to help further catalog transactions and financial information. See Chapter 3 for more information.

You can create new categories as you create items or, if you prefer, you can click the Manage Categories button and create categories so that they are available as you create items. Yes, you can do both.

From the Product Categories page shown in Figure 4-20, you can click the New Category button to add a category; the Category Information panel appears on the right side of your screen and you simply supply the category name. If the category is a sub-category of an existing category, check the Is a Sub-Category box and select the name of the existing category. Click Save at the bottom of the panel to set up your category.

TIP

You can create sub-categories up to four levels deep. That is, you can create a category called Clothing and then create a sub-category of Clothing called Shoes. For the Shoes sub-category, you can create a sub-category called Women's Shoes, and, for the Women's Shoes category, you can create one last sub-category called Sneakers. You can't create a sub-category for Sneakers, but you can create another sub-category for Women's Shoes called Dress Shoes.

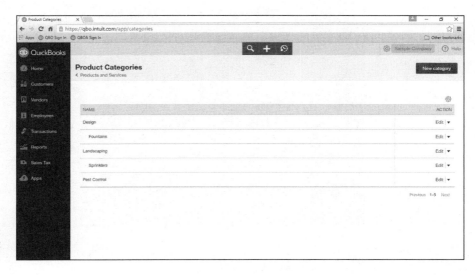

FIGURE 4-20:
The Product
Categories page.

If necessary, you can edit an existing category; click the Edit link beside the category you want to modify in the table on the Product Categories page. Once again, the Category Information panel appears, displaying the category's current information. Make changes and click Save; alternatively, you can click Remove to remove a category.

REMEMBER

The effect on items of removing a category depends on whether you remove a sub-category or a category. If you remove a sub-category, QBO moves the items assigned to it up one level. If you remove a category (with no sub-categories) QBO reclassifies the items as uncategorized.

Adding service and non-inventory items

You can create inventory, non-inventory, and service items, and you can edit batches of items to change their type; I'll show you how to change an item's type after I show you how to add an item to the list.

1. **To display the Products and Services list, click Gear⇨Products and Services.**

2. **Click the New button.**

QBO displays the Product/Service Information panel on the right side of your screen (see Figure 4-21) where you select whether you're creating an inventory item, a non-inventory item, or a service.

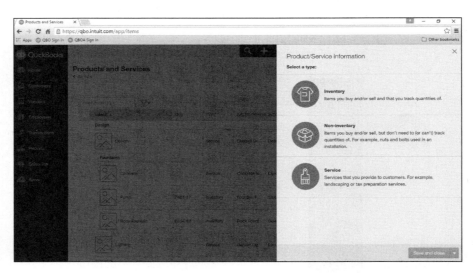

FIGURE 4-21:
Select a type of item to create.

3. **Click a type to select it.**

For this example, I chose Non-inventory item. You create a service item the same way you create a non-inventory item, supplying the same kind of information shown in these steps. See the next section, "Creating an Inventory Item," for details on the additional information you supply when creating an inventory item.

QBO then displays the panel for the type of item you chose; Figure 4-22 shows the Non-inventory panel.

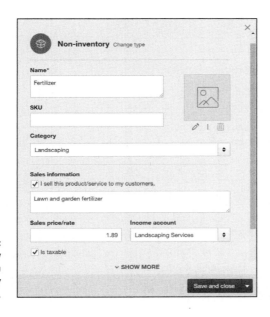

FIGURE 4-22:
Use this window
to create a
non-inventory
item.

4. **Supply a name for the item and, if appropriate, a stock keeping unit (SKU).**

    You also can select the item's category.

TIP

    You can upload a picture of the item by clicking the Upload button and navigating to the location where you store the picture.

5. **In the Sales Information section, you can:**

    a. **Select the I Sell This Product/Service to My Customers check box and supply a default description,**

    b. **Supply the price you charge when you sell this item,**

    c. **Select the income account associated with the item, and**

    d. **Select the Is Taxable check box if appropriate.**

    QBO uses this information when you select this item on sales transactions.

6. **Click the Show More link at the bottom of the window to display the Purchasing Information section (see Figure 4-23).**

7. **If appropriate, place a check in the I Purchase This Product/Service From a Vendor check box. Then, supply a default description, the cost you pay when you purchase the item, and the expense account associated with the item.**

   QBO uses this information when you select this item on expense transactions.

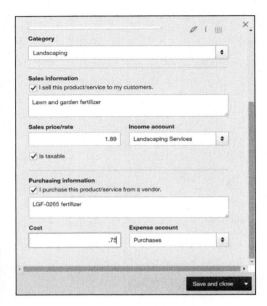

FIGURE 4-23:
Add purchasing
information for
the item.

8. **Click Save and Close.**

   QBO saves the item and redisplays the Products and Services list; the new item appears in the list.

Creating an inventory item

Creating an inventory item has a few additional types of information you need to supply. As you can see in Figure 4-24, in addition to the other information you supply when you create a service or non-inventory item, for an inventory item you supply quantity on hand information as well as the inventory asset account that tracks your inventory items.

Supply the quantity you have on hand and the date on which you determined the quantity on hand. Remember, before you can sell an item, you must own some of it. If you don't own any at the time you create the item, you'll probably buy some of it using an expense transaction, and that will update your quantities for you.

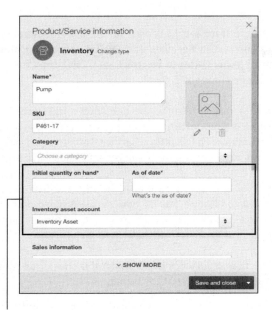

FIGURE 4-24:
Supply quantity
on hand and
inventory asset
account
information for
inventory items.

Supply this additional information.

Changing item types

You can change a service or non-inventory item's type individually or you can select several items and change their item types simultaneously.

TYPES OF CHANGES YOU CAN MAKE

Be aware that you can change item types with some limitations. Specifically, you cannot change Inventory items to any other item types. You can make the following types of changes:

- Non-inventory and Service items to Inventory items,

- Service items to Non-inventory items or Inventory items, and

- Non-inventory items to Service items

When changing item types, you change several items at one time only if you are changing Non-inventory items to Service items or Service items to Non-inventory items. If you need to change either a Service item or a Non-inventory item to an Inventory item, you can make the change only one item at a time.

To change any single item's type, edit that item by clicking Edit in the Action column of the Products and Services list; QBO displays the item in the Product/Service information panel (refer to Figure 4-21). Click the Change Type link at the top of the panel above the item's name.

QBO displays a panel very similar to the one shown in Figure 4-20; the only difference you'll notice is that current item type contains a check. Click the new item type, and QBO redisplays the Product/Service Information panel using the new item type. Make any other necessary changes and click Save and Close.

Changing the type of a single item using the method just described works well when you only need to change one or two items. But, when you need to change multiple items, use a different approach to save time when changing items of the same type to a different type; follow these two steps:

1. **On the Products and Services page, select the check box that appears to the left of each item you want to change.**

REMEMBER

Make sure that you select either service items or non-inventory items, but not both.

QBO displays two buttons above the table of items (see Figure 4-25).

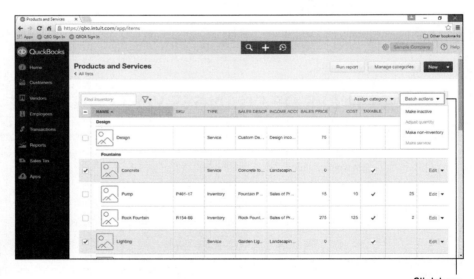

FIGURE 4-25:
Changing the type of multiple items simultaneously.

Click here.

2. **Click the Batch Actions button and select the new type for the selected items.**

QBO whirs a bit and then redisplays the Products and Services list, showing the new item types for the items you selected in Step 1.

TIP

Note the Assign Category button at the top of the Products and Services list; this button appears when you select multiple items, and you can use it to simultaneously assign the same category to multiple items.

Adjusting inventory item information

On occasion, you might need to make adjustments to inventory item information. Specifically, you might need to adjust inventory item quantities on hand or starting values.

TIP

You can edit any item to change descriptive information, such as its name or description; just click the Edit link in the Action column beside its name on the Products and Services page to view the item's information in the panel shown previously in Figures 4-22, 4-23, and 4-24. In this section, I'm talking about adjusting inventory item information, which encompasses more than editing descriptive information.

Adjusting inventory quantities

You might discover, particularly after physically counting inventory, that you have a different number of an inventory item than reported in QBO. In this case, you need to adjust the quantity in QBO to match what you actually have in stock.

REMEMBER

Remember to use the Physical Inventory Worksheet report in QBO to record item quantities on hand as you count inventory. The report information can help you determine the adjustments you need to make. See Chapter 10 for details on working with QBO reports.

To create an adjustment for a just a few inventory items, follow these steps:

1. **Click the Create menu (+ at the top of the QBO window) and choose Inventory Qty Adjustment (see Figure 4-26).**

REMEMBER

Don't forget that the Create menu plus sign changes to an X when the menu is open.

QBO displays the Inventory Quantity Adjustment window (see Figure 4-27).

2. **If necessary, change the adjustment date and the Inventory Adjustment Account.**

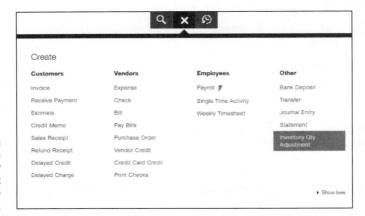

FIGURE 4-26:
Starting an
inventory
item adjustment
for a single
inventory item.

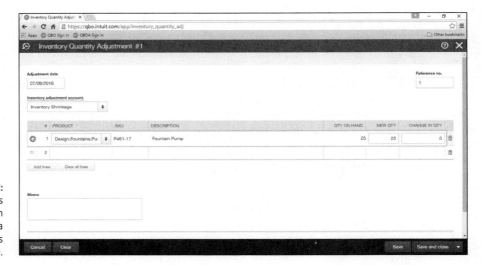

FIGURE 4-27:
You can use this
window when
you have just a
few adjustments
to make.

3. In the table, click the Product field, click the drop-down arrow that appears, and select an inventory item.

QBO fills the inventory item's SKU, description, and quantity on hand. QBO also suggests the Qty On Hand value for the New Qty value.

REMEMBER

If you've enabled class and location tracking, you can supply information for those fields as you complete the Inventory Quantity Adjustment window.

4. Enter either a new quantity or a change in quantity.

Suppose that the Qty On Hand field indicates you own 25 of your item and you need to reduce the quantity you own by 5. You do either of the following:

a. Enter 20 in the New Qty field, or

b. Enter -5 in the Change in Qty field.

5. **Repeat Steps 3 and 4 for each inventory item you need to adjust.**

6. **In the Memo field, enter a description that explains why you made this adjustment.**

7. **Click Save.**

If you have a lot of inventory items to adjust, you can save some time by preselecting them and adjusting them as a batch. Choose Gear⇨Products and Services to display the Products and Services page (see Figure 4-28).

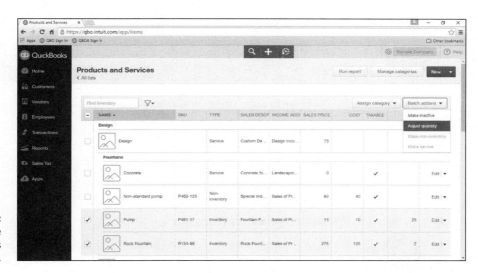

FIGURE 4-28:
Selecting multiple
inventory items
to adjust.

Then, select the inventory items you want to adjust by placing a check in the column to the left of the item name. Click the Batch Actions button and choose Adjust Quantity. QBO displays the Inventory Quantity Adjustment window shown previously in Figure 4-27, but prefills the window with the information about the inventory items you selected. Complete Steps 4, 6, and 7 above for each item in the window.

Editing an inventory quantity adjustment

If you need to edit an inventory quantity adjustment you previously saved (hey . . . it happens), follow these steps:

1. **Click the Create menu plus sign (+)⇨Inventory Qty Adjustment to display the Inventory Quantity Adjustment window.**

2. **In the upper left corner of the window, click the Recent Transactions button (see Figure 4-29).**

   QBO displays recent inventory adjustment transactions.

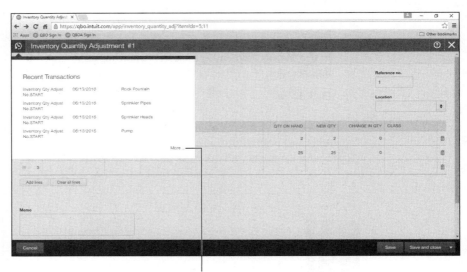

FIGURE 4-29:
Searching for a
recent inventory
adjustment
transaction
to edit.

Click here to search for more inventory adjustment transactions.

3. **If the adjustment appears in the list, click it.**

   If the adjustment doesn't appear, click More to display the Search page, where you can expand your search for the transaction. In most cases, changing the date range will do the trick.

4. **Make the necessary changes.**

   You can remove a line from an adjustment by clicking its Delete button at the right edge of the row.

   TIP

5. **Click Save and Close.**

Adjusting an inventory item's starting value

Suppose that you made a mistake when you set up the starting value for an inventory item; you can edit the item's starting value as long as you created the inventory item after the November 2015 QBO release.

WARNING

Changing an item's starting value can have wide-ranging effects, and QBO will display a warning to this effect when you start your inventory item starting value adjustment. If you're not sure about what you're doing, ask your accountant. Please.

To adjust an inventory item's starting value, follow these steps:

1. **Choose the Gear⇨Products and Services.**

2. **In the Action column beside the inventory item you want to adjust, click the drop-down arrow and select Adjust Starting Value (see Figure 4-30).**

QBO displays a warning explaining that changing an inventory item's starting value may affect the initial value of your inventory.

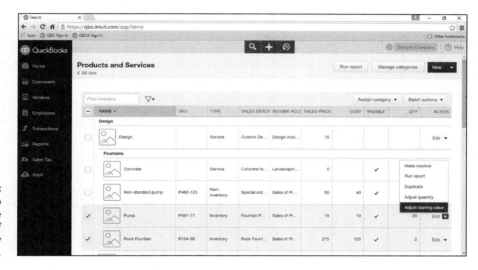

FIGURE 4-30:
Getting ready to adjust the starting value of an inventory item.

3. **Assuming you've heeded the warning above and know what you're doing, click Got it!**

QBO displays the Inventory Starting Value window (see Figure 4-31).

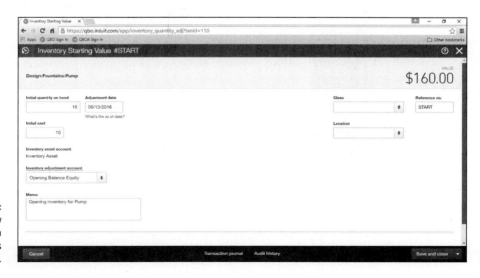

FIGURE 4-31:
Use this window to adjust an inventory item's starting values.

TIP

If you've enabled class and location tracking, note that you can supply information for those fields along with other fields that affect the inventory item's starting value.

4. Make the necessary changes.

REMEMBER

You can't change an item's inventory asset account from the Inventory Starting Value window. To change the item's inventory asset account, display the Products and Services page and click the Edit link for the item to display the item's information in the Inventory Item Product/Services Information panel shown previously in Figure 4-24.

5. Click Save and Close.

A Look at Other Lists

Just as QuickBooks desktop has other lists besides lists of people and items, QBO also has other lists. To find them, click the Gear icon beside the company name and, from the menu that appears, click All Lists in the second column from the left. QBO displays the Lists page shown in Figure 4-32.

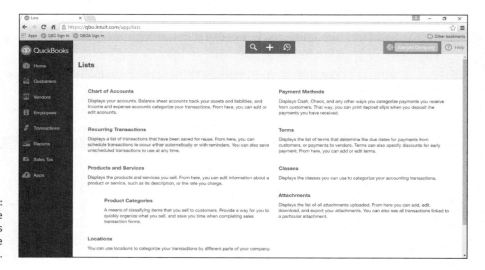

FIGURE 4-32: The Lists page contains links to all available lists in QBO.

Click any list name to open that list and work with it. You can add new entries, select and edit existing entries, and select and delete entries that have never been used. The steps to create any new list element are pretty much the same as the steps you've seen in this chapter to create people, items, and product categories.

Chapter **5**

Dealing with the Outflow of Money

I t's always more fun to make money than to spend it, but paying bills is part of life — unless you're living in *Star Trek: The Next Generation*, where they have no bills — but, I digress. This chapter explores the transactions you use in QBO to meet your financial obligations.

To record most expense-related transactions, you can choose Transactions ⇨ Expenses to display the Expense Transactions page shown in Figure 5-1. Click the New Transaction button to select a transaction type.

If the transaction type you want to record isn't available, click the Create plus sign (+) icon at the top of QBO and choose the type of transaction you want to record from the Create menu that appears; expense-related transactions show up in the Vendors column (see Figure 5-2).

REMEMBER

The Create icon changes to an X when you open the menu.

GETTING UP-AND-RUNNING

If you start using QBO after you've been in business for a while and have some outstanding bills you haven't yet paid, you can use those bills as a learning tool and enter them as described in this chapter. If you recorded an opening bank account balance back in Chapter 3, be sure to enter into QBO the checks you've written that haven't yet cleared your bank. If you didn't record an opening bank account balance back in Chapter 3, or you recorded a bank account balance as of December 31 of last year, be sure to enter into QBO all the checks you've written this year, even if they have cleared the bank.

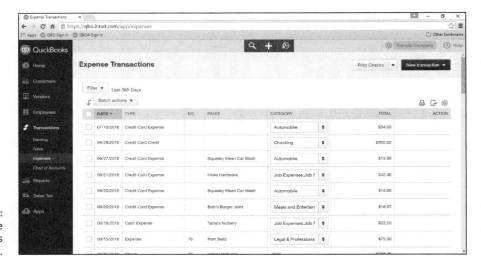

FIGURE 5-1:
The Expense Transactions page.

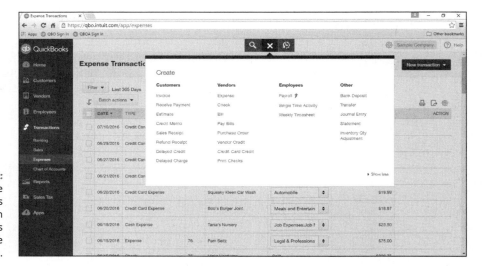

FIGURE 5-2:
Expense transactions appear in the Vendors column of the Create menu.

Writing a Check

Typically, you enter a check transaction when you intend to print a check to pay for an expense. Suppose that the UPS guy has just made a delivery for which you owe money and you want to give him a check: Use the Check transaction. You can print the check immediately or at a later time.

Assigning a check to accounts or items

When you write a check, you need to assign the expense for which you're writing the check to either an account or an item, and you can assign one check to both accounts and items. Follow these steps to enter and print a check:

1. **On the Expense Transactions page, click the New Transaction button.**

2. **From the list that appears, click Check.**

   QBO displays the Check window, which is divided into four sections:

   - **The Header section:** Shown in Figure 5-3, this section displays the balance in the selected checking account, the selected payee and the payee's mailing address, the payment date, the check amount and number, and the option to print the check later.

   - **The Account Details section:** You use this table when the expense is not related to an item you've defined.

   - **The Item Details section:** You use this table when you're writing a check to pay for a product or service you purchased. If you don't see this table, its preference isn't enabled. To display the table, choose Account and Settings ➪ Expenses ➪ Bills and Expenses and edit the Show Items Table on Expense and Purchase Forms option.

REMEMBER

   You typically write a check using *either* the Account Details section or the Item Details section, but not both. However, you can use both sections. If you won't be using a section, you can hide it by clicking the downward-pointing arrow beside the section name.

   - **The Footer section:** Contains the check total, the Memo box, and the box you use to attach an electronic document to the check.

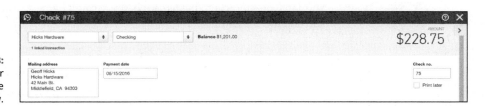

FIGURE 5-3:
The Header section of the Check window.

3. **Choose a payee and an account from which to make the payment.**

Along with the payee's address information, QBO displays information from previously entered transactions unless you haven't entered any transactions for that payee yet, or you have disabled the setting to display previously entered transaction information in Account and Settings.

TIP

If a pane appears on the right side, it displays transactions you might want to link to the check you're writing — and, if that's the case, see the next section, "Writing a check for an outstanding bill." On the other hand, if the check you're writing has nothing to do with any transaction that appears in the pane, just ignore the pane; you can hide it as described in the next section.

4. **Double-check the payment Date, and Check Number, and make an appropriate selection in the Print Later check box.**

5. **Assign part or all of the check to an expense account or an item using the Account Details section or the Item Details section (see Figure 5-4).** To assign a portion to an expense account:

FIGURE 5-4:
The Account Details and Item Details sections of the Check window.

a. **Click in the Account column and select an appropriate expense account for the check you are recording.**

TIP

You can type characters that appear in the account name and QBO will help you find the account.

b. **In the Description column, describe the expense you're paying.**

c. **In the Amount column, supply the amount of the check that you want to apply to the selected account.**

d. **If you incurred the expense on behalf of a customer and you want to bill the customer for the expense, check the Billable box — and, if appropriate, the Tax box — and select the customer's name in the Customer column.**

e. **Repeat Steps a to d to add more lines to the check.**

6. **To assign part or all of the check to items or services you have defined, use the Item Details section (also shown in Figure 5-4):**

a. **Click in the Product/Service column and select an appropriate item for the check you are recording.**

You can type characters in the Product/Service column and QBO will help you find the item.

b. **Optionally, edit the Description column for the selected item.**

c. **Use the Qty, Rate, and Amount columns to supply the quantity of the selected item you are purchasing, the rate you're paying for each item, and the amount you're paying.**

TIP

When you supply any two of the Qty, Rate, and Amount values, QuickBooks calculates the third value.

d. **If you purchased the item on behalf of a customer and you want to bill the customer for the item, check the Billable box — and, if appropriate, the Tax box — and select the customer's name in the Customer column.**

e. **Repeat Steps a to d to add more items to the check.**

7. **You can scroll down in the Check window to the Footer section, type a message to the payee, and attach an electronic document (such as the payee's invoice) to the check.**

TIP

To attach an electronic document to the check, click in the Attachments box; a standard Open dialog box appears that you can use to navigate to the document. Alternatively, you can drag and drop the electronic copy into the Attachments box.

8. **At the bottom of the window, you can**

- **Cancel your action or clear the window and start again.**

- **Click Print Check to print the check.**

TIP

The first time you print checks, QBO walks you through the process of selecting the type of checks you use and aligning them for your printer.

- **Click Order Checks to visit the Intuit Marketplace and order check stock.**

- **Click Make Recurring to set up the check as a recurring payment you intend to make on a schedule you specify.**

- **Click More to see additional actions, such as voiding the check or viewing its audit history.**

- **Click Save and New to save the check and redisplay the Check window so that you can write another check.**

REMEMBER

The Save and New button is a sticky preference. That means, if you click the drop-down arrow to the right of the button and select Save and Close, the next time you open the window to write a check, the default button will be the Save and Close button.

Writing a check for an outstanding bill

You can use the Check window to write a check to pay a bill you previously entered — something that you cannot do in the QuickBooks desktop product.

TIP

Don't use the Check transaction if you're planning on paying several bills. Instead, see the section "Paying bills" at the end of this chapter.

If you select a payee for whom an outstanding bill exists, QBO displays a pane at the right side of the Check window (see Figure 5-5) that shows all transactions linked to the selected payee; each transaction appears as a separate entry. If nothing in the pane applies to your transaction, you can hide the pane by clicking the button shown in Figure 5-5.

If you're writing the check to pay a bill that appears in the pane, click Add in the bill transaction you want to pay. That way, QBO appropriately applies the check you're writing to the outstanding bill and correctly reduces your outstanding obligations.

WARNING

If you write a check to pay a bill and you *don't* apply the check to the bill, your reports show that you continue to owe the bill amount to the payee, which really messes things up.

Click here to hide the pane.

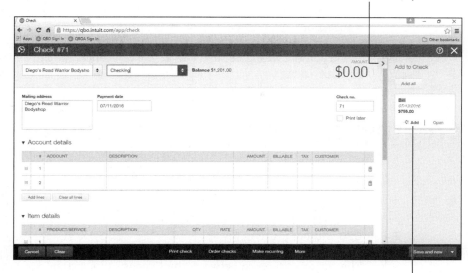

FIGURE 5-5:
If you select a payee for whom you previously entered a bill, the outstanding bill appears in the pane on the right side of the Check window.

Click here to use the check to pay an outstanding bill.

When you click Add, QBO adds that bill to the check and switches to the Bill Payment window, essentially converting the check to a bill payment transaction. In Figure 5-6, you see the Bill Payment window after I added an outstanding bill to a check in the Check window. If you compare Figures 5-5 and 5-6, you'll notice that the original check number was 71, and it's still 71 in the Bill Payment window.

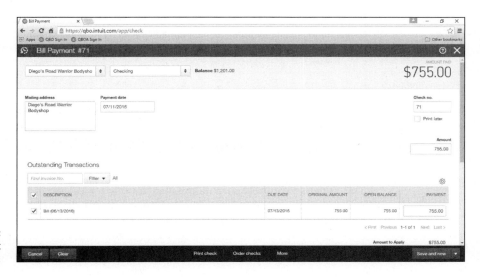

FIGURE 5-6:
The Bill Payment window.

You complete the Bill Payment transaction the same way you complete a Check transaction; follow Steps 7 and 8 in the preceding section.

TIP

If you add the wrong bill to a check, you can cancel the Bill Payment transaction without saving it.

Creating an Expense Transaction

You use an Expense transaction when you're trying to record an expense without printing a check. For example, you record Expense transactions in QBO to account for a payment you make using a credit or debit card. And, you use an Expense transaction if you have manually written a check that you now need to record in QBO without printing it.

The major difference between the Expense transaction window and the Check transaction window is the lack of any tools to help you print an Expense transaction; compare Figures 5-4 and 5-7.

FIGURE 5-7:
You can use the Expense transaction window to record making a payment without writing a check.

The Expense transaction window also contains a Payment Method list box that you don't find in the Check transaction window. Other than those two differences, the windows appear and function the same way.

QBO AND CREDIT CARD TRANSACTIONS

By default, QBO treats Credit Card account transactions as cash transactions, a conservative approach that recognizes expenses as they occur. To account for credit card transactions, set up both your credit card company as a vendor and a Credit Card account for the credit card in your Chart of Accounts, and use Expense transactions to record credit card purchases to the account as you make each purchase. If you need to record a credit card return, use the Credit Card Credit transaction.

When the credit card bill arrives, you can pay it in a number of ways:

- To pay by check, use the Check transaction, select your credit card company as the vendor, and, in the Account Details section, select your credit card account.

- To pay by transfer (where you transfer money electronically or manually from a bank account to your credit card account, which reduces both accounts), use the Transfer transaction, selecting the bank account you'll use to pay the bill as the Transfer Funds From account and the credit card company/vendor you're paying as the Transfer Funds To account.

- To pay the bill while reconciling the credit card account, follow the steps in Chapter 8 to reconcile the account. When you click Finish, you'll be given the option to write a check to pay the amount due, enter a bill to pay the bill later, or do nothing about paying the bill now (and later, on your own, enter a check or a bill for the amount due).

If you want to recognize credit card expenses when you pay your credit card bill (rather than when you make a purchase using your credit card), *do* set up a vendor for your credit card company, but *don't* set up a Credit Card account in the Chart of Accounts, and don't enter Expense transactions or Credit Card Credit transactions in QBO for credit card transactions as they occur. Instead, when you receive your credit card statement, enter a Bill transaction, as described later in this chapter, and allocate each line on the credit card statement to the appropriate account or item; record credit card refunds as negative lines on the Bill transaction. QBO then treats your credit card account as an Accounts Payable vendor. And when you're ready to pay the credit card bill, you can write a check, transfer funds, or use the Pay Bills page to pay the credit card statement. Remember, this is the less conservative approach to tracking credit card expenses; if you are a heavy user of your credit card, do yourself a favor and use the first approach so that you can effectively manage your credit card spending.

If you want to download credit card transaction information into QBO, see Chapter 8.

Entering a Purchase Order

Businesses that order lots of stuff from vendors often use purchase orders to keep track of the items on order. Purchase orders in QBO do not affect any of your accounts; instead, they simply help you keep track of what you order. And, when the order arrives, you can compare the goods that come in the door with the ones listed on the purchase order to make sure they match.

If you plan to use purchase orders, then your ordering process typically happens in the following way:

>> You place an order with a vendor and you enter a purchase order in QBO that matches the order you placed.

>> You receive the items you ordered, typically along with a bill for the items; you then match the items you receive to the purchase order and enter a bill for the items. Note that sometimes you receive the bill without the items or the items without the bill.

>> You pay the vendor's bill.

You enter a purchase order using the Purchase Order transaction window; you can open this window either from the Expense Transactions page or from the Create menu (the plus sign). A typical purchase order looks like the one shown in Figure 5-8, and you'll notice the window closely resembles the Check window shown earlier in Figure 5-4.

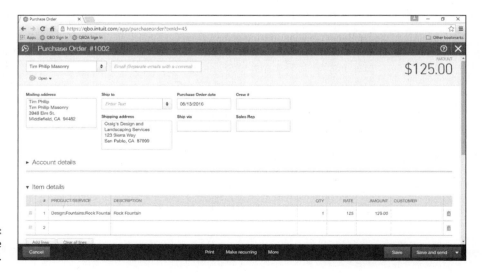

FIGURE 5-8:
The Purchase Order window.

As you fill in the Purchase Order transaction window, QBO assigns a status of Open to the purchase order; the status appears just below the vendor's name in the upper left corner of the transaction window.

When you receive the goods, the vendor's bill, or both, you record a bill as described in the next section, or a check, an expense transaction, or a credit card charge as described earlier in this chapter, showing what you paid (or what you owe) the vendor.

When you select a vendor who has open purchase orders on any of these types of transactions, a pane appears on the right side of the window, showing available purchase orders. You add a purchase order to the transaction the same way you add a bill to a Check transaction: by clicking the Add button. In Figure 5-9, I've opened a Check transaction and selected a vendor who has open purchase orders.

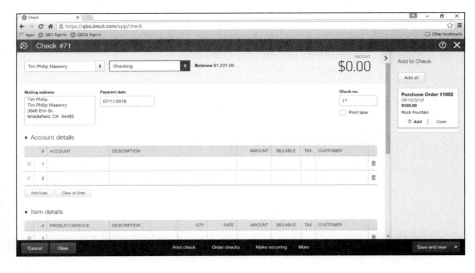

FIGURE 5-9:
The Check window, with a vendor selected who has open purchase orders.

When I click Add to add the purchase order to my transaction, QBO adds the purchase order lines to the first available line in the Item Details section of my Check transaction. QBO also indicates, immediately below the vendor name, that the Check transaction has one linked transaction (see Figure 5-10).

If you save the Check transaction and then reopen the purchase order, QBO has changed the purchase orders status from open to closed so that you don't accidentally add the purchase order to another transaction.

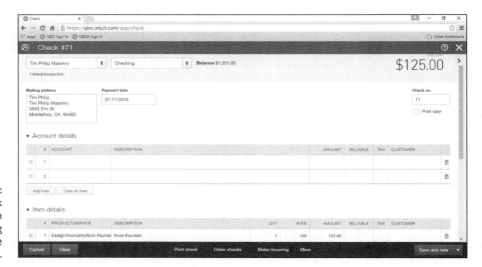

FIGURE 5-10:
A Check transaction after adding a purchase order to it.

TIP

If you add the wrong purchase order to a transaction, you can remove the purchase order line in the Item Details section by clicking the Trash Can icon at the right edge of the line.

QBO can't add only part of a purchase order to a transaction. So, if you receive only part of a purchase order, add the purchase order to your transaction and then record a payment for the part of the purchase order you received by deleting lines from the check for items you didn't receive. To continue to track the outstanding part of the purchase order, you can manually close the original purchase order and create a new purchase order that contains the remaining outstanding items; when you create the second purchase order — essentially a back order — try to assign a number to it that helps you track it in relation to the original purchase order.

TIP

You can use your own custom purchase order numbers if you choose Gear ⇨ Account and Settings ⇨ Expenses. Then click in the Purchase Orders section to edit purchase order settings, select the Custom Transaction Numbers check box, and then click Save. You also can convert Estimate transactions to Purchase Order transactions; see Chapter 6 for details.

When you need to identify open purchase orders, use the Open Purchase Order List report. For more on reports, see Chapter 10.

Entering and Paying Bills

You use QBO's Bill transaction to enter a bill from a vendor that you don't want to pay immediately. QBO tracks the bill as a *payable*, which is a liability of your business — money you owe but have not yet paid. Most companies that enter Bill transactions do so because they receive a fair number of bills and want to sit down and pay them at one time, but they don't want to lose track of the bills they receive. They also want to be able to easily determine how much they owe; if you enter Bill transactions, you can print the A/P Aging Summary and Details reports to find that information.

REMEMBER

Depending on the version of QBO that you use, the Bill transaction might not be available to you; if that's the case, pay your bills using the Check or the Expense transaction.

Entering a bill

To enter a bill you receive from a vendor, use QBO's Bill transaction. Follow these steps:

1. **Choose Transactions ⇨ Expenses.**

2. **Click the New Transaction button in the upper right corner of the Expenses page and select Bill.**

   QBO displays the Bill transaction window shown in Figure 5-11.

FIGURE 5-11:
The Bill transaction window.

3. **Select the vendor from whom you received the bill.**

   QBO fills in the vendor's mailing address information.

4. **Check and, if necessary, change the bill date and the due date.**

5. **Use the Account Details section, the Item Details section, or both to record information about the bill.**

   See the section "Writing a Check" for details on filling out the Account Details section and the Item Details section. Be aware that I hid the Account Details section in Figure 5-11 so that you could see the information in the Item Details section.

6. **Optionally, scroll down to the Footer section (which isn't shown in Figure 5-11) and enter information in the Memo field and attach electronic documents to the bill.**

7. **Click Save.**

Recording a vendor credit

You enter a vendor credit to record returns to vendors or refunds from vendors. A vendor might supply you with a credit document that indicates you no longer owe the amount stated on the document, or the vendor might issue a refund check to you.

If a vendor issues a credit document, you enter a vendor credit and then apply it when you pay the vendor's bill. If a vendor issues a refund check to you, you still enter a vendor credit, but you also enter a deposit and then link the deposit to the vendor credit.

Follow these steps to enter the vendor credit:

1. **On the Expense Transaction page, click New Transaction⇨Vendor Credit.**

   QBO displays the Vendor Credit window shown in Figure 5-12.

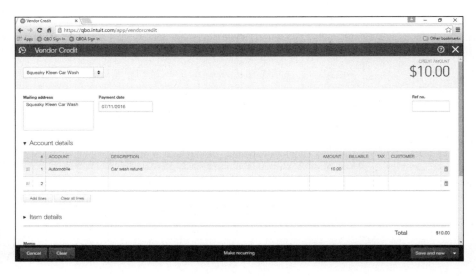

FIGURE 5-12:
A Vendor Credit transaction.

2. **Select the vendor who issued the credit.**

3. **Enter the date of the credit.**

4. **Enter the credit amount.**

5. **In the Account Details section, select the account used on the original bill.**

   If you received the credit because you returned items to the vendor, select the items you returned in the Item Details section.

6. **You can optionally scroll down and attach an electronic copy of the credit to the Vendor Credit transaction.**

7. **Click the arrow beside Save and New and choose Save and Close.**

TIP

   The Save option referenced in Step 7 is called a *sticky preference*, which means that after you select Save and Close, it will appear as the default Save option the next time you display this screen.

If the vendor issued only a credit document, read the section "Paying bills" to learn how to use the vendor credit you just entered to reduce the amount you owe the vendor when you pay the vendor's bill.

RECORDING A REFUND TO A CARD CREDIT

If a vendor issues a credit to your credit card, the way you handle it depends on how you track credit cards in QBO.

If you haven't set up a credit card account and you wait to enter credit card transactions when you receive and record the credit card vendor's bill, enter a line on the Bill transaction using the account associated with the refund and make the amount negative.

However, if you *have* set up a credit card account, record a Credit Card Credit transaction, whether you manually record Expense transactions or download them; when you record a Credit Card Credit, QBO lets you post the transaction to any of your available credit cards. In the Account Details section, select the account associated with the refund. Note that when you download transactions, you'll be able to match both Expense transactions and Credit Card Credit transactions to downloaded information.

When a vendor issues a refund check . . .

If the vendor issued a refund check to you, you need to complete the previous steps to enter a vendor credit. Then, follow these steps to enter a deposit to record the refund check in your bank account and then link it to the vendor credit:

1. **Click the Create plus (+) sign and, from the Other section of Create menu that appears, choose Bank Deposits.**

QBO displays the Deposit transaction window shown in Figure 5-13.

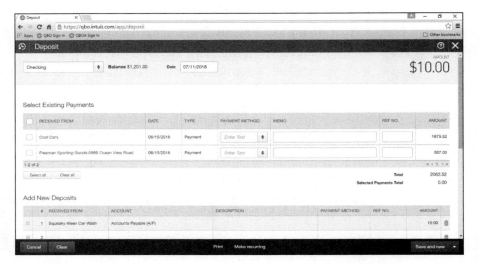

FIGURE 5-13: The Deposit transaction window.

2. **In the Add New Deposits section, enter the following information:**

- **In the Received From column, select the vendor who issued the check.**

- **In the Account column, select the Accounts Payable account.**

- **In the Amount column, enter the amount of the check.**

3. **Click the arrow beside Save and New and choose Save and Close.**

The Save option functions as a sticky preference and you might not see Save and New because you previously made a different choice.

REMEMBER

4. **Click the Create plus (+) sign and, from the Create menu that appears, choose Expense.**

5. **Select the vendor whose refund check you deposited.**

QBO displays available deposits, credits, and bills (see Figure 5-14).

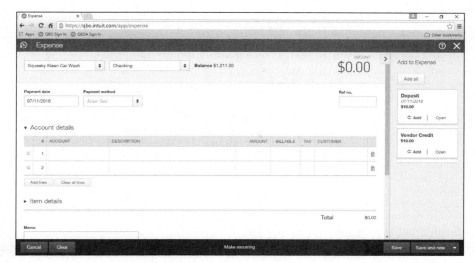

FIGURE 5-14:
Open transac-
tions for the
selected vendor
appear.

6. **Click Add in the Deposit transaction.**

7. **Click Add in the outstanding Vendor Credit transaction.**

   When you add these two transactions, in this order, to the Expense, QBO
   creates a Bill Payment transaction with a net value of $0 because QBO applies
   the deposit to the vendor credit; Figure 5-15 focuses on the Details section of
   the transaction.

8. **Click the arrow beside Save and New and choose Save and Close.**

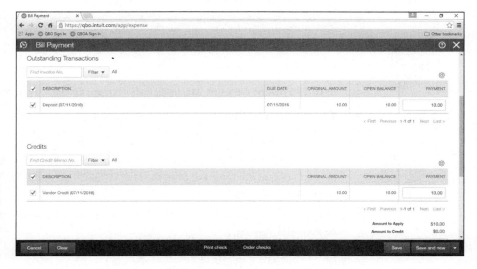

FIGURE 5-15:
Adding the
vendor credit and
the bank deposit
of the vendor's
check results in a
$0 bill payment
transaction.

Paying bills

If you've been entering bills from vendors, then, at some point, you need to pay those bills. Most people sit down once or twice a month and pay outstanding bills. To pay bills in QBO, follow these steps:

1. **Click the Create plus (+) sign and, from the Create menu that appears, choose Pay Bills in the Vendors column.**

   QBO displays the Pay Bills page shown in Figure 5-16.

Overdue bills

FIGURE 5-16:
The Pay Bills page
lists bills you
owe but have
not yet paid.

TIP

Overdue bills display a red flag.

2. **In the Payment Account list, select an account to use to pay the bills.**

3. **Provide a payment date at the top of the screen.**

4. **Enter the number of the first check you'll use to pay bills.**

REMEMBER

You can select the Print Later button to identify bills to pay and schedule them to print later; at the time you print the checks, QBO lets you establish the starting check number.

5. **In the Filter list, select an option to specify the outstanding bills you want to consider paying.**

   By default, QBO displays unpaid bills for the last year, but you can limit what appears onscreen for your consideration by a variety of dates and even for selected payees.

6. **By clicking the appropriate column heading, you can opt to sort the listed bills by Payee, Reference Number, Due Date, or Open Balance.**

7. **Select the check box in the column at the left side of each bill you want to pay.**

   As you select bills to pay, QBO updates the Payment column using the bill amount as the default payment amount (see Figure 5-17). You can change the payment amount of any bill by typing in the Payment column.

   If a vendor credit exists, QBO assumes you want to apply outstanding vendor credits to reduce the amount you owe a particular vendor.

REMEMBER

FIGURE 5-17:
QBO uses the bill amount less any vendor credits to calculate a payment amount.

8. **Click Save and Print, or click the arrow beside Save and Print to choose either Save or Save and Close.**

   Click Save or Save and Close to mark the bills paid without printing any checks. Click Save and Print to print checks and mark the bills paid.

TIP

If you choose to pay the bills using a credit card instead of a bank account, the window looks the same except that no options appear related to printing checks, just as you'd expect.

If you opted, in Step 4, to print checks later, you can print those checks by choosing Create ⇨ Print Checks. The Print Checks option appears in the Vendors column of the Create menu.

Chapter **6**

Managing the Inflow of Money

This is where the fun starts. "Why?" you ask. Because this chapter covers stuff related to bringing money into the business, which, from any businessperson's perspective, is the reason you started your business — and therefore the most fun part!

To record most sales-related transactions, you can choose Transactions ⇨ Sales to display the Sales Transactions page shown in Figure 6-1; then click the New Transaction button. If the transaction type you want to record isn't available on the Sales Transactions page, open the Create menu by clicking the Create button — the plus sign (+) icon at the top of QBO, which changes to an X after you click it. Then, choose the type of transaction you want to record; sales-related transactions appear in the Customers column (see Figure 6-2).

GETTING UP-AND-RUNNING

If you've been in business while when you start using QBO, and you have some invoices you've issued but customers haven't yet paid, you can use those invoices as a learning tool and enter them as described in this chapter. If you recorded an opening bank account balance back in Chapter 3, be sure to enter into QBO the deposits you've made since your last bank statement. If you didn't record an opening bank account balance back in Chapter 3, or you recorded a bank account balance as of December 31 of last year, be sure to enter into QBO all the deposits you've made this year, even if they have cleared the bank.

Click here to start a new sales transaction.

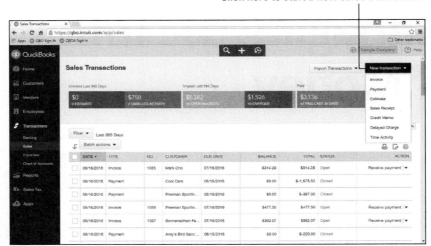

FIGURE 6-1:
The Sales Transactions page.

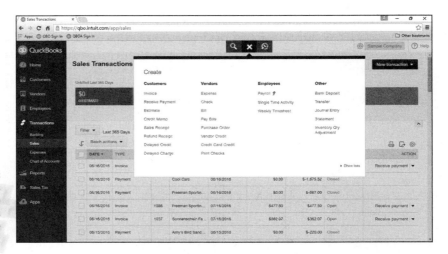

FIGURE 6-2:
Sales transactions appear in the Customers column of the Create menu.

Customizing Forms to Handle Subtotals

Before we dive into preparing various types of forms, you should address a house-keeping task: setting up sales forms so that you can include subtotals on them. If you have no need to subtotal information on your sales forms, you can skip this section and move on to the next one.

You can subtotal lines on an invoice, an estimate, or a sales receipt. First, turn on the feature; for this example, I turn on the feature for the Invoice form. Follow these steps:

1. **Choose Gear ⇨ Custom Form Styles.**

    The Custom Form Styles page appears, which displays the form styles you have set up.

    REMEMBER

    In Chapter 3, you saw how to customize forms. If you opted not to set up any custom forms, you might not see anything listed on the Custom Form Styles page. In that case, click the New Style button and continue with these steps.

2. **Select a form to customize, and then click Edit in the Action column.**

    The Customize Form Style dialog box appears.

3. **On the left side of the dialog box, click the Activity Table section.**

4. **In the More group, select the Group Activity By check box and make a selection from the list.**

    For my example, shown in Figure 6-3, I chose Type.

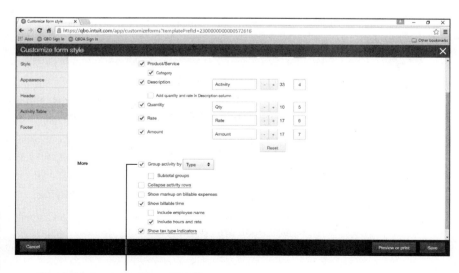

FIGURE 6-3:
Turn on the setting to enable grouping on the selected sales form.

Check this box to enable subtotaling.

TIP

You can select Subtotal Groups if you want QBO to group specifically by the grouping type you select in Settings. Not selecting the option gives you more flexibility on the forms.

5. **Save the settings.**

REMEMBER

You'll need to repeat the preceding steps for each type of form (invoice, estimate, and sales receipt) on which you want to be able to subtotal information.

Preparing an Invoice

You enter invoices in QBO to inform customers that they owe you money for goods you sold them or services you performed for them. In QBO, you can prepare invoices and send them using email or using the U.S. Postal Service.

When you prepare an invoice, you include information about what you're selling to the customer by including items on the invoice. You create items for both services and products using the Products and Services list, as described at the end of Chapter 4. To enter an invoice, follow these steps:

1. **Choose Transactions ⇨ Sales to display the Sales Transactions page.**

2. **Click the New Transaction button and, from the list that appears, click Invoice.**

3. **Choose a customer.**

QBO displays the customer's mailing address, payment terms, invoice date, due date, and Send Later option.

TIP

If a pane appears on the right side, it displays transactions you might want to link to the invoice you're creating; you can see examples in the sections "Preparing an Estimate" and "Creating Billable Time Entries."

4. **Double-check the Invoice Date, Due date, and Terms, and make an appropriate selection in the Send Later check box.**

If you want to send invoices via email, you can set up your preferences; from the QBO Home page, click the Gear button beside your company name and choose Account and Settings.

5. **Fill in the products and services the customer is buying:**

a. **Click in the Product/Service column and select an appropriate item for the invoice you are creating.**

TIP

You can type characters in the Product/Service column and QBO will help you find the item.

b. Optionally, edit the Description column for the selected item.

c. Use the Qty, Rate, and Amount columns to supply the quantity of the selected item you are selling, the rate you're charging for each item, and the amount the customer should pay. When you supply any two of the Qty, Rate, and Amount values, QBO calculates the third value.

d. If appropriate, check the Tax box.

e. Repeat Steps a to d to add more items to the invoice.

6. To add a subtotal in the proper place on the invoice:

a. Click the last line on the invoice that should be subtotaled; in Figure 6-4, I clicked the third line of the invoice.

b. Click the Add Subtotal button, which appears below the lines on the invoice.

QBO adds a line that subtotals the ones above it. You can continue adding lines to the invoice, and you can add more subtotals.

7. You can scroll down in the Invoice window, as shown in Figure 6-5, and select a sales tax rate and, if appropriate, a discount amount or percent.

You see the Sales Tax Rate option on invoices only if you have turned on the Sales Tax feature by choosing Sales Tax ➪ Set Up Sales Tax Rates.

Click the last line to include in the subtotal.

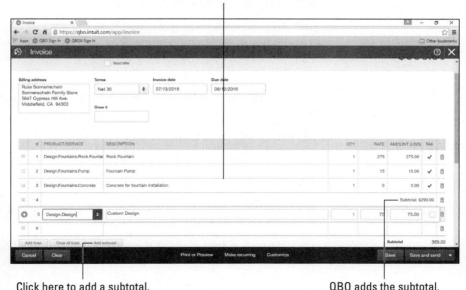

FIGURE 6-4:
Click the last line that should be part of the subtotaled group, and then click Add Subtotal.

Click here to add a subtotal.

QBO adds the subtotal.

Click here to control whether a discount is pre- or post-taxable.

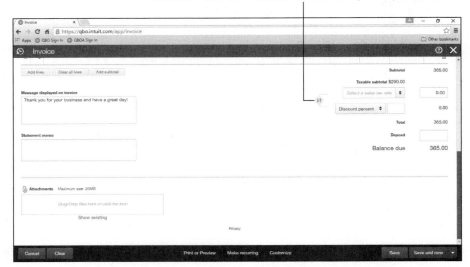

FIGURE 6-5:
Use the bottom of the Invoice window to handle sales tax, discount information, messages, and attachments.

You can also apply a discount to the invoice if you have turned on the company preference to display the Discount box; type a message to the customer; type information in the Statement Memo box, which QBO transfers directly to any statement you create in the future; and attach an electronic document to the invoice.

TIP

You can control whether the discount is a pre-tax or after-tax discount by clicking the switch that appears to the left of the Discount and Sales Tax Rate boxes. Clicking the switch swaps the position of the two boxes; when the Discount box appears on top, the discount is pre-tax.

If, in the Account and Settings dialog box, you turn on the preference to display the Deposit box at the bottom of the invoice, you can use it to reduce the amount of the invoice by a deposit amount paid by the customer.

8. **To attach an electronic document to the invoice, click in the Attachments box and navigate to the document or drag and drop the electronic copy into the Attachments box.**

9. **At the bottom of the window, you can**

   - **Cancel the invoice or clear the window and start again.**

   - **Click Print or Preview to print or preview the invoice.**

   - **Click Make Recurring to set up the invoice as a recurring invoice you intend to send on a schedule you specify.**

   - **Click Customize to customize the invoice form as described in Chapter 3.**

- **Click Save to assign an invoice number and save the invoice in QBO.**

- **Click Save and Send to assign an invoice number, save the invoice, and email a copy to the customer.**

  A window appears, in which you can write an email message and look at a preview of the invoice. After you send your invoice, the email time and date-stamp information appears in the header.

TIP

You can click the arrow beside Save and Send and then choose Save and New to save the invoice and start a new one, or choose Save and Close to save the invoice and close the Invoice window. The option you choose will appear the next time you display the Invoice window. In fact, in any transaction window, the choice you make appears the next time you open the window.

Recording a Customer Payment

When you receive a payment from a customer, you record it in QBO. You can display the Receive Payment window in the following ways:

» You can click the Create menu and select Receive Payment.

» You can click the New Transaction button on the Sales Transactions page and select Payment.

» In the Sales Transactions list, you can find the invoice for which you want to record a payment and click Receive Payment in the Action column.

If you use either of the first two methods, QBO displays an empty Receive Payment window. You then select a customer, and QBO displays all the customer's open invoices in the Outstanding Transactions section, at the bottom of the window (see Figure 6-6).

If you choose the third method in the previous list, QBO displays the Receive Payment window, prefilled with the information for the invoice you selected in the Sales Transactions list.

At the top of the screen, select a Payment Method and select the account in which you want QBO to place the customer's payment. In the Outstanding Transactions section, place a check beside each invoice being paid by the customer's payment.

So, what happens differently if you use the third method and opt to find the invoice on the Sales Transaction list, shown in Figure 6-7, and click the Receive Payment button in the Action column? If you work from the list, QBO automatically fills in the customer name; displays and selects, in the Outstanding

Transactions section, the invoice you chose in the Sales Transaction list; and fills in a proposed payment amount. The window you see when you click the Receive Payment button looks just like the window shown in Figure 6-6.

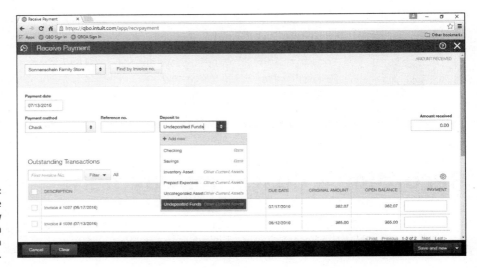

FIGURE 6-6:
The Receive Payment window after selecting a customer with open invoices.

Click here to open a blank Receive Payments window.

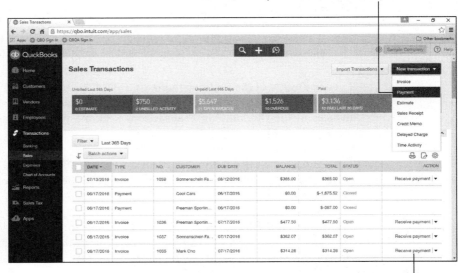

FIGURE 6-7:
You can open the Receive Payments window from the Sales Transaction list.

Click one of these buttons to receive payment for a specific invoice.

TIP

QBO interfaces with QuickBooks Payments, Intuit's online merchant service offering, so that you can accept ACH and credit card payments from your customers. Visit `http://payments.intuit.com/` or contact Intuit for details.

At the bottom of the Receive Payment window, click Save and New to enter additional customer payments, or click the arrow beside Save and New and choose Save and Close.

USING THE UNDEPOSITED FUNDS ACCOUNT

If you receive more than one customer payment on any given day, you'll find the Undeposited Funds account a convenient way to handle the money that comes into your business. If you take several checks to your bank on a given day and deposit all of them as a single deposit, most banks typically don't record the individual checks as individual deposits. Instead, the bank records the sum of the checks as your deposit — pretty much the same way you sum the checks on the deposit ticket you give to the bank teller.

"And why is this important?" you ask. This fact is important because, when you receive your statement from your bank, you need to reconcile the bank's deposits and withdrawals with your own version of deposits and withdrawals. If you track each customer payment you receive as a deposit in the bank, then your deposits won't match the bank's deposits. And, if you don't use the Undeposited Funds account — and instead record customer payments directly into your QBO Bank account — your deposits definitely *won't* match the bank's version of your deposits.

Herald the arrival of the Undeposited Funds account in QBO, which acts as a holding tank for customer payments before you've prepared a bank deposit slip. If you place customer payments in the Undeposited Funds account, you can then use the Bank Deposit feature in QBO to sum up the payments you receive and intend to deposit at your bank simultaneously — and, if you don't go to your bank daily to make deposits, there's no problem. QBO records, as the deposit amount in your QBO Bank account, the amount calculated in the Bank Deposit window, which will match the amount you actually deposit at your bank. Then, your bank reconciliation process becomes quick and easy — well, okay, maybe not quick and easy, but certainly quicker and easier than if you were trying to figure out which customer payments made up various bank deposits.

See Chapter 8 for details on preparing a bank deposit and reconciling a bank statement.

Working with Estimates

You can use estimates to prepare a document that estimates what you need to charge a client to complete a project; estimates don't update your QBO accounts but do enable you to keep track of proposals you make to customers. If a customer decides to buy, based on your estimate, you can copy the estimate to a purchase order to easily order the items needed to complete the job. You also can copy the estimate to an invoice.

WARNING

You can copy only those estimates with a status of Pending. Copying an estimate to an invoice automatically changes the estimate's status from Pending to Closed. Therefore, if you want to copy an estimate to both a purchase order and an invoice, make sure you copy the estimate to the purchase order first.

NON-POSTING TRANSACTIONS

Estimates and purchase orders are two examples of non-posting transactions. Non-posting transactions don't affect your accounts in any way, but they are helpful because they enable you to enter potential transaction information you don't want to forget. In addition to the estimate and the purchase order, QBO Essentials and Plus also enable you to record two other non-posting transactions: the Delayed Charge and the Delayed Credit.

You can use a Delayed Charge transaction pretty much the same way you use an estimate. The Delayed Charge transaction records potential future revenue, and you can convert a Delayed Charge to an invoice in the same way you convert an estimate to an invoice. For details, see the section "Converting an estimate to an invoice."

The Delayed Credit transaction enables you to record a potential future credit memo. When you prepare an invoice for a customer for whom you've entered a Delayed Credit transaction, QBO displays the Delayed Credit in the pane on the right side of the Invoice window, and you can add the credit to the invoice. A Delayed Credit transaction differs from a Credit Memo transaction because a Credit Memo transaction updates your accounts when you enter it, but a Delayed Credit transaction updates your accounts only when you include it on an invoice.

You fill out both forms the same way you create an invoice; for details, refer to the section "Preparing an Invoice."

Preparing an estimate

You prepare an estimate in much the same way you prepare an invoice. To display the Estimate window, click the Create menu and choose Estimate. Or, if you prefer to work from the Sales Transactions page, choose Transactions ➪ Sales, click the New Transaction button, and, from the menu that appears, click Estimate. QBO displays the Estimate window (see Figure 6-8).

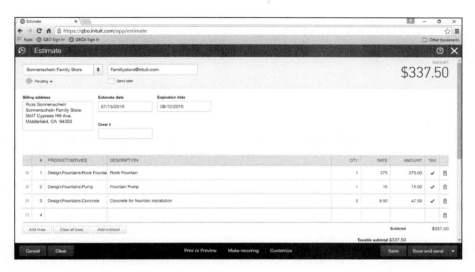

FIGURE 6-8:
Creating an estimate.

Choose a customer, and QBO displays the customer's address information and the estimate date. You supply the estimate's expiration date and optionally select the Send Later option. Figure 6-8 also shows a Crew # field that appears because the estimate was customized. You can read more about customizing forms in Chapter 3.

REMEMBER

QBO sets an estimate's status as Pending as long as the estimate is open and has not expired or been converted to an invoice. The status appears just above the customer's billing address.

To fill in the products and services the customer is considering for purchase, click in the Product/Service column and select an item. You can type characters in the Product/Service column and QBO will help you find the item. QBO fills in any default information stored about the item. You can change the description, quantity, rate, amount, and taxable status of the item. Repeat this process to add more items to the estimate.

If you scroll down in the Estimate window, you see the additional fields shown in Figure 6-9.

Click here to control whether a discount is pre- or post-taxable.

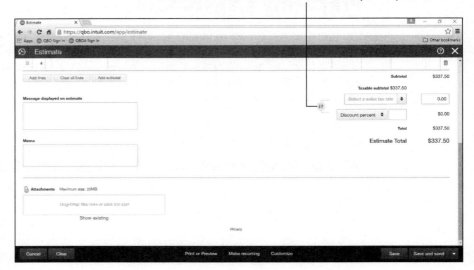

FIGURE 6-9:
The bottom of
the Estimate
window.

You can select a sales tax rate, apply a discount percentage or dollar amount to the estimate if you have the company preference turned on to display the Discount box, type a message to the customer, type information in the Memo box, and attach an electronic document to the estimate.

TIP

To attach an electronic document to the estimate, click in the Attachments box and navigate to the document or drag and drop the electronic copy into the Attachments box.

REMEMBER

You control whether the discount is a pre-tax or post-tax discount by clicking the switch that appears to the left of the Discount and Sales Tax Rate boxes. Clicking the switch swaps the position of the two boxes; when the Discount box appears on top, the discount is pre-tax.

At the bottom of the window, you can

>> Cancel the estimate or clear the window and start again.

>> Click Print or Preview to print or preview the estimate.

>> Click Make Recurring to set up the estimate as a recurring estimate you intend to send on a schedule you specify.

>> Click Customize to set up a custom form style for the estimate.

>> Click Save to assign a number to the estimate and save it in QBO.

>> Click Save and Send to assign a number to the estimate, save it, and email a copy to the customer. A window appears, in which you can write an email message and look at a preview of the estimate. After you send your invoice, the email time and date-stamp information appears in the header.

TIP

You can click the arrow beside Save and Send and then choose Save and New to save the estimate and start a new one, or choose Save and Close to save the estimate and close the Estimate window.

Copying an estimate to a purchase order

So, you did a good job on your estimate, and now your customer wants to purchase based on the estimate you provided. In this case, you often want to use the estimate information to prepare a purchase order for a vendor. QBO Plus enables you to copy an estimate with a status of Pending to a purchase order if you turn on the feature.

WARNING

An estimate's status determines whether it can be copied. If the estimate is open and has not expired or been converted to an invoice, the estimate's status is Pending. Converting an estimate to an invoice automatically changes the estimate's status to Closed. So, copy an estimate to a purchase order before you convert the estimate to an invoice.

Be aware that QBO includes on purchase orders only those items for which you have selected the "I Purchase This Product/Service From a Vendor" option. If you include items on the estimate for which you have not selected this option, those items won't copy to the purchase order. To solve this problem, you can edit your items and make sure you select the option.

To give yourself the option of copying an estimate to a purchase order, follow these steps:

1. **Click Gear ⇨ Account and Settings.**

   QBO displays the Account and Settings dialog box.

2. **Click Expenses on the right side of the dialog box.**

3. **Click in the Purchase Orders section.**

   QBO enables editing for the options in that section.

4. **Select the Copy Estimates to Purchase Orders option (see Figure 6-10).**

5. **Click Save.**

6. **Click Done.**

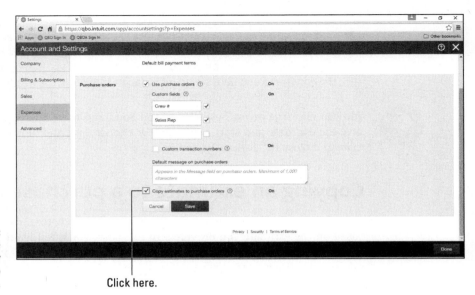

FIGURE 6-10:
Enabling the
option to copy
estimates to
purchase orders.

Click here.

At this point, you'll find you can copy any estimate with a Pending status to a purchase order. Follow these steps:

1. **Create and save a new estimate using the steps in the preceding section, "Preparing an estimate," or open an existing pending estimate.**

2. **At the top of the Estimate window, click the down arrow beside the Copy to Invoice button and choose Copy to Purchase Order (see Figure 6-11).**

Click here.

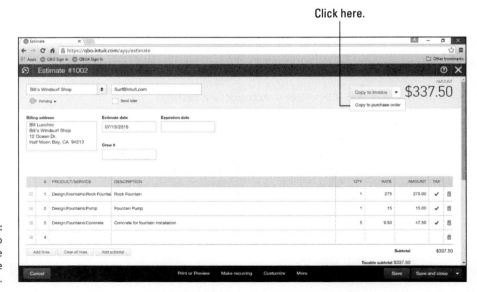

FIGURE 6-11:
Getting ready to
copy an estimate
to a purchase
order.

You might see the message that explains that some items on the estimate might not carry over to the purchase order. The message appears because some items on the estimate are set up without the "I Purchase This Product/Service From a Vendor" option selected.

3. **If the message appears, click OK to dismiss it.**

   QBO creates a purchase order using the information from your estimate and displays it in the Purchase Order window (see Figure 6-12).

FIGURE 6-12:
A purchase order
QBO created
from an estimate.

4. **Edit the purchase order as necessary, selecting a vendor and adding any more items to the purchase order.**

5. **Save the purchase order.**

Converting an estimate to an invoice

When you're ready to prepare an invoice for a customer based on an estimate you previously created, save yourself some time and effort and convert the estimate's information to an invoice. You can, if necessary, make adjustments to such an invoice by adding or removing lines. You can convert an estimate's information to an invoice using any of several approaches.

REMEMBER

Converting an estimate to an invoice in QBO automatically changes the estimate's status from Pending to Closed.

First, you can open the Invoice window and select the customer with the open estimate. QBO displays available documents you can link to the invoice, including any estimates (see Figure 6-13). Click the Add button at the bottom of an estimate, and QBO automatically adds the estimate information to the Invoice window.

Click here to add estimate information to the invoice.

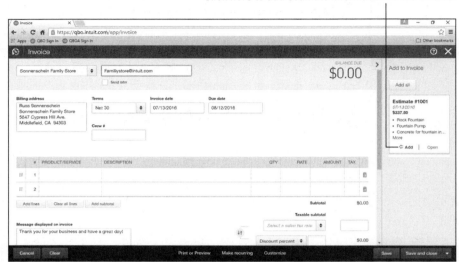

FIGURE 6-13: Converting an estimate to an invoice from the Invoice window.

Second, you can filter the Sales Transactions page to display only estimates, and click the Start Invoice link in the Action column beside the estimate you want to convert (see Figure 6-14). QBO displays an invoice that contains all the lines available on the estimate.

Third, from the Sales Transactions page, you can click the estimate to open it (and review its content, if you want). In the Estimate window of any estimate with a status of Pending, you'll find a Copy to Invoice button, as shown in Figure 6-15; click that button, and QBO displays the Invoice window containing all the information from the estimate.

Regardless of the method you use, after you have converted an estimate on an invoice, QBO changes the estimate's status from Pending to Closed. Be aware that QBO closes the estimate even if you don't invoice the customer for all lines on the estimate. Also be aware that you can change an estimate's status from Closed to Pending, but, if you do, you are making all lines on the estimate available for invoicing — and you could then accidentally invoice your customer twice for the same goods. So, if your customer buys only some lines on the estimate but intends to buy other lines at a later point in time, your best bet to ensure that you have the right information available for a future invoice is to let QBO close the original estimate and create another estimate for only the lines the customer didn't yet buy.

Filtering to view only estimates

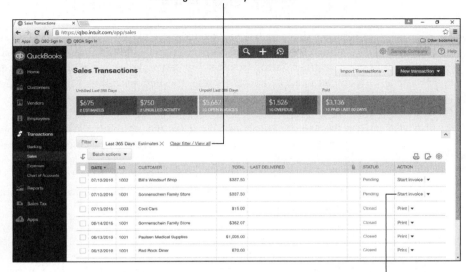

FIGURE 6-14:
Click the Start
Invoice link to use
estimate
information on
an invoice.

Click this link to start an invoice based on an estimate.

Click here to copy estimate information to an invoice.

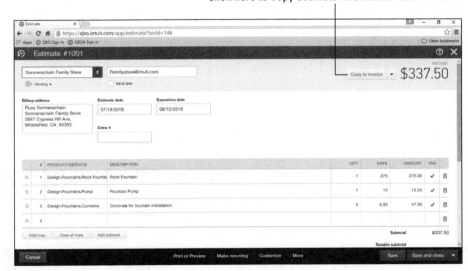

FIGURE 6-15:
Click Copy to
Invoice to display
estimate
information on
an invoice.

Copying an existing estimate

Suppose that you have an existing estimate — even one you've already converted to an invoice — and you want to create a new estimate using most of the information on the existing invoice. You can make a copy of the existing estimate, edit the copy as needed, and then save the new estimate. Making a copy saves you time because you don't need to reenter a lot of information.

On the Sales Transactions list, click the estimate you want to copy to open it in the Estimate window. Notice that, in Figure 6-16, I've displayed an estimate with a status of Closed.

At the bottom of the window, click the More button and, from the menu that appears, click Copy.

The estimate's status is Closed.

FIGURE 6-16:
Click Copy to duplicate an estimate, even if it's closed.

Click here to copy the estimate.

QBO opens a new estimate that already contains the information of the estimate you copied. Just above the Billing Address information, you see a message that explains that the estimate you're viewing is a copy and you should make any changes you need (see Figure 6-17). For example, change the customer, and QBO updates the Billing Address information. Feel free to add or delete lines as needed. When you finish making changes, click Save or Save and Send, as appropriate.

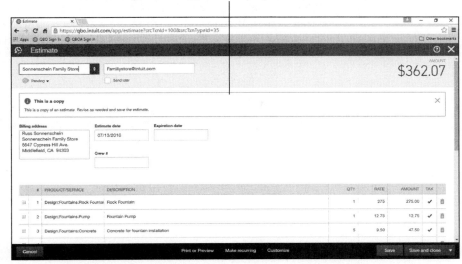

The message indicating you're working in a duplicate estimate

FIGURE 6-17: Edit the duplicated estimate and save it.

Working with Sales Receipts

You use invoices when you need to track money that a customer owes you but hasn't yet paid. But suppose that your customer pays you at the time you sell goods or render services. In these situations, you don't need to enter an invoice; instead, you can enter a sales receipt. And, if you're shipping the items to the customer, you can print a packing list, which shows the quantities of the items the customer purchased without price information.

Entering a sales receipt

To enter a sales receipt, click Create ⇨ Sales Receipt or, from the Sales Transactions page, click New Transaction ⇨ Sales Receipt to display the window shown in Figure 6-18.

The sales receipt form closely resembles other sales forms you've seen in this chapter: You select a customer — QBO fills in customer billing address information and assigns today's date to the transaction — enter a payment method and optional reference number, and select the account into which QBO should place the funds. See the sidebar in this chapter, "Using the Undeposited Funds account," for information on selecting an account from the Deposit To list.

You fill out the rest of the Sales Receipt transaction the same way you fill out an invoice transaction; if you scroll down in the window, you'll find the same fields at the bottom of the Sales Receipt window as the ones that appear at the bottom of the Invoice window.

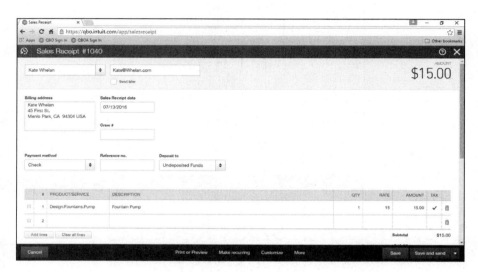

FIGURE 6-18:
A sales receipt.

Printing sales receipts and packing slips

You can print both the sales receipt and, if appropriate, a packing list. To print either document, click the Print or Preview button at the bottom of the Sales Receipt window. Regardless of the document you opt to print, QBO saves the sales receipt and then displays a preview window. If you opt to print the sales receipt, QBO displays a preview window you can use to scroll through the appearance of the sales receipt. But, a better preview appears when you click the Print button (see Figure 6-19).

Notice that the sales receipt displays all pertinent information, including the prices of items.

If you opt to print the packing slip, QBO again saves the sales receipt if you haven't already saved it. Then, QBO again displays a preview window you can use to scroll through the appearance of the packing slip, but, a better preview appears when you click the Print button (see Figure 6-20).

Notice that the packing slip identifies only what the customer bought and not how much the customer paid.

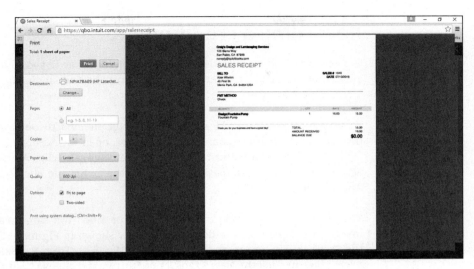

FIGURE 6-19:
The Print Preview window for a sales receipt.

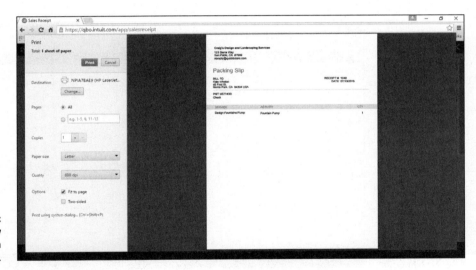

FIGURE 6-20:
The Print Preview window for a packing slip.

Giving Money Back to a Customer

It happens. It's a bummer, but, it happens. Occasionally, you need to return money you have received from a customer.

If a customer returns merchandise to you, issue a credit memo. Alternatively, if you need to refund money to a customer — perhaps because goods arrived damaged and the customer doesn't want to reorder them — issue a refund receipt.

Recording a credit memo

If a customer returns goods previously purchased or if you and your customer agree that the customer's outstanding or future balance should be reduced, record a credit memo in QBO.

TIP

By default, QBO automatically applies credit memos to outstanding or future invoices. If you want to change that behavior, open the Account and Settings dialog box (choose Gear menu ⇨ Account and Settings) and click Advanced on the left. Scroll down to the Automation section on the right, and click the Automatically Apply Credits option.

You enter a Credit Memo transaction pretty much the same way you enter an invoice; to display the Credit Memo window shown in Figure 6-21, you can click the Create menu button and choose Credit Memo or, from the Sales Transactions page, you can click the New Transaction button and choose Credit Memo.

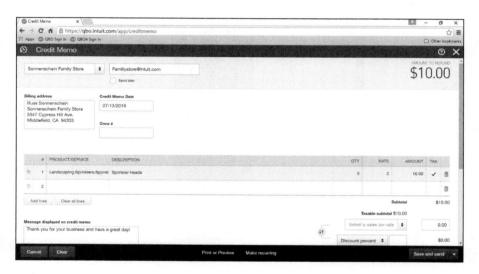

FIGURE 6-21:
Entering a credit memo.

Select the customer, fill in the products or services for which you are issuing a credit memo, fill in the bottom of the Credit Memo window with appropriate information, and save the transaction. This transaction window is very similar to the Invoice transaction window: Refer to the section "Preparing an Invoice" for details.

You can enter a credit memo for a customer even if that customer currently has no outstanding invoices; when you enter the customer's next invoice, QBO will apply the credit memo to the invoice.

When you enter a credit memo for a customer who has outstanding invoices, QBO applies the credit memo to an outstanding invoice; if you view the Sales

Transactions list for that particular invoice, you'll notice that its Status is Partial, meaning that the invoice is partially paid (see Figure 6-22).

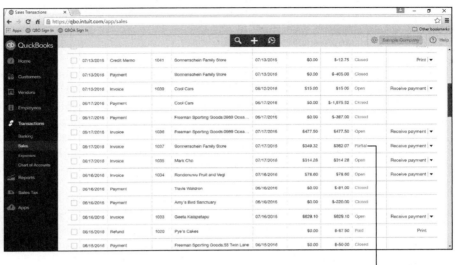

FIGURE 6-22:
An invoice to which QBO has applied a credit memo.

Invoice with a credit memo applied

If you click the invoice to view it, you'll see the credit amount on the Amount Received line at the bottom of the invoice (see Figure 6-23).

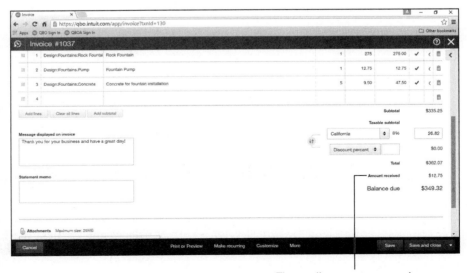

FIGURE 6-23:
By default, QBO applies credit memos to an existing outstanding invoice.

The credit amount appears here.

Issuing a refund to a customer

Use QBO's Refund Receipt transaction if you need to refund money to a customer instead of reducing an outstanding or future balance. In this example, I'm going to issue a refund check to a customer, which will deduct the amount of the refund from a Bank account and reduce an Income account. The customer didn't return any items.

TIP

To account for refunds you issue when a customer doesn't return an item, first set up an account called something like Returns and Allowances and assign this account to the Category Type of Income and a Detail Type of Discounts/Refunds Given. Then set up a service on the Products and Services list and call it something like Customer Refunds or even Returns & Allowances. Do *not* select Is Taxable for the service. Assign the service to the Returns and Allowances account and don't assign a default Price/Rate.

Filling in the Refund Receipt window is very similar to filling in the Invoice window, so, if you need more details than I supply here, see the section "Preparing an Invoice." To display the Refund Receipt window shown in Figure 6-24, click the Create button — the plus (+) sign — and choose Refund Receipt in the Customers column. Select a customer, and QBO fills in related customer information.

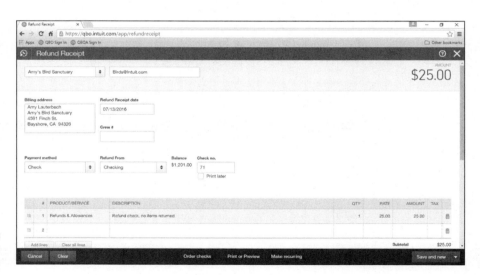

FIGURE 6-24: Issuing a refund check.

Select a payment method and an account; if you select a Bank account like I did, QBO lists the Bank account's current balance and the next check number associated with the account. If you want, click the Print Later check box.

In my example, the customer isn't returning any items, so I selected the Refunds & Allowances service. If your customer is returning items, select the item in the

Product/Service column that the customer is returning in exchange for the refund and don't select the Refunds and Allowances service shown in Figure 6-24.

You can scroll down to the bottom of the Refund Receipt transaction window and fill in all the same information available at the bottom of an invoice.

Creating Billable Time Entries

Your employees might work directly for you on activities needed to run your company (such as preparing customer invoices or entering accounting information into QBO), and they might also perform work directly related to your customers. In the latter case, you might want to track the time employees spend on client-related projects and then bill your customers for your employees' time.

To track time, you use either the Time Activity window or the Weekly Timesheet window; regardless of the window you use, QBO tracks the time entered and, when you prepare an invoice for a client for whom time was recorded, QBO prompts you to add the time to the invoice.

In this section, you'll learn to enter time using both the Time Activity window and the Weekly Timesheet window, and you'll see how QBO prompts you to include the billable time on a customer's invoice. Note that a time entry that you can bill back to a customer is called, cleverly, *billable time.*

Entering a single time activity

Open the Time Activity window using the Create plus (+) sign menu at the top of QBO. Follow these steps:

1. Click the Create plus (+) sign button to open the Create menu.

2. In the Employees column, click Single Time Activity.

   QBO displays the Time Activity window shown in Figure 6-25.

3. From the Name list, select the employee or vendor who performed the work.

4. Enter the date the work was performed.

5. From the Customer list, select the customer for whom the work was performed.

6. From the Service list, select the service that was performed.

7. Place a check in the Billable box, which changes to the Bill At box, and supply an hourly rate.

FIGURE 6-25:
The Time Activity
window.

8. **If the work performed is subject to tax, place a check in the Taxable box.**

9. **In the Time box, enter the amount of time spent on this activity.**

You can enter start and end times, including any break time, by checking the Enter Start and End Times box; QBO calculates the time spent and displays it below the Description box.

10. **Enter a description of the work that will appear, by default, on an invoice.**

You can change the description after adding the time entry to the invoice.

11. **Click Save to save the entry or Save and New to enter another time activity.**

If you click the arrow beside Save and New, you can choose Save and Close.

Using a timesheet to record time

If you prefer to enter time in a grid format that shows the days and dates for a week, then the Weekly Timesheet, shown in Figure 6-26, is for you. To enter time using this window, follow these steps:

1. **Click the Create button — the plus (+) sign — to open the Create menu.**

2. **In the Employees column, click Weekly Timesheet.**

3. **Select the name of the person whose time you're recording.**

4. **Select the week for which you want to record time.**

5. **In the Details section, select a customer name, a service item, and, if appropriate, supply a description.**

FIGURE 6-26:
The Weekly
Timesheet.

6. **To bill the time back to a customer, select the Billable check box and provide a rate at which to charge the time.**

7. **Fill in the time worked on the appropriate day.**

8. **Click Save, Save and New, or click the arrow beside Save and New and select Save and Close.**

Adding a billable expense to an invoice

You can add billable time entries to an invoice in a couple of ways. For example, if you view any customer's page, QBO displays a list of outstanding transactions, as shown in Figure 6-27. In the Action column of any billable time entry, QBO displays a Start Invoice button that you can click to start an invoice to the customer and include the billable expense on the invoice. To view a customer's page, click Customer in the Navigation bar and then click a customer's name.

But you don't need to go looking for billable time entries. QBO prompts you to add them to any invoice you create for a customer for whom billable time entries exist. Start an invoice (from the Create menu — the plus sign — click Invoice) and select a customer. If the customer has billable time entries, they appear in the pane on the right side of the screen (see Figure 6-28).

Click the Add button in each billable time entry that you want to add to the invoice. Or, to add all the entries, click the Add All button at the top of the pane on the right. QBO enters each billable time entry's information on a line on the invoice, filling in the service, description, quantity, rate, and total amount. You can edit any information on the line as needed. Fill in the rest of the invoice as described in the section "Preparing an Invoice," adding other lines that might not pertain to time entries.

TIP

Don't forget that you can add a subtotal for time entries, if you choose. See the first section in this chapter, "Customizing Forms to Handle Subtotals," for details.

Click here to display your customer list and select a different customer.

These lines contain billable expenses.

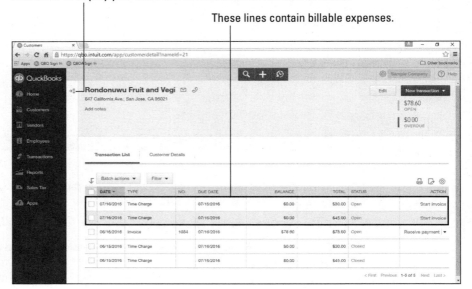

FIGURE 6-27:
Viewing a customer's page in QBO.

Click here to add all entries to the invoice.

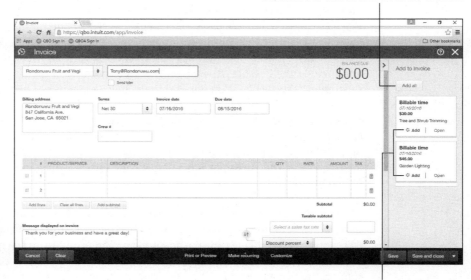

FIGURE 6-28:
Creating an invoice for a customer with billable time entries.

Click here to add a single entry to the invoice.

Chapter **7**

Working in Registers

C hapters 5 and 6 show you how to enter transactions such as checks, sales receipts, invoices, and customer payments using various QBO transaction windows. You also see ways to find and filter for certain transactions.

But transaction windows and lists aren't the only way to work with transactions in QBO. You can use registers. Some people are more comfortable entering transactions, particularly checks, into a register.

And many people find it easy to use a register to quickly view the transactions that affect a particular account and find particular transactions, as described at the end of this chapter.

Understanding Registers

You use registers to see every transaction that affects a particular account. Registers in QBO contain much of the same information you find in the paper registers that banks give you along with handwritten checks. To view the register for a particular account, click Gear ⇨ Chart of Accounts. Then use the View Register link in the Action column to display the register of a particular account (see Figure 7-1).

Click here.

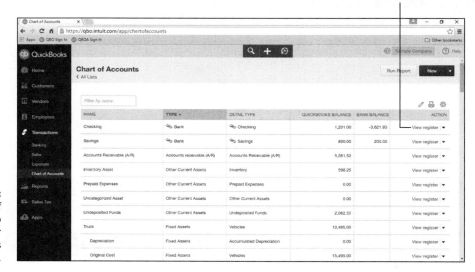

FIGURE 7-1:
Use the Chart of
Accounts page to
open a particular
account's
register.

When you switch to a register, QBO assumes you want to enter a new transaction and displays a new transaction window at the bottom of the register. In Figure 7-2, I've closed that new transaction window so that you can see a Bank account register in QBO as it appears by default.

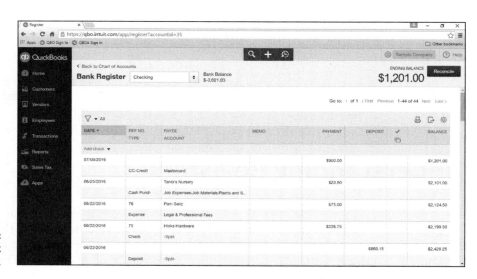

FIGURE 7-2:
A typical Bank
account register.

The register page displays the name of the account — in this case, Checking — and its ending balance at the top of the register.

Because the bank account register shown in Figure 7-2 is electronically connected to its counterpart at a banking institution, you also see the balance in the account as that financial institution reports it — and in this case, the balance at the bank is negative.

One rule you need to remember about registers: They are *not* available for all accounts. You'll find that registers are available for all *balance sheet* accounts except Retained Earnings. Balance sheet accounts fall into the following QBO account category types:

>> Bank

>> Accounts Receivable

>> Other Current Assets

>> Fixed Assets

>> Other Assets

>> Accounts Payable

>> Credit Card

>> Other Current Liabilities

>> Long Term Liabilities

>> Equity

You see these account category types when you add a new account to the Chart of Accounts or when you view the Chart of Accounts page in QBO.

TIP

If you use account numbers, then typically all asset accounts begin with 10000, all liability accounts begin with 20000, and all equity accounts begin with 30000. This numbering scheme is *not* carved in stone, but most accountants recommend that you follow these guidelines when you assign numbers to the accounts in your Chart of Accounts.

Within the register, you see column headings that identify the information contained in each column for every transaction and, at the right edge of a register page, you see a running balance for the account. All the transactions in a Bank account register affect a Bank account — along with some other account, as dictated by the rules of accounting (*double-entry bookkeeping*, a founding principle of accounting, means that every transaction affects at least two accounts). The amount shown in the Balance column is a running balance for the account as long as the register is sorted by date.

TIP

At the end of this chapter, in the section "Other Things You Can Do in a Register," you learn how to sort a register so that it appears in some order other than the default transaction date order. Be aware that if you sort by any column other than the Date column, the Balance column won't display any information because the information wouldn't make any sense.

By default, the latest transactions appear at the top of the register, but, if you prefer, you can change the appearance of the register to use Paper Ledger Mode, as shown in Figure 7-3. In Paper Ledger Mode, QBO lists transactions from earliest to latest — similar to the way transactions appear when you use a paper bank account register. In a paper register, you enter your transactions as they occur, so the earliest transactions appear at the top of the register and the latest transactions appear at the bottom of the register.

Click here.

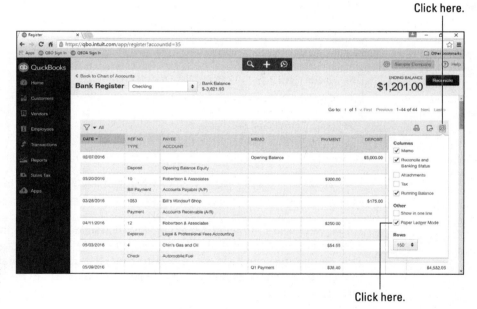

Click here.

FIGURE 7-3:
A bank account register in Paper Ledger Mode.

REMEMBER

When you switch to Paper Ledger Mode, QBO assumes you want to enter a new transaction, as described later in this chapter in the section "Entering a transaction," and automatically displays a new transaction window at the bottom of the register page.

To switch to Paper Ledger Mode, follow these steps:

1. **Click the Table Settings gear above the Balance column.**

Refer to Figure 7-3.

2. **From the drop-down menu that appears, click Paper Ledger Mode to select it.**

QBO reorders the transactions in the register so that they appear in date order from oldest to newest.

In addition, QBO displays a new transaction window at the bottom of the register.

To switch back to the register's regular appearance, repeat the steps above; when you remove the check beside Paper Ledger Mode, QBO reorders the transactions in the register in date order with the latest transaction at the top of the register page.

TIP

QBO remembers the setting you select for the register's appearance; if you choose to display the register in Paper Ledger Mode, the next time you display any register, QBO displays it in Paper Ledger Mode.

In addition to using Paper Ledger Mode, you can control the appearance of a register in a few other ways; you can

» Change the size of columns

» Control the number of rows on a page in your QBO company

» Reduce each register entry to a single line

TIP

QBO remembers adjustments you make in registers, even after you navigate away from the register. Further, if you open a different register, QBO applies your adjustments to that register.

To change the size of any column, slide the mouse pointer into the column heading area on the right boundary of the column. In Figure 7-4, I'm resizing the Ref No. Type column. When the mouse pointer changes to a pair of left- and right-pointing arrows connected to a pair of vertical bars, drag the pointer. Dragging to the left makes the column narrower, and dragging to the right to makes the column wider. As you drag, a solid vertical line helps you determine the size of the column. Release the mouse button when the column reaches the size you want.

If resizing columns doesn't satisfy your viewing needs, you can save space horizontally by removing columns from the register. To do so, you use the options on the Table Settings gear. Click the Gear button above the Balance column (see Figure 7-5). In the Columns section, remove the checks beside any options you don't need to view; by default, QBO displays the Memo, Reconcile and Banking Status, and Running Balance columns. Remove the checks beside these options and QBO removes their columns from the register.

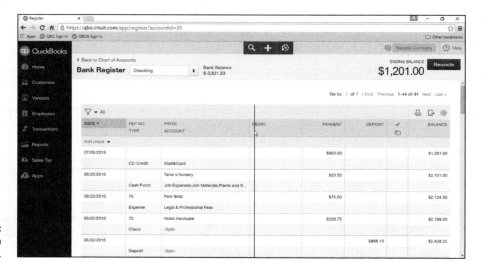

FIGURE 7-4:
Resizing a
column.

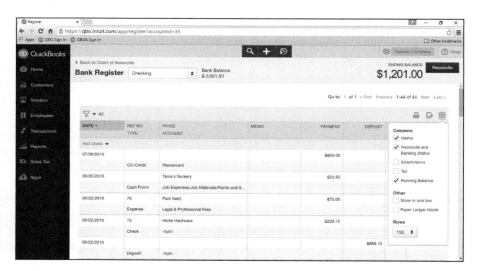

FIGURE 7-5:
Options you can
use to control the
appearance of
the register.

To save space vertically, place a check mark in the Show in One Line box and change the number of rows that appear on a page. You can display 50 rows, 150 rows, or 300 rows. Figure 7-6 shows a register displaying a single line for each transaction.

REMEMBER

By default, if you opt to show transactions on a single line in the register, QBO hides the Memo and the Reconcile and Banking Status columns.

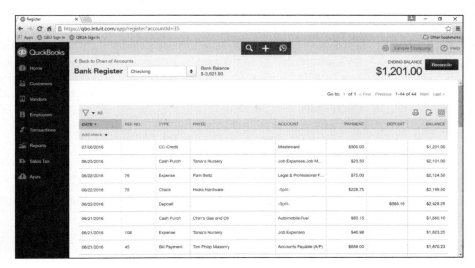

FIGURE 7-6:
A register
displaying one
line for each
transaction.

Entering and Editing Transactions

Many people are comfortable using a Bank account register to enter a check or a bill payment; some people are also comfortable entering a bill in the Accounts Payable register or an invoice in the Accounts Receivable register. But, even if you're not comfortable entering transactions in a register, many people find viewing a transaction in a register very easy and helpful.

You open a register from the Chart of Accounts page. To open the Chart of Accounts page, click the Gear button beside your company's name and, from the menu that appears, click Chart of Accounts in the Settings column. From the Chart of Accounts page (shown earlier in Figure 7-1), you click the View Register link in the Action column beside any account that displays the link to display that account's register; all accounts displaying the link are balance sheet accounts.

Entering a transaction

Because checks are the transaction most often entered using a register, I'm focusing the discussion in this section on Bank account registers. After you click the View Register link of a Bank or Credit Card account, you can enter a transaction into the register.

REMEMBER

If you need to add attachments to transactions you enter, display the Attachment column in the register; click Table Gear Settings ⇨ Attachments. You can see the open Table Gear Settings menu in Figure 7-5. Displaying the Attachments column automatically gives you the option to add an attachment as you enter a transaction.

By default, when you first open a register, QBO assumes you want to add a transaction and opens the window you use to enter the most common transaction type for that register — in the case of a Bank account, QBO opens the Add Check window. But let's suppose that you've already entered a transaction and now you want to enter another transaction. To start a new transaction and enter it, follow these steps:

1. **Click the down arrow beside the Add button.**

   The Add button, which appears just below the Date column heading, is named Add Check in Bank accounts and Add CC Expense in Credit Card accounts.

   After you open the list box, QBO displays the list of available transaction types (see Figure 7-7).

TIP

   For you keyboard fans, you can press Ctrl+Alt+N to open the Add list box.

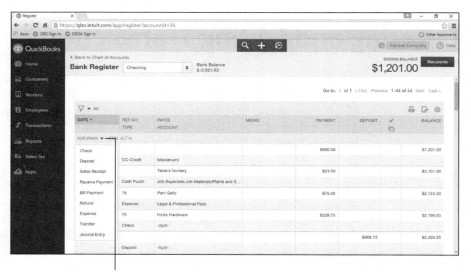

FIGURE 7-7:
Select the type of transaction you want to enter.

Click here to display the available transaction types.

REMEMBER

QBO displays only those types of transactions available in the account register you opened. For example, you can record a customer payment in a Bank account register, but you cannot enter a customer invoice. Similarly, you can record a check or a bill payment in a Bank account register, but you cannot enter a vendor bill.

2. **From the list that appears, select the type of transaction you want to enter.**

   QBO fills in today's date and displays lines so that you can complete the transaction (see Figure 7-8).

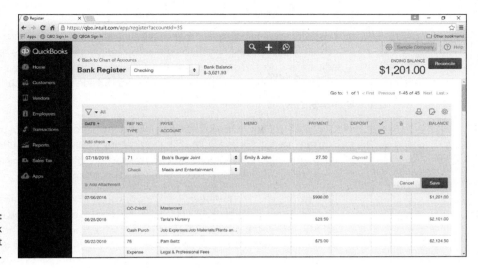

FIGURE 7-8:
Entering a check
in a Bank account
register.

3. **If necessary, change the transaction date.**

4. **Press Tab and, if appropriate, change the check number for the transaction.**

5. **Press Tab and supply a Payee name.**

   For example, if you're recording a payment you received from a customer, select the customer's name. If you're writing a check, select the check recipient's name.

6. **Press Tab and, in the Memo column, supply any memo information you want to record for the transaction.**

7. **Press Tab and, in the appropriate column, provide the amount of the transaction.**

   In a Bank account register, record a payment you're making in the Payment amount box and an amount you're depositing in the Deposit amount box.

8. **Press Tab.**

   QBO places the mouse pointer in the Reconcile and Banking Status column. This column displays a character representing the status of the transaction: C for Cleared or R for Reconciled. When the column is blank, the transaction is neither cleared nor reconciled. Typically this column is updated when you download or reconcile transactions.

   If the account is also connected electronically to your financial institution, this column also indicates whether a transaction was added or matched when transactions were downloaded via the account's bank feed.

WARNING

Don't be tempted to adjust the reconciliation status of a transaction from this screen because doing so adjusts the account's reconciled balance but the adjustment doesn't show up on reconciliation reports. You'll have a mess on your hands if you modify the reconciliation status outside the reconciliation process.

9. **Press Tab.**

QBO's placement of the insertion pointer depends on the type of transaction you're entering. For example, if you're entering a Sales Receipt, a Receive Payment, a Bill Payment, or a Refund transaction, QBO places the insertion point in the area where you can save the transaction.

If, however, you're entering a Check, a Deposit, an Expense, a Transfer, or a Journal Entry transaction, QBO places the insertion point in the Account column. Select the other account affected by the transaction (in addition to the account whose register you have opened). For example, if you're entering a check, select an Expense account. If you enter an account and press Tab, you can enter a memo for the transaction.

TIP

To add an attachment to the transaction, click the Add Attachment button in the lower left corner of the window. QBO opens a standard "Open" dialog box, where you navigate to the electronic document you want to attach to the transaction. Once you find it, click it and click Open to attach it to the transaction.

10. **Click the Save button that appears in the transaction.**

Keyboard fans, press Ctrl+Alt+S.

QBO saves the transaction and starts another of the same type. You can click Cancel to stop entering transactions.

Editing a transaction

You can edit the transaction in the register by clicking the transaction and then making changes. Or, if you prefer to use the transaction window for the type of transaction you selected, click the Edit button. For example, if you opt to edit an Expense transaction in an account register, QBO displays the transaction in the Expense window. If you opt to enter a Check transaction, QBO displays the transaction in the Check window. See Chapter 5 for examples of transaction windows.

Other Things You Can Do in a Register

Registers wouldn't be all that useful if you could only add and edit transactions. You need to be able to find transactions easily. And, it's always helpful to be able to print a register.

Sorting transactions

After a while, the number of transactions in a register can make the Register page very long, especially in a Bank account register. Looking for a transaction by skimming through the register — or *eyeballing* — can be a nonproductive way of finding a transaction. Instead, sort to help you find a particular transaction.

You can sort by any column in the register simply by clicking that column heading. In Figure 7-9, the transactions are sorted by date, in descending order from latest to earliest; note the downward-pointing arrow in the Date column.

Click a column heading to sort by that column.

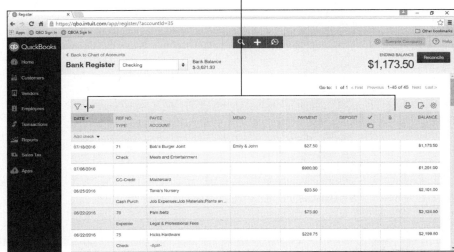

FIGURE 7-9:
Sorting transactions by date, from latest to earliest, is the default order QBO uses to display transactions.

To sort the transactions by date from earliest to latest, click the Date column; the arrow changes direction and points upward. Or suppose you want to search for transactions for a particular payee. You can click the Payee column heading to sorting transactions in alphabetical order by payee, and you can click the column heading a second time to sort in reverse alphabetical order.

WARNING

You can sort by any column heading *except* the Account, Balance, Memo, and Attachment columns. And, if you sort by any column other than Date, the Balance column won't display any information because the information wouldn't make any sense.

Filtering transactions

When sorting seems like the long way to find a transaction, try working with filters. Click the Filter button that appears just above the Date column, and QBO displays a variety of ways you can filter register transactions (see Figure 7-10).

Click here to view filter options.

Currently selected filter

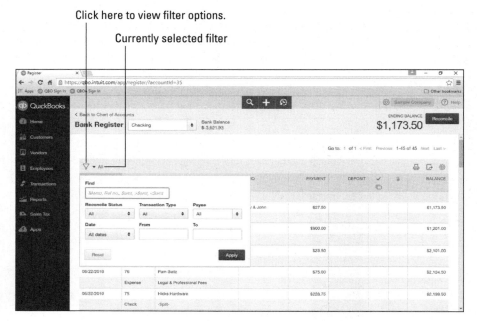

FIGURE 7-10:
Displaying
available filters.

TIP

The current filter appears just beside the Filter button. When you haven't selected any filters, you see All beside the Filter button.

If you're looking for a transaction of a certain dollar amount, enter the amount, making sure that you don't forget the currency symbol. When you filter by amounts, use these examples as a guideline:

>> 1234 will find all checks or reference numbers with 1234.

>> $500 will find all transactions that equal $500.

>> >$25 will find all transactions with amounts over $25.

To display transactions for a specific transaction date, use the All Dates box to select one of the predefined date ranges (such as Last Week) or use the Date From and To dates to view transactions only within that timeframe.

You also can filter by a transaction's reconciliation status, transaction type, or payee.

Any transactions that meet the criteria you specify in the Filter window appear in the register after you click Apply. In addition, the selected filter appears beside the Filter button (see Figure 7-11). You can click the Clear Filter/View All link to clear the filter and redisplay all transactions in the register.

The current filter appears here.

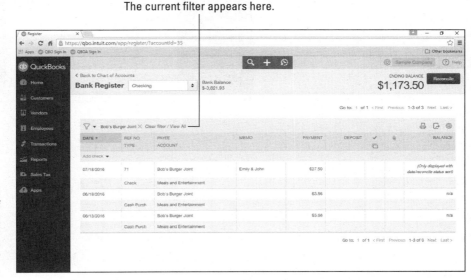

FIGURE 7-11:
A list of transactions QBO found based on criteria specified in the Filter window.

Printing a register

When doing research, many people find it easiest to print the information that appears in the register. To do so, click the Print button beside the register's Table Gear button (at the right edge of the register, just above the Balance column). QBO displays the Print tab, with your register formatted for printing (see Figure 7-12).

Select the printer you want to use and make any other necessary selections, such as the pages to print, the number of copies, and the layout orientation. When you finish selecting settings, click Print. When the report finishes printing, you can close the Print tab to redisplay your register in your QBO company.

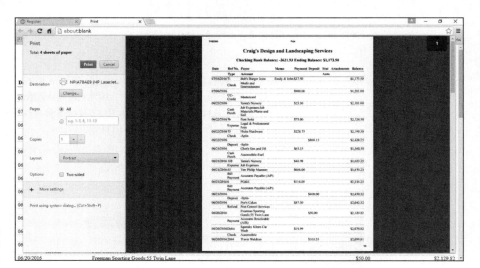

FIGURE 7-12:
Printing a
register.

IN THIS CHAPTER

» Managing the order and appearance
of Bank accounts

» Connecting QBO Bank and
Credit Card accounts to accounts
at financial institutions

» Making bank deposits

» Reconciling a Bank account

Chapter **8**

Handling Bank and Credit Card Transactions

The real title of this chapter should be "Handling Bank and Credit Card Transactions and Other Banking Tasks," but my editors said that title, although accurately descriptive, was too long.

So, in a nutshell, this chapter covers the ways you can connect Bank and Credit Card accounts in QBO to their counterparts at financial institutions. You also find out how to make bank deposits and reconcile your bank statement.

Controlling the Appearance of Bank Accounts

Before diving in to using Bank accounts, let's take a look at a few things you can do to make your life easier while working with Bank accounts.

Bank accounts (and Credit Card accounts) appear on the QBO Home page and also on the Bank and Credit Cards page. You can control the order in which your accounts appear on these pages. For example, perhaps you'd like your accounts to appear in alphabetical order. Or maybe you'd like them to appear in most used order. Whatever works for you.

On the QBO Home page, click the pencil that appears to the right of Bank Accounts (see Figure 8-1). The pencil changes to the Save button. Then using the icon that appears to the left of an account, drag up or down to move the account. Once the accounts appear in the order you want, click the Save button. Changes you make will appear on both the Home page and on the Bank and Credit Cards page.

Click here to change the order in which bank accounts appear.

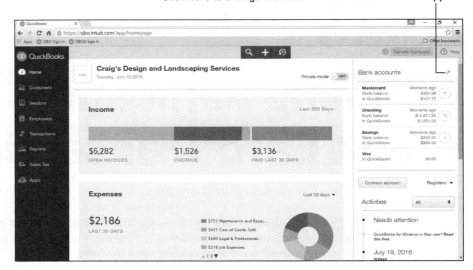

FIGURE 8-1:
Drag accounts to
place them in the
order you want.

In addition to changing the order of accounts, you can, to some extent, control the information that appears in the table on the Bank and Credit Cards page. For example, you can opt to

>> Display check numbers

>> Display Payee names

>> Make the date field editable so that you can change it if necessary

>> Display more detailed information about a transaction by displaying information provided by the bank

>> Copy bank detail information into the Memo field

You can display the Memo field in an individual bank register; see Chapter 7 for details.

TIP

To display the Bank and Credit Cards page, choose Transactions⇨Banking. To make changes to the page's appearance, click the Gear button that appears just above the Action column (see Figure 8-2).

Click here.

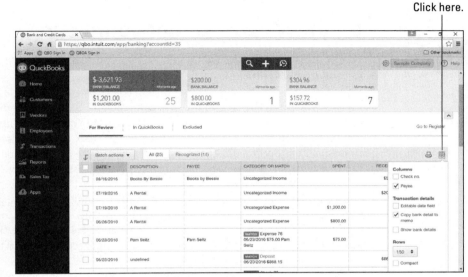

FIGURE 8-2:
Use the table
Gear button
to make changes
to the Bank and
Credit Card
page table.

You also can make adjustments to the column widths in the table on the Bank and Credit Cards page, and QBO will remember any column width adjustments you make, even after you sign out of QBO and then sign back in.

Connecting QBO Accounts to Financial Institutions

QBO offers three ways to connect QBO Bank and Credit Card accounts to corresponding accounts at financial institutions:

>> Connect directly if your bank supports a direct connection.

>> Use QuickBooks Web Connect.

>> Import transactions stored in an Excel file.

You have a fourth option: You don't have to connect at all. If you choose this fourth option, skip to the end of this chapter, where I discuss making bank deposits and reconciling bank statements. If you aren't sure whether to connect, read through this section until you make up your mind.

Connecting . . . or not connecting

I don't think Shakespeare would mind if I paraphrased Hamlet: "To connect or not to connect, that is the question."

In QBO, you might be able to directly connect QBO Bank and Credit Card accounts to their counterparts at financial institutions. I say "might" because not all financial institutions support directly connecting to QBO. If you bank at an institution that doesn't support a direct connection, you can use the QuickBooks Web Connect method to export transactions from the financial institution's website into QBO.

Before I dive into connecting, it's important to understand that you *don't have to connect.* You can work along quite happily in QBO without ever connecting an account at a financial institution to one in QBO. You simply enter transactions that affect the appropriate account and, monthly, you reconcile the accounts.

So, why connect? Most people connect to accounts at financial institutions so that they can electronically verify (by matching) the transactions recorded in QBO with the ones recorded at the financial institution. Connecting is, therefore, primarily a matter of convenience.

CONNECTING AS A FORM OF DATA ENTRY . . . NOT!

Don't be tempted to use connecting as a method for entering information into QBO. You might think you'll save time because you won't have to fill out transaction windows in QBO, but, in reality, you won't save time. As you see later in this chapter, you need to review every downloaded transaction and confirm that it is properly assigned in QBO. And, even if you review transactions daily, you won't have an up-to-date version of your accounting information, because you will know about transactions that have not yet cleared your financial institution. That means that the account balances in QBO won't really be up-to-date unless you enter transactions in QBO and use connecting as a method of confirming that your QBO balances match financial institution balances. Long story short: It's safer to enter transactions and use connected account information to confirm QBO balances.

Connecting Bank or Credit Card accounts

When you add a new Bank or Credit Card account, you can opt to connect it to a financial institution — or you can choose not to connect to a financial institution, as you read in the preceding section. The method you choose to add a new account depends on whether you want to connect it to a financial institution.

REMEMBER

Just a reminder: See Chapters 5 and 6 for details on entering transactions that affect a Bank account. You typically use an Expense transaction to record credit card purchases and sales receipts to record refunds to a credit card.

Adding but not connecting

In Chapter 3, I show you how to create a new Bank account in QBO. The technique I use in Chapter 3 assumes that you do not want to connect the QBO Bank account to its corresponding account at a financial institution. If you want to set up and not connect a Credit Card account, you use the same technique. For example, follow these steps to set up a Credit Card account that you don't intend to connect to a financial institution:

1. **Click the Gear button beside your company's name and, from the left side of the menu that appears, choose Chart of Accounts.**

   QBO displays the Chart of Accounts page.

2. **Click the New button on the Chart of Accounts page to open the Account dialog box (see Figure 8-3).**

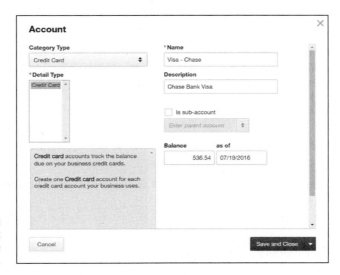

FIGURE 8-3:
The dialog box you use to create an account.

3. Open the Category Type list and choose Credit Card.

4. If you're using account numbers, supply a number for the new account.

5. Optionally, you can enter your account's balance as it appears on the last statement.

WARNING

If you enter a balance, QuickBooks updates both the account balance and the Opening Balance Equity account, and your accountant probably won't be happy with you. I suggest that you not enter a balance.

6. Click Save and Close.

QBO redisplays the Chart of Accounts page and your new account appears in the list.

REMEMBER

You'll need to enter expense transactions that have occurred since you received the last statement for this credit card account.

Adding and directly connecting

If, on the other hand, you want to create an account that is connected to a financial institution, you can do so if your financial institution offers the option to connect directly to QBO accounts. Gather up the user ID and password you use to log in to the financial institution online and follow these steps:

1. In the Navigation bar, choose Transactions ➪ Banking.

QBO displays the Bank and Credit Cards page.

2. In the upper right corner, click Add Account (see Figure 8-4).

QBO starts a wizard that helps you connect to a financial institution.

3. On the first wizard page, shown in Figure 8-5, you either provide your financial institution's website address, or you click your financial institution's name if it appears on the page.

TIP

To expand the search for banks, click the Search Global Banks option at the right edge of the website address box.

The screen that appears next depends on whether you typed a web address or clicked one of the popular banks onscreen. I clicked Chase.

4. Supply your user ID and password and click the Log In button.

Follow any additional onscreen prompts you see to finish setting up the account.

Click here.

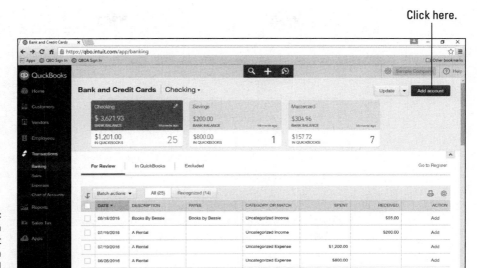

FIGURE 8-4:
Adding an
account
connected to a
financial
institution.

Type a web address here.

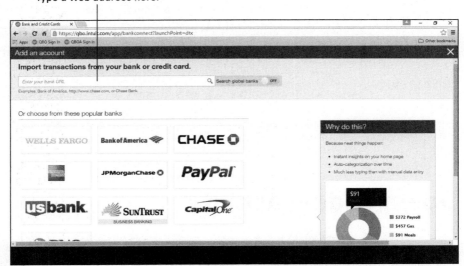

FIGURE 8-5:
Identify your
financial
institution.

DIRECTLY CONNECTING AFTER THE FACT

Suppose that you originally decided that you didn't want to connect a Bank or Credit Card account to a financial institution, but now you've decided that you do want to connect, and your bank supports direct connection. You're not out of luck.

If you follow the steps outlined for setting up an account that is connected to a financial institution, you'll end up with two accounts on your QBO Chart of Accounts for the same account. And that's okay because you can then merge the accounts so that the connected account ends up containing all the transactions from the unconnected account.

But I think you'll find it easier to connect after the fact by following these steps, which don't involve merging accounts; instead, you get the opportunity to identify accounts at your bank that should correspond to accounts in QBO:

1. **Choose Transactions ⇨ Banking.**

2. **Click the Add Account button.**

    QBO displays the page shown previously in Figure 8-5, where you select the bank with which you want to connect.

3. **Select your bank, supply the user ID and password you use to sign in to your bank's website, and click Log In.**

    A page appears, listing the accounts you can connect.

4. **Select the accounts you want to connect to QBO and choose Connect.**

You'll then be given the option to select accounts in QBO to tie to the selected online accounts.

Downloading activity

Once you've connected a Bank or Credit Card account to QBO, you download activity from the bank so that you can compare transactions you've entered in QBO with those the bank has cleared. The method you use to download activity depends on the method you use to connect to your financial institution.

Downloading information for a directly connected account

This is kind of a silly heading for the book, but I need a way to get your attention. You see, if you connect your account directly to a financial institution as described in the preceding section, transactions download automatically whenever

>> You sign in to QBO,

>> You manually update connected accounts to check for new transactions,

>> The bank automatically downloads transactions, which can happen periodically while you're working in QBO,

>> You upload transactions to QBO that you obtained via QuickBooks Web Connect (see the next section for details on QuickBooks Web Connect), and

>> You create or change an *auto-add rule* (you can read more about auto-add rules later in this chapter, in the section "Establishing rules to accept transactions."

So, if you connect your account directly to a financial institution, you don't need to take any action to download transactions.

You can view downloaded transactions by choosing Transactions⇨ Banking to display the Bank and Credit Cards page, from which you can compare transactions and resolve any issues. Later sections in this chapter cover more about using the Bank and Credit Cards page to review and, if necessary, resolve any questions.

Downloading information using QuickBooks Web Connect

If you can't connect your account directly to QBO, perhaps because your financial institution doesn't yet support QBO, you're not out of luck. Instead, you can use QuickBooks Web Connect, which has been around for years. If you were previously a QuickBooks desktop user, you might have used QuickBooks Web Connect. When you use QuickBooks Web Connect, you download transactions from your financial institution's website to your computer, and then you upload the downloaded transactions from your computer to QBO.

WARNING

Because QuickBooks Web Connect files are not encrypted, you should not use a public computer to download information using QuickBooks Web Connect.

To use QuickBooks Web Connect, follow these steps:

1. **Log in to your financial institution's website and look for a link that enables you to download to QuickBooks.**

Some banks have a "Download to QuickBooks" link. If you can't find the link, contact your financial institution and let them direct you to the link. After you find it, make note of where it appears on your financial institution's website for future use.

2. **Using the link you found in Step 1, select any of the following file formats:**

   - qbo: QuickBooks
   - .qfx: Quicken
   - .ofx: Microsoft Money

   If you save your file to some other format, QBO won't be able to upload it.

3. **Select the dates for the transactions you want to download.**

   If you download transactions with dates that precede the opening balance you entered for the account in QBO, the account's opening balance will change.

4. **Save the file to a location on your computer where you'll be able to find it later.**

   Many people download to the Downloads folder or to their Windows desktop.

5. **To upload the file to QBO, log in to QBO and, in the Navigation bar, choose Transactions ⇨ Banking.**

   QBO displays the Bank and Credit Cards page.

6. **At the right side of the page, click the arrow beside the Update button and choose File Upload (see Figure 8-6).**

   QBO starts the Upload Bank File wizard and displays the screen shown in Figure 8-7.

Click here to access the File Upload option.

FIGURE 8-6:
Click the File Upload button or click the arrow beside the Update button and select File Upload.

FIGURE 8-7:
Use this screen to navigate to the transactions you download from your financial institution.

7. Click the Browse button, navigate to the location where you saved the transactions you downloaded in Step 2, and select the downloaded file.

8. Click Next.

QBO displays a screen where you select the QBO account into which you want to upload the transactions.

9. Select the QBO account where the transactions should appear and click Next.

QBO uploads the transactions to the selected QBO account (The process can take a few minutes.)

10. When you see the confirmation screen, click Finish.

WARNING

After you successfully upload a QuickBooks Web Connect file, you should delete it because it is not encrypted and it contains your account information.

Importing transactions via Excel

If your bank supports downloading transactions to a CSV format (a *comma-separated values* format that can be read by Excel), you can download your banking activity to a CSV format and then import it into your QBO Bank account. First, log in to your bank's website and save your banking transactions. QBO can import CSV files formatted in either three or four columns, as shown in Tables 8-1 and 8-2.

TABLE 8-1 An Acceptable Three-Column Format

Date	Description	Amount
1/1/20‾9	Example payment	-100.00
1/1/20‾9	Example deposit	200.00

TABLE 8-2 An Acceptable Four-Column Format

Date	Description	Credit	Debit
1/1/2019	Example payment	100.00	
1/1/2019	Example deposit		200.00

Open your CSV file using Excel and make sure it matches one of these formats; if necessary, edit it. Then, follow these steps to import the transactions:

1. Choose Transactions ➪ Banking in the Navigation bar.

2. Click the arrow beside the Update button and, from the menu that appears, click File Upload.

   The Upload File page, shown earlier in Figure 8-7, appears.

3. Click the Browse button, select the CSV file you downloaded from your bank's website, and click Next.

4. Select the account into which you want to import transactions and click Next.

5. On the Map CSV Columns screen that appears, match the fields in QBO to the fields in your CSV file and then click Next (see Figure 8-8).

   The transactions you can import from your CSV file appear, with a check box to the left of each transaction. To avoid importing a particular transaction, select its check box.

6. Click Next.

   QBO displays the number of transactions that will be imported and asks if you want to import the transactions.

7. Click Yes to import the transactions.

   When QBO finishes importing the transactions, a confirmation screen appears.

8. Click Finish.

   The Bank and Credit Cards page appears, and the transactions you imported appear on the New Transactions tab.

FIGURE 8-8: Match QBO fields to the fields in your CSV file.

Handling downloaded activity

After you download transactions using either download method, you evaluate each transaction and, as appropriate, use them to update QuickBooks. From the Bank and Credit Cards page, you match, exclude, or add transactions downloaded from a financial institution to your QBO company.

REMEMBER

Don't worry; if you make a mistake, you can fix it, as described later in this chapter in the section titled (what else?) "Fixing mistakes."

Choose Transactions ➪ Banking to display the Bank and Credit Cards page (see Figure 8-9) and, if necessary, select an account by clicking it at the top of the page.

TIP

You match transactions the same way for bank accounts and for credit card accounts.

Just below the accounts, QBO displays three transaction status tabs:

>> If you click For Review, transactions appear that you have downloaded but have not yet specified how you want to handle.

>> If you click In QuickBooks, transactions appear that you have downloaded and added to QBO.

>> If you click Excluded, transactions appear that you have downloaded and decided not to include in QBO.

Transaction Status tabs

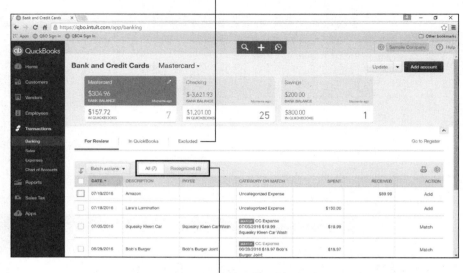

FIGURE 8-9:
Use this page to
specify how QBO
should handle
each downloaded
transaction.

Tabs used to view and filter downloaded transactions

To view the transactions you need to consider, click For Review. QBO displays a button you can use to take batch actions — I'll discuss that button in a moment — and two additional tabs:

» The All tab lets you view all downloaded transactions for the selected account.

» The Recognized tab displays downloaded transactions that QBO thinks it knows how to handle.

Both the All tab and the Recognized tab display the same information; think of the Recognized tab as a filtered version of the All tab.

In the Category or Match column, QBO suggests a way to assign each transaction. Using both information from other businesses like yours and your past behavior, QBO tries to identify downloaded transactions that potentially match transactions you entered in QBO. If you have previously accepted a transaction from a vendor, QBO assumes that you want to assign the same category to subsequent transactions for that vendor. And, if you change the payee on a transaction, QBO will suggest that change the next time a transaction appears for that payee.

TIP

Although the suggestions are helpful, after a while, you might find yourself wishing that QBO would stop suggesting and just record the transaction — and you can use *auto-add rules* to accomplish that behavior. See the section "Establishing rules to accept transactions" later in this chapter for details.

When QBO finds no matches, the words "Uncategorized Expense" or "Uncategorized Income" appear in the Category or Match column. When QBO finds only one possible match, QBO assumes the match is accurate and assigns the transaction accordingly; transactions like these appear in green in the Category or Match column; you can still make changes to the transaction before you accept it. If QBO finds multiple possibilities, QBO doesn't actually assign information to the transaction but notifies you of possible matches by displaying the match information in the Category or Match column in gray.

Read on to learn how to handle these situations.

Excluding transactions

Let's examine that Batch Actions button now. As you evaluate new transactions, you need to decide first whether they belong in QBO. I suggest that you identify transactions to exclude and then exclude them before you deal with transactions you intend to include in QBO. That way, you eliminate transactions that need no further consideration. When might you exclude a transaction from QBO? Suppose that you accidentally used a business credit card to pay for groceries. This transaction is not a business expense and shouldn't be part of your QBO transactions. So, you can exclude the transaction from QBO.

REMEMBER

When you reconcile your statement, remember that the statement balance will include all transactions, not just those you included in QBO.

To exclude a transaction, follow these steps:

1. On the For Review tab, select the check box beside each transaction you intend to exclude.

2. Click the Batch Actions button above the list of transactions.

3. From the menu that appears, click Exclude Selected.

QBO moves the selected transactions to the Excluded tab.

Including transactions

The remaining transactions fall into two categories: those that don't have an obvious matching transaction in QBO and those that do. And, you can identify the category into which a transaction falls using the Action column. If you see Add in the Action column, QBO couldn't find an obvious matching transaction; if you see Match in the Action column, QBO did find a potentially matching transaction (refer to Figure 8-9). QBO makes its best guess for adding or matching transactions, but it isn't perfect.

When QBO guesses correctly . . .

You need to confirm or change each transaction before you include it in QBO. If the listed transaction information is correct, you don't need to individually add or match transactions as described in the rest of this section. Instead, you can follow the steps in the preceding section except, in Step 3, click Accept Selected.

TIP

If you need to make the same change to a number of transactions, select those transactions and choose the Modify Selected option in the Batch Actions list.

When QBO doesn't know . . .

QBO might not know how to handle a transaction (for these transactions, QBO displays the words "Uncategorized Expense" or "Uncategorized Income" in the Category or Match column), or QBO might simply guess wrong. In these cases, you need to change the transaction before you accept it.

When you click any transaction that you intend to add to QBO, QBO expands the transaction information so that you can change the details of the transaction (see Figure 8-10). For example, you can use the option buttons above the transaction information to specify whether you want to add the transaction, search for a matching QBO transaction, or transfer the transaction information to another account. You also can change the category QBO suggests to one you deem more appropriate, and you can click the Split button to distribute the transaction among multiple categories. After you make your changes, you can click the Add button to add the transaction to QBO.

TIP

If you're working with a bank account transaction, be aware that you can change the check number if needed.

If you change the transaction's category, QBO will assume, in the future, that all transactions for the selected vendor should be assigned to the category you choose. You can change this behavior by clicking the Edit This Setting link just below the vendor's name. When you click the link, you can choose to leave future transactions uncategorized or to create a custom rule; I talk about rules in the next section, "Establishing rules to accept transactions."

You also can add attachments to any transaction using the Add Attachment link at the bottom of the expanded transaction information window.

When you click a downloaded transaction that QBO suggests you match to an existing QBO transaction, QBO displays a different set of details (see Figure 8-11). You can select the correct matching transaction, search for other matching transactions, add the transaction (and supply account information for it), or transfer the transaction to a different account. After you make your choices in this window, you can click the Match button at the right edge of the window.

Click here to change QBO's behavior when assigning categories.

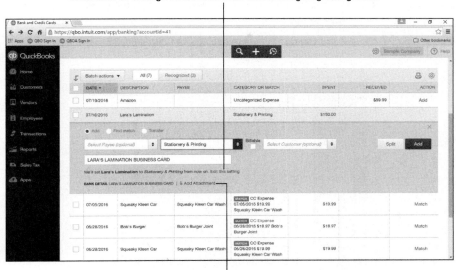

FIGURE 8-10:
When you click a transaction, QBO displays transaction details.

Click here to add an attachment.

FIGURE 8-11:
The transaction details QBO displays when you click a transaction you plan to match to an existing QBO transaction.

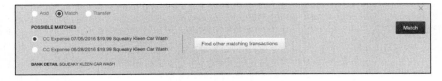

Repeat the process of adding and matching until you've handled all downloaded transactions.

Establishing rules to accept transactions

We've already established that QBO tries to learn your habits as you review downloaded transactions; you can help the process along by establishing rules for QBO to follow. When you set up rules, you speed up the review process because, effectively, you tell QBO in advance how to treat certain types of transactions.

THE ORDER OF RULES

The order of the rules you establish matters. QBO uses your rules in the order they appear on the Rules page and applies only one rule to any particular transaction. To ensure that QBO applies the correct rule to a transaction, you can reorder the rules. Drag the waffle icon that appears to the left of the rule on the Rules page.

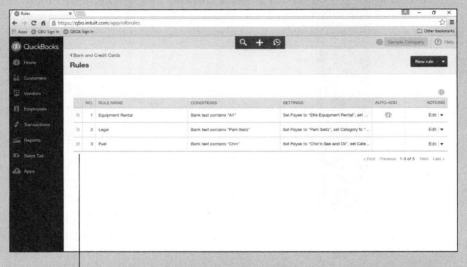

Drag here to reorder rules.

Suppose that you set up two rules in the following order.

- Rule 1: Categorize all transactions under $10 as Miscellaneous Expenses.
- Rule 2: Categorize all McDonald's transactions as Meals & Entertainment.

If a $12 dollar transaction from McDonald's appears, QBO applies Rule 2. But if a $7.50 transaction from McDonald's appears, QBO applies Rule 1.

How rules work

Suppose, for example, that you purchase gas for business-use cars from Shell gas stations and you always pay using a credit card you've connected to a financial institution in QBO. Effectively, you want to categorize all transactions at Shell stations to your Fuel expense account.

You can manually assign the category to one of these transactions and wait for QBO to "learn" your preference, or you can set up a rule for QBO to follow. When you establish a rule, you specify information such as the accounts and the types of transactions (money in or money out) to which the rule should apply.

TIP

You can create a rule that affects all accounts or a rule that affects specific accounts.

You then identify criteria that individual transactions should meet before QBO acts on the transactions. Last, you stipulate the information QBO should assign to transactions that meet the criteria. For example, you can specify a transaction type and a category.

The rules you establish can work in one of two ways:

» QBO can use your rule to suggest changes to downloaded transactions that you then review and approve. Or

» You can opt to have QBO automatically apply the rule to all transactions that it determines match the rule's conditions and add those transactions to QBO.

When you use the first approach, QBO identifies, on the For Review tab of the Bank and Credit Cards page, transactions for which it finds and expects to apply a rule. You can identify these transactions because, in the Category or Match column, they display a Rule icon, as shown in Figure 8-12.

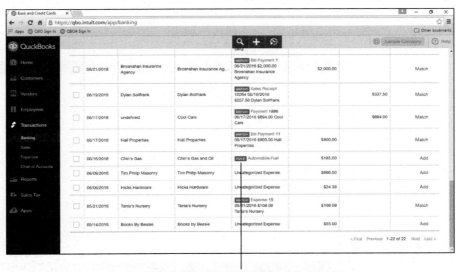

FIGURE 8-12:
QBO displays a Rule icon for transactions for which it finds a rule.

A transaction to which QBO applied a rule

TIP

QBO uses different icons to identify transactions matched by rules but not yet added to your company and transactions added automatically by rules; you can read more about these icons in the section "Fixing mistakes."

The second approach might seem risky, but it really isn't. Even though QBO automatically applies the rule, you can still make changes to transactions that QBO automatically accepts.

Creating a rule

You set up either type of rule — the one that suggests changes and you must review them, and the one that automatically adds transactions based on a rule — using the same steps. There's only one step where you do things differently; I'll point out that step when I get there.

1. **Choose Transactions ⇨ Banking.**

   The Bank and Credit Cards page appears.

2. **On the right side of the page, click the down arrow beside the Update button and choose Manage Rules.**

   QBO displays the Rules page, which appears in the figure in the sidebar "The order of rules."

3. **Click the New Rule button in the upper right corner of the Rules page.**

   QBO displays the Rule dialog box shown in Figure 8-13.

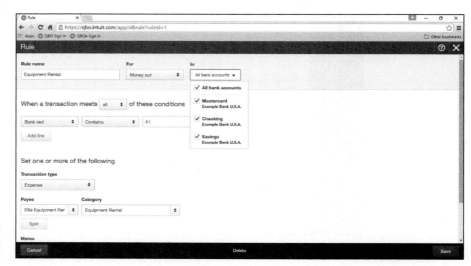

FIGURE 8-13:
The Rule dialog box.

4. Assign the rule a name — one that will be meaningful to you.

5. Identify whether the rule applies to money coming into QBO or money flowing out of QuickBooks, and select the accounts to which you want the rule to apply.

6. Use the "When a Transaction Meets" section to set criteria QBO should use when examining downloaded transactions to determine whether to apply the rule to them.

You can set multiple criteria using the Add Line button, and you can specify that a transaction should meet all or any of the criteria. Specifying "all" is more stringent and QBO is more selective about applying the rule.

TIP

The first list box in the section enables you to specify whether QBO should compare the transaction description, the bank text, or the transaction amount to a condition you set. For those inquiring minds out there, Description (the transaction description) refers to the text that appears in the Description column of the Bank and Credit Cards page. The Bank Text option refers to the Bank Detail description the bank downloads; you can view the Bank Detail description if you click any downloaded transaction. The Bank Detail description appears at the bottom left of the transactions being edited back in Figures 8-10 and 8-11.

7. At the bottom of the Rule dialog box, shown in Figure 8-14, set the information you want QBO to apply to transactions that meet the rule's criteria. You can select one or more of the following:

FIGURE 8-14:
Set the information you want QBO to apply to transactions when it uses the rule.

a. **Select the Transaction Type QBO should assign to the transaction.**

b. **Select the Payee and one or more categories to apply to transactions that meet the rule's conditions.**

c. **Optionally, add a Memo to each transaction that meets the rule's conditions.**

See the sidebar, "The Memo field and transactions rules" for a way you might want to use the Memo field.

d. **Select the Automatically Add to My Books check box if you want QBO to automatically add transactions that meet the rule's conditions to your company.**

TIP

REMEMBER

This is the "different" step I refer to in the introduction to these steps. If you select this box, you don't need to approve transactions to which QBO applies this rule. But you can always make changes to automatically added transactions.

8. **Click Save.**

Once you create a rule, you can use the Actions column of the Rules page to copy it (so that you don't have to create similar rules from scratch) and to delete rules you no longer want. And, if you need to edit a rule, click the Edit button in the Actions column to reopen the Rule dialog box and make changes.

TIP

Accountants, you can help your clients and save some time if you export and import rules between QBO companies. See Chapter 13 for details.

THE MEMO FIELD AND TRANSACTION RULES

QBO uses different special icons to identify transactions added using rules and transactions automatically added using rules. These icons follow the transactions into QBO registers. But, at the present time, you can't filter a register to show you only those transactions added by a rule (automatically or not).

You can, however, filter registers using the Memo field. So, if you anticipate needing to filter a register for transactions added by rules and transactions added automatically by rules, use the Memo field in the Rule dialog box to distinguish them. You might include text such as, "Added by Rule" and "Added Automatically by Rule" to appropriate rules.

Fixing mistakes

You can easily identify transactions to which QBO has applied rules. In Figure 8-12, you see that the Rule icon appears in the Category or Match column when QBO finds a transaction to which QBO wants to apply a rule. And you can see how QBO handles each downloaded transaction in your company when you click the In QuickBooks tab on the Bank and Credit Cards page (see Figure 8-15).

REMEMBER

QBO uses different icons to identify transactions added by rules and transactions added automatically by rules.

Click the QuickBooks tab to find transactions.

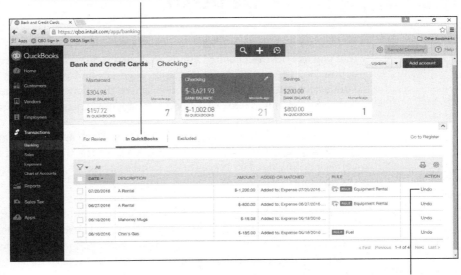

FIGURE 8-15:
Use the In QuickBooks tab to find transactions you've accepted into QBO.

Click here to undo an accepted transaction.

Suppose that you accidentally include a transaction in QBO that you meant to exclude. Or suppose that QBO assigned the wrong category to a transaction. You can easily correct these mistakes using the In QuickBooks tab on the Bank and Credit Cards page.

REMEMBER

The method used to match and add a transaction — manually, through a rule, or automatically through a rule — doesn't matter. You can make changes to any downloaded transaction. Be aware, though, that QBO treats downloaded transactions as having cleared your bank; so, if you edit a downloaded transaction in the register, QBO will ask you if you're sure.

If you include a transaction in QBO that contains mistakes — for example, the transaction was automatically added by a rule to the wrong category — you can undo the action. Undoing an accepted transaction places it back on the For Review tab, where you can make changes and accept it again as described earlier in this chapter in the sections "Excluding transactions" and "Including transactions."

To undo an accepted transaction, click the In QuickBooks tab on the Bank and Credit Cards page. Find the transaction and click the Undo link in the Action column. QBO displays a message explaining that it will place the transaction on the For Review tab, where you can click it, edit it, and accept it again — or, you can exclude it from QBO, if appropriate.

Making a Bank Deposit

In Chapter 6, I show you how to record payments from customers, and I suggest that you use the Undeposited Funds account as you record a Receive Payment transaction. So, after receiving a customer payment and placing it in the Undeposited Funds account, your Bank account — where the money will eventually show up — hasn't yet been updated. That updating happens when you prepare a bank deposit.

You can think of the Undeposited Funds account as a temporary holding place until you prepare a bank deposit. "So, why use the Undeposited Funds account?" you ask. "Why not just place the customer payments into the Bank account where they belong?"

Excellent questions. And the answers revolve around making sure that the bank deposits in QBO match the ones at your bank, because if the deposits match, bank statement reconciliation — everybody's least favorite task — becomes quite easy. But if they don't match . . . well, you don't want to go there.

For example, if you receive more than one customer payment on any given day, you'll take several checks to your bank that day. And you'll probably deposit all of them as a single deposit. Most banks typically don't record the individual checks that make up a deposit as individual deposits. Instead, the bank records the sum of the checks as your deposit — pretty much the same way you sum the checks on the deposit ticket you give to the bank teller.

"And why is this important?" you ask. This fact is important because, when you receive your statement from your bank, you need to match the bank's deposits and withdrawals with your own version of deposits and withdrawals. If you track each customer payment you receive as a deposit in the bank, then your QBO deposits *won't* match the bank's deposits. But if you record customer payments into the Undeposited Funds account, your deposits *will* match the bank's version of your deposits because you'll move multiple checks from the Undeposited Funds account to create a single deposit to your bank account.

So, assuming that you're following my advice and using the Undeposited Funds account before you prepare a bank deposit slip, you then use the Bank Deposit feature in QBO to sum up the payments you receive and intend to deposit simultaneously at your bank. QBO records, as the deposit amount in your QBO Bank account, the amount calculated in the Bank Deposit window, which will match the amount you actually deposit at your bank. Then your bank reconciliation process becomes quick and easy — okay, maybe not quick and easy, but certainly quicker and easier than if you were trying to figure out which customer payments make up various bank deposits.

To set up a bank deposit, follow these steps:

1. **Click the Create button — the plus (+) sign — and, from the Create menu, select Bank Deposit.**

QBO displays the Deposit transaction window shown in Figure 8-16. Existing payment transactions appear at the top of the window in the Select Existing Payments section of the window. You can use the lines in the Add New Deposits section to add a new payment transaction that is not associated with an outstanding invoice.

FIGURE 8-16:
Use the Deposit window to select payment transactions to deposit.

WARNING

Don't try to record a payment from a customer for an outstanding invoice in the Add New Deposits section. QBO is unlikely to match the line on the Deposit transaction to the outstanding invoice. Instead, record the Receive Payment transaction; the transaction will then appear in the Select Existing Payments section of the Deposit transaction window.

2. **At the top of the window, select the account into which you plan to deposit the payments.**

3. **In the Select Existing Payments section, click the check box beside each transaction you want to include on the deposit.**

4. **For each transaction you intend to deposit, select the Payment method.**

TIP

Credit card companies often deposit credit card transaction receipts into your Bank account, and most of them make a daily deposit. To keep bank statement reconciliation as simple as possible, I suggest that you record separate QBO deposits for each credit card you accept. You can group the checks and cash payment methods on the same deposit.

5. **Optionally, you can supply a memo and a reference number.**

The total of the selected payments — and the amount you intend to deposit unless you add entries in the Add New Deposits section — appears below the Select Existing Payments list.

6. **Scroll down the Deposit transaction window.**

Optionally, supply a memo for the deposit.

Optionally, supply a cash back amount — money from the deposit total that you don't intend to deposit — along with an account in which to place the cash back amount and a memo to describe the purpose of the cash back amount.

Optionally, you can attach an electronic document to the deposit, such as a scanned copy of the deposit ticket you take to the bank.

TIP

To attach an electronic document to the deposit, click in the Attachments box and navigate to the document or drag and drop the electronic copy into the Attachments box.

7. **Click Save and Close.**

QBO moves the deposited amount from the Undeposited Funds account to the account you selected in Step 2.

All that's left to do is take a trip to the bank. Or if you're mobile-savvy, you might be able to remotely deposit checks via your cellphone; talk to your banker.

Reconciling a Bank Account

Most people's least favorite task is reconciling the bank statement. But, if you're diligent about entering transactions in QBO and recording bank deposits as described in the preceding section, reconciling your bank statement should be a fairly easy process.

To reconcile an account, follow these steps:

1. **Click the Gear button beside your company name and, from the Tools portion of the menu that appears, select Reconcile.**

2. **From the Reconcile page that appears, select the account you want to reconcile and click the Reconcile Now button.**

   QBO displays the Start Reconciling dialog box shown in Figure 8-17.

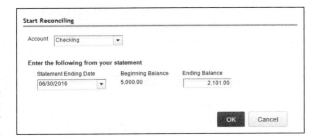

FIGURE 8-17: Enter information found on your bank statement.

3. **Enter the ending date and balance found on your bank statement, and then click OK.**

   QBO displays the Reconcile page shown in Figure 8-18.

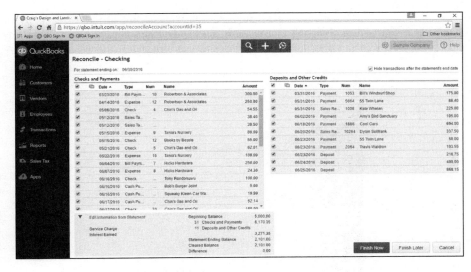

FIGURE 8-18: Match transactions found on your bank statement with those shown on the Reconcile page in QBO.

4. **Select each transaction that appears on your bank statement and in the Reconcile page.**

By selecting a transaction, you're marking it as having cleared the bank. Your goal is to have the Difference amount at the bottom of the Reconcile window equal $0.

TIP

If you have lots of transactions, make sure that a check appears in the Hide Transactions After the Statement's End Date check box (upper right corner of the window). Hiding those transactions can help you find transactions to clear. If the Difference amount isn't $0, then deselect the box to look for additional transactions to mark as cleared.

5. **When the Difference amount equals $0, click the Finish Now button.**

QBO redisplays the Reconcile page that appeared in Step 2 but wasn't shown. The reconciliation you just performed now appears in the Reconciliation History part of the screen (see Figure 8-19).

FIGURE 8-19:
A history of reconciliations for the selected account appears on the Reconcile page.

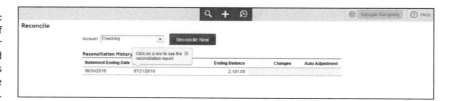

You can click any reconciliation on this page to see its Reconciliation report, which resembles the one shown in Figure 8-20.

You can drill down to view any transaction in the window where you created it; just click the transaction. And to produce a paper copy, click the Print button in the upper left corner of the report window.

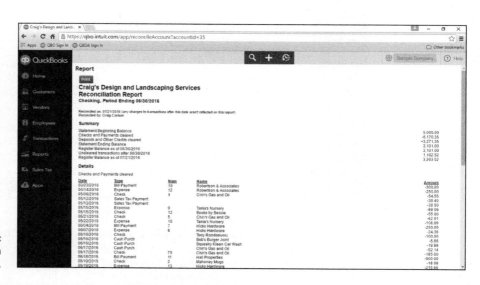

FIGURE 8-20:
A Reconciliation report.

Chapter **9**

Paying Employees

I t's important to understand that QBO users can prepare payroll in one of two ways: using QuickBooks Online with Enhanced Payroll (which I'll call QBOP) or using QuickBooks Online with Full Service Payroll. Although both of these options work in QBO, this chapter explores using QBOP, where you use QBO to do the work yourself. There isn't much point for me to describe QuickBooks Online with Full Service Payroll because Intuit does the work for you.

REMEMBER

A third alternative is to use Intuit Online Payroll; using this option, Intuit prepares payroll, manages all payroll tax payments, and prepares and files all payroll tax returns (including W-2s at the end of each year) for you — for a fee, of course. You can explore this option at `http://payroll.intuit.com/payroll-services/fullservice-payroll/`. Be aware that Intuit Online Payroll doesn't integrate with QBO.

"So, what's the difference between this and QuickBooks Online with Full Service Payroll?" you ask. If you or your accountant opt to use Intuit Online Payroll, you prepare payroll outside of QBO, and you can import the data you enter using Intuit Online Payroll into QBO. Generally speaking, Intuit Online Payroll is a pretty straightforward online payroll processing tool; you can take a tour at `http://payroll.intuit.com/online-payroll/`, and you can watch videos that show you the basics of using it. You also can sign up for a 30-day free trial.

UNDERSTANDING THE PAYROLL PROCESS

Just so you understand the job you're undertaking, be aware that running payroll is more than just issuing paychecks to your employees (although your employees will tell you that's the most important part of payroll). Yes, you first need to prepare accurate paychecks that account for withheld payroll taxes, deductions for benefits such as health insurance, and company contributions to, for example, retirement plans. But then, after you've prepared paychecks, you also need to electronically deposit withheld payroll taxes, remit amounts withheld for deductions and benefits to the appropriate parties, and file payroll tax returns with the appropriate taxing authorities. And all this work needs to be done according to a timetable that the IRS has established based on the size of your business's payroll tax liability.

Getting Started with QBO Payroll

When you prepare payroll, the process involves setup work so that you can accurately calculate payroll checks. You must also account for payroll taxes withheld from each employee's paycheck. You will remit federal and state payroll taxes to the appropriate tax authorities. You will also remit any required deductions and contributions that affect each employee's paycheck to appropriate agencies.

This section examines the payroll setup process in QBOP.

ENTERING PAYROLL HISTORY

If you've been using QuickBooks for Windows desktop and preparing payroll in it, you can import your company as described in Chapter 12. In that case, your employees will appear in QBO; but, assuming you're using QBOP, you'll have some setup work to complete, such as the work described in this section. When entering payroll history, you'll find two payroll reports useful:

- **The Payroll Summary report** for each employee for the current year, which you use to add year-to-date wages and taxes withheld for every W-2 employee.

- **The Payroll Summary report** for every payroll run for the current tax period, which you use to add payroll totals for past pay dates during the current tax period.

Turning on QBOP

QBOP uses a wizard to walk you through the setup process. You start by first turning on payroll in QBO. Then, the wizard walks you through setting up your company so that you can pay your employees.

Click the Employees link in the Navigation bar, and then click the Get Started with Payroll button (see Figure 9-1).

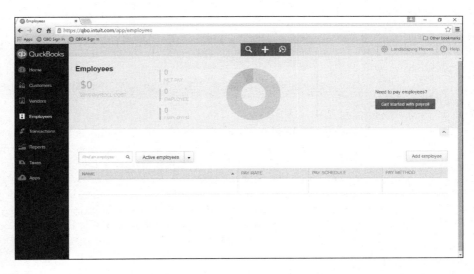

FIGURE 9-1:
Turning on QBOP.

The Get Ready for Payroll wizard starts. On the first page, QBO fills in information you provided when you initially set up your company. Double-check the information and click the Continue button in the lower right corner of the screen.

On the next screen of the wizard, you indicate whether you've been paying employees during the current year or whether you are about to start paying employees for the first time.

If you indicate that you have previously done payroll and are now switching to QBOP, the wizard displays two additional questions for you to answer, as shown in Figure 9-2. Answer the questions and click the Continue button in the lower right corner of the screen. If you indicate that you've not previously paid employees, no additional questions appear, so you can just click Continue.

REMEMBER

For this example, I'm going to assume that you've not previously paid any employees. If you have, I suggest that you use the payrolls you have completed as your learning tools and enter them into QBOP as described in the section "Preparing Payroll." That way, you'll learn how to prepare payroll and simultaneously get your payroll accounts up to date.

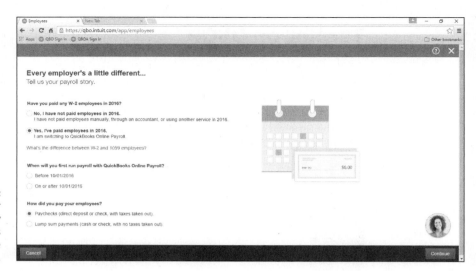

FIGURE 9-2:
Indicate whether
you've previously
paid employees
during the
current year.

The next page of the wizard asks if you have collected completed W-4 forms from your employees. W-4 forms are the Internal Revenue Service's form that employees complete to specify their withholding allowance. If you need to complete Form W-4 for any employee, you can click the Need W-4 Forms link in the Payroll Setup wizard to display and print or save a PDF version after printing the form; the form QBO displays is not an editable form. For an editable form that you can complete using your computer, visit www.irs.gov and click the W-4 link in the Forms & Pubs section to display editable PDF forms.

After you indicate that you have received completed W-4 forms from your employees, click Continue. The wizard prompts you to enter one of your employees. Provide the information for one of your employees and click Continue. QBO displays a screen like the one shown in Figure 9-3.

Provide the information for which the wizard prompts you:

>> Name

>> Form W-4 information

This information includes the employee's address, social security number, marital status, withholding amount, and state payroll tax — which varies from state to state, but QBOP prompts you to supply information for the state in which your business operates. The prompts for all this information appear when you click the Enter W-4 Form button.

To identify your state's payroll tax requirements, visit your state's website and search for *payroll taxes*.

TIP

FIGURE 9-3:
Provide
information
for the first
employee.

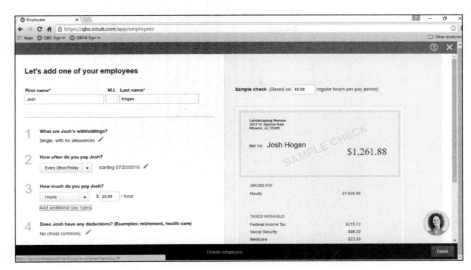

>> The frequency with which you pay the employee and the next expected pay date. When you supply pay frequency information, QBO creates a pay schedule that you can apply to subsequent employees you create.

>> The amount you pay the employee.

>> Whether the employee has any deductions.

>> The method you want to use to pay the employee (such as paper check or direct deposit).

After you answer questions 2–5, if you need to make changes, click the pencil icon beside the answer. As you supply information, QBOP updates the preview of the sample check on the right side of the window.

When you finish supplying the employee's information, click Done, and QBO displays the Employees page shown in Figure 9-4; the employee you set up appears in the list, and you can click the employee to edit the information, or you can click the Add employee button to add additional employees. You can display the Employees page at any time and click the Add employee button to set up additional employees.

TIP

If QBO displays a page with a Preview Payroll button in the bottom right corner, you can click the down arrow beside the button and opt to do so later.

Setting payroll preferences

In addition to adding employees, you should review payroll preferences and set up payroll taxes.

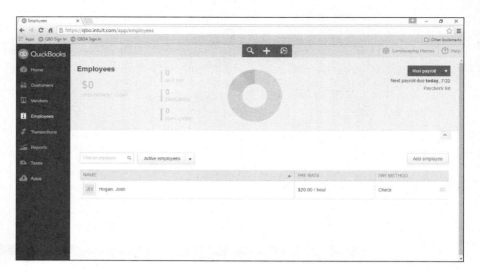

FIGURE 9-4:
Add or edit employees.

To review payroll preferences, click the Gear button beside your company's name and, from the menu that appears, click Payroll Settings (in the Settings column) to display the Preferences page shown in Figure 9-5. The page contains a series of links that you can click to review or establish various settings related to payroll. Understanding this page might make you feel less overwhelmed by what you see.

Additional links to settings pages   Column headings

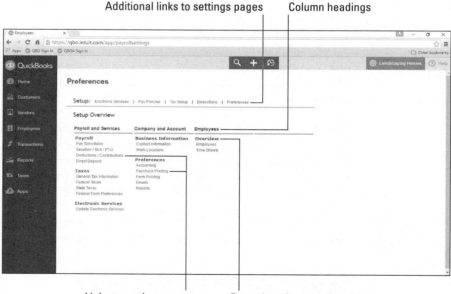

FIGURE 9-5:
The Payroll Preferences page.

Links to settings pages   Examples of section headings

The Setup Overview page is divided into three columns: Payroll and Services, Company and Account, and Employees. Within each column, you find additional headings — I'll refer to these additional headings as *section headings* — that summarize the types of settings you find as you click each link in that section. For example, under the Company and Account column, you find section headings for Business Information and Preferences. In the following bullets, I describe the kind of information you find as you click the links under each section heading on the Setup Overview page.

In addition, links appear above the Setup Overview heading; good news here — these aren't additional settings that you need to review. Instead, these links lead to the same pages as some of the links listed in the columns and section headings on the Setup Overview page. For example, the Electronic Services link at the top of the page displays the same page as the Update Electronic Services link in the Electronic Services section under the Payroll and Services column heading. And clicking the Pay Policies link displays the same page as clicking the Pay Schedules and Vacation/Sick/PTO links in the Payroll section under the Payroll and Services column heading.

In the bullets that follow, you find a description of the pages that appear as you click the links beneath each section heading:

>> In the Payroll section (under Payroll and Services), you can set up additional pay schedules; establish vacation, sick, and paid time off policies; define deductions and contributions used by your company during payroll; and set up direct deposit.

>> In the Taxes section, you establish general company tax information (such as your company's legal organization); set up your federal tax ID number and your filing and tax deposit schedule requirements; set up your state's payroll requirements, which vary from state to state; and designate whether you have a third-party or paid form preparer. To identify your state's payroll tax requirements, visit your state's website and search for *payroll taxes*.

>> Use the Electronic Services section to enroll in electronic services for filing and paying payroll taxes.

>> Use the Business Information section to ensure that your contact information is accurate.

>> Use the Preferences section to establish the following:

- Wage and tax accounts for payroll

- Paycheck and W-2 form printing settings

- Payroll-related email preferences such as receiving reminders about preparing payroll, making tax payments, and filing tax forms

- Report settings to identify reports you want available after you prepare payroll

>> In the Overview section, the Employees link takes you to the Employees page; clicking Employees on the Preferences page has the same effect as clicking Employees in the Navigation bar.

>> Use the Time Sheets link in the Overview section to establish the way you want to enter employee hours.

Setting up payroll taxes

Before you start using payroll, you should use the wizard QBOP provides to set up payroll tax form and filing information. The wizard asks you for federal and state tax details such as your federal Employer ID number (EIN) and your corresponding state account number, how often you're required to remit payroll taxes, and whether you want to file and pay taxes electronically or manually using paper coupons. Choose Taxes ⇨ Payroll Tax in the Navigation bar to display the Payroll Tax Center before you set things up (see Figure 9-6).

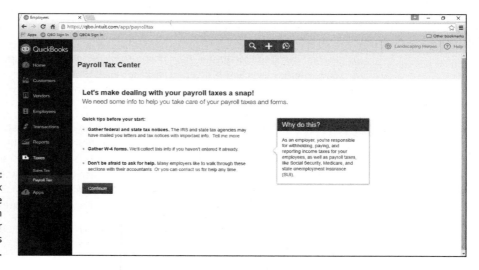

FIGURE 9-6:
The Payroll Tax Center before you establish settings for payroll tax forms and payments.

Click Continue, and the wizard displays the Employee Details page, which lists each of your employees. Fill in a birth date and hire date (in mm/dd/yyyy format) and click the W-4 Info link to confirm that the employee's W-4 details are correct.

After you check each employee, click Continue. On the next screen, the wizard displays the Business Details page. Confirm or change information the wizard supplies about your business, including the address you use when filing tax forms, the first time you'll be running payroll using QBOP, the timeframe during which you hired your first employee, and your workers' compensation insurance status.

See the "Getting up-and-running" sidebar for information about the date you intend to run your first QBOP payroll. Then, click Continue.

The Payroll Tax setup wizard next displays the Federal Tax Details page shown in Figure 9-7. Supply your federal Employer Identification Number (EIN), and confirm the payroll tax form you use and how often you must remit payroll taxes. You should also specify whether your company is a federally recognized non-profit organization that is not required to pay federal unemployment taxes (FUTA).

Click Continue, and the Payroll Tax setup wizard displays the State Tax Details page. This page is the state counterpart of the Federal Tax Details page. On the State Tax Details page, you supply details about your state payroll account, including the number, the State Unemployment Insurance (SUI) rate assigned to your business, and your state payroll tax deposit schedule. You also supply details for other taxes, if any, in your state.

Click Save, and QBO displays the E-pay and E-file Setup page, where you specify whether you want to file and pay payroll taxes electronically or manually, using paper coupons. If you opt to file and pay electronically, you then supply information about the bank account from which you want to pay, including your routing and account number.

When you finish supplying information about how you want to file and pay your taxes, click Next. QBO confirms that you've finished setting up your payroll taxes. Click Done, and QBO redisplays the Payroll Tax Center screen (see Figure 9-8).

GETTING UP-AND-RUNNING

The date you start using QBOP determines the "as of" date of historical information you need to collect. Try to start using QBOP on January 1 of any year — that way, you don't need to enter any historical information. If you can't start using QBOP on January 1, try to start using it on the first day of an accounting period — either on the first day of your company's fiscal year or on the first day of a month.

If you are starting on a date other than January 1 and have issued payroll checks during the current year and prior to using QBOP, I suggest that you use these prior payrolls as a learning tool. You can enter the paychecks and then record the tax payments and prepare the tax forms without e-filing anything you've already filed; that way, this year's payroll history will be recorded in QBOP.

Chapter 3 includes the sidebar, "Proper account balances." If you opted to set an opening balance on the bank account from which paychecks are paid, you can't use prior payrolls as your learning tool because you'll mess up your bank account balance. Instead, I suggest that you contact Intuit QuickBooks Support for help entering historical payroll information.

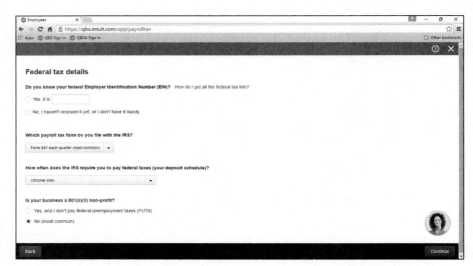

FIGURE 9-7:
The Federal Tax
Details page.

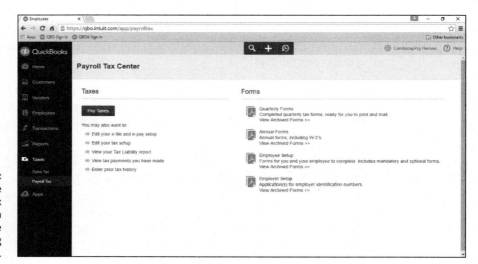

FIGURE 9-8:
The appearance
of the Payroll Tax
Center screen
now that you've
finished setting
things up.

You can use the links on the Payroll Tax Center screen to make changes to any of the settings you provided as you worked through the wizard.

Preparing Payroll

After you get past the setup work, you're ready to process payroll — essentially a three-step process:

>> Record paycheck information

>> Review paycheck information

>> Generate paychecks

TIP

Mobile users: Consider trying out the Intuit Online Payroll Mobile app, which works with both QBOP and with QuickBooks Online with Full Service Payroll (as well as other Intuit payroll products). You can use it to pay your employees and your payroll taxes, file payroll tax forms electronically, and review employee information and paycheck history. Data syncs automatically between the mobile app and your Intuit payroll account. Download the mobile app from the Apple App Store or from the Google Play Store; it's free with a payroll subscription.

Recording payroll information

To start preparing paychecks, click the Employees link in the Navigation bar. On the Employees page, click the Run Payroll button on the top-right side of the page.

QBOP starts the Run Payroll wizard by displaying the window shown in Figure 9-9, which lists all your employees (I have only two employees in this company, so my list is short).

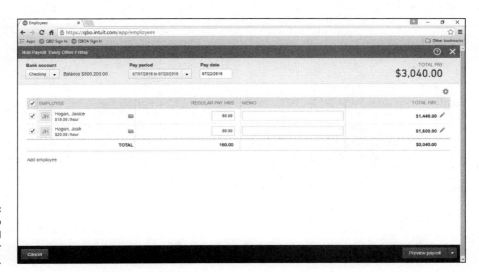

FIGURE 9-9:
Use this screen to
enter payroll
information for
your employees.

At the top of the window, select the bank account from which you'll pay employees and double-check pay period and pay date information. Then, place a check to the left of each employee you intend to pay and, for each employee paid on an hourly basis, supply the hours worked during the pay period.

TIP

LETTING EMPLOYEES USE TIMESHEETS

If you use QBO Plus, you can set up *time tracking users* who can log in with limited privileges that enable them to complete timesheets (and do nothing else).

To add a time tracking user, follow these steps:

1. **Click the Gear button beside your company name and, from the menu that appears, click Manager Users.**
2. **Click the New button and, from the window that appears, click Time Tracking Only.**
3. **Click Next and select the employee (or vendor) you want to fill out timesheets.**
4. **Supply the employee's (or the vendor's) email address.**
5. **Click Next and then click Finish.**

QBO sends to the user an email containing a link that he clicks to complete the Time Tracking Only setup process. If the user already has a QBO sign-in name and password, he can use it. Otherwise, he needs to create a sign-in name and password.

Once the user has signed in, the Single Activity Time Sheet screen appears; if the employee prefers to use the Weekly Timesheet screen, she can click the tab at the top of the screen. Because most employers don't pay their employees based on hours reported on timesheets — employers instead use timesheets to bill clients for time spent on client projects — see Chapter 6 for details on entering time.

You can view hours entered on timesheets by time-tracking employees. Before you start payroll, click the Create (+) button at the top of QBO, select Weekly Timesheet, and then select the employee. If you prefer, you can print information: Run a Time Activity by Employee report (click the Reports link in the Navigation bar and then search for "Time Activities by Employee Detail." Then, customize the report to display the payroll time-frame. For information on reports, see Chapter 10.

TIP

If you have lots of employees and want to see more of them onscreen, click the gear on the right side of the screen above the table and choose Compact. QBO reduces the amount of screen real estate it allots to each employee.

Reviewing and generating payroll checks

Once you finish entering hours and, if appropriate, memos for each employee you plan to pay, click the Preview Payroll button in the lower right corner of the Run

Payroll window (shown previously in Figure 9-8). The Run Payroll wizard displays the Review and Submit page, similar to the one shown in Figure 9-10.

FIGURE 9-10:
Reviewing paychecks before generating them.

When you're satisfied with the information on this page, click the Submit Payroll button in the lower right corner of the screen. If you're unsure about the payroll or you don't have time to complete it now, click the down arrow beside the Submit Payroll button and choose Save for Later to save the work you've done so far.

TIP

You can click the pencil at the right edge of the line for any employee to see the details associated with the employee's paycheck. If necessary, you can make changes to some paycheck details; for example, for hourly employees, you can change the hours an employee worked and the Federal and State income tax amounts.

QBO displays the last screen of the Run Payroll wizard, which confirms that you've completed payroll. If you don't directly deposit paychecks for your employees, QBO gives you the option to print paychecks and stubs. You can supply a starting check number and click Print Pay Stubs to preview paychecks and stubs and print them.

On the last screen of the Run Payroll wizard, click Finish Payroll to record the payroll information in QBO.

Printing payroll reports

After you complete payroll, you might want to print payroll-related reports. Click the Reports link in the Navigation bar to display the Reports page (see Figure 9-11).

Then click the All Reports link on the page and QBO displays the All Reports page. Scroll down the page to find the Manage Payroll link and click it.

Click here.

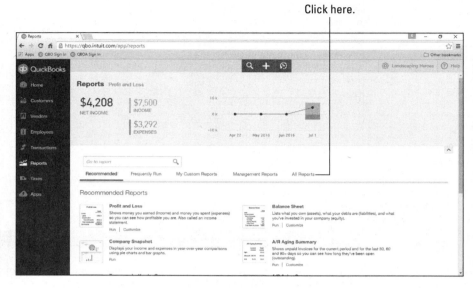

FIGURE 9-11:
From the Reports page, display all reports.

You can click any payroll report to print it to the screen and, subsequently, to your printer. To preview the type of information that appears on a report, slide the mouse pointer over the icon beside the report, and QBO displays a sample of the information on the report (see Figure 9-12). To customize reports, see Chapter 10.

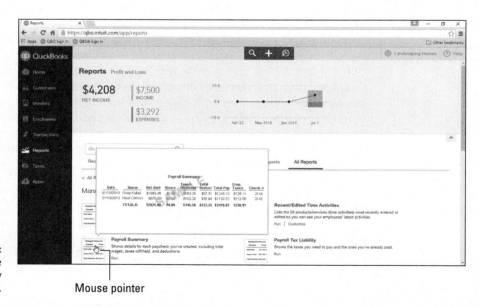

FIGURE 9-12:
Preview the content of any report.

Mouse pointer

Managing Payroll Taxes

As I mention at the beginning of this chapter, the payroll process doesn't end with preparing and producing paychecks. On a schedule determined by the IRS, you need to remit payroll taxes and file payroll tax returns.

Paying payroll taxes

Using rules established by the IRS, you pay payroll taxes weekly, monthly, or quarterly, depending on the amount you owe (called your *payroll tax liability*).

You must make Federal tax deposits by electronic funds transfer. Most people make Federal tax deposits using the Electronic Federal Tax Payment System (EFTPS), a free service provided by the United States Department of Treasury, and QBOP makes use of the EFTPS.

To pay your payroll taxes, choose Taxes ⇨ Payroll Tax to display the Payroll Tax Center (shown earlier in Figure 9-8). Once you've paid employees, the Payroll Tax Center displays taxes that are due, along with their due dates and e-payment cut-off dates. You can preview how much you owe by printing the Payroll Tax Liability report; click the View Your Tax Liability Report link on the Payroll Tax Center page.

PAYROLL-RELATED DUE DATES

Payroll and unemployment tax payments are due on a different schedule than the corresponding tax forms. To summarize, payroll tax payments are due weekly, monthly, or quarterly, depending on the size of your payroll tax liability. The payroll tax form (Federal Form 941) is due quarterly.

Federal unemployment tax payments are typically due quarterly, but the federal unemployment tax return (Federal Form 940) is typically due annually.

If you do business in a state that imposes a personal income tax, then you also have state payroll tax obligations. In addition, most states impose an unemployment tax.

Last, but not least, localities within any given state might also impose payroll tax obligations.

The due dates for these state and local payments and their corresponding returns vary from state to state; to determine the due dates for your state and locality, check at the state's website.

When you click the Pay Taxes button, QBO displays the Pay Taxes page (see Figure 9-13), which shows payroll tax amounts that you owe to various taxing authorities and when the payments are due.

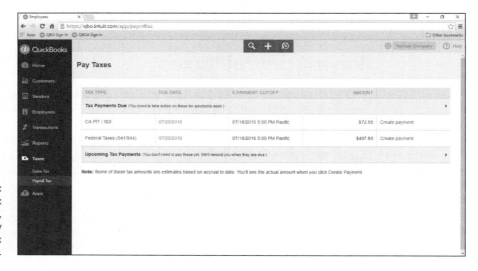

FIGURE 9-13:
Your payroll tax liabilities, separated by payroll tax authority.

TIP

If you "look ahead" — that is, opt to view payroll tax liabilities before their due date — the amounts you see are estimates of your liabilities.

When you click the Create Payment link beside a line, QBO shows you the amount you owe, allocated by tax item (see Figure 9-14). At the top of the screen, you can opt to pay the liability electronically using EFTPS or make the payment yourself. If you're entering historical payrolls to set up accurate payroll information for the current year, choose to make the payment yourself (because you've probably already made the payment and you simply want to record it in QBOP).

REMEMBER

I'm working in the sample company, and I'm showing you this potential payment a few days after it was due. So, QBO displays a note at the top of the screen indicating that late payments might be subject to interest and penalties and providing information on what action I should take.

When you finish reviewing the details for the payment, including the payment method (electronic or manual), the bank account from which you'll make the payment, and the payment date, click the E-pay button or the Record Payment button (depending on whether you're paying electronically or making the payment yourself) in the lower right corner of the screen. QBO displays a payment confirmation window that describes the payment method, type, liability, due date, payment date, and payment amount.

Repeat this process for each payroll tax liability.

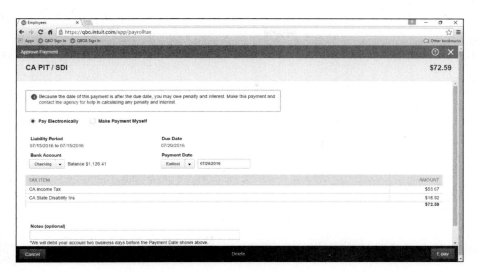

FIGURE 9-14:
A payroll tax
payment.

Preparing payroll tax forms

Quarterly, you must complete and submit a federal payroll tax return using Federal Form 941, which identifies the total wages you paid, when you paid them, and the total taxes you withheld and deposited with appropriate taxing authorities throughout the quarter. The IRS permits you to file the form electronically or to mail the form.

TIP

If you live in a state that imposes a personal income tax, then you typically must also file a similar form for your state; check your state's website for the rules you need to follow for payroll tax reporting. Your state probably has a state unemployment form you need to prepare and submit as well.

When you click Quarterly Forms on the Payroll Tax Center page (refer to Figure 9-8), QBOP displays the reports you need to prepare and submit (see Figure 9-15).

Click the link to the right of each form, and QBOP displays a page where you can opt to file the form electronically and preview the form. Click the View button to preview the form, and it appears onscreen, prefilled with information (see Figure 9-16). The form preview also includes a set of tools that you can use to review, save, and print the form. And, as you scroll to the bottom of the form, filing instructions appear.

Repeat the process of reviewing and printing each form as appropriate.

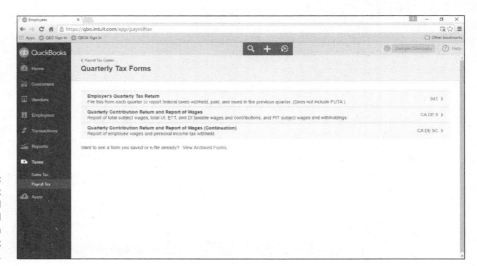

FIGURE 9-15:
The payroll tax returns you need to prepare and submit appear on the Quarterly Tax Forms page.

FIGURE 9-16:
A sample Federal Tax Form 941 used to report payroll tax information to the Federal Government.

Chapter **10**

How's the Business Doing?

No big surprise here: To help you measure and evaluate your business's health, you use reports. The reports reflect the information in QBO, so, keeping QBO up to date with your daily activities helps ensure that accurate information appears on the reports you run.

Quickly Review Income and Expenses

When you click Reports on the Navigation bar, you see a page like the one shown in Figure 10-1.

The graphic at the top of the page shows profit and loss information and is interactive; for example, if you click anywhere in the graphic — on the Net Income number, on either the Income or the Expenses number, or on any of the bars in the chart — QBO displays the Profit and Loss report shown in Figure 10-2. This version of the Profit and Loss report breaks down income and expenses by week for the period of the graphic.

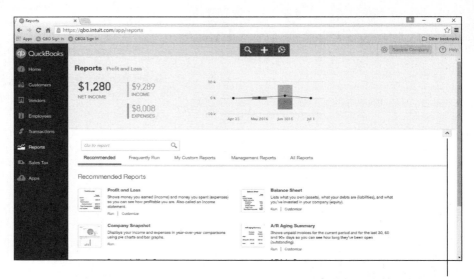

FIGURE 10-1:
The Reports page.

Click here to hide the graphic.

FIGURE 10-2:
A Profit and Loss
report by week.

You can click Reports in the Navigation bar to redisplay the Reports page shown in Figure 10-1, or you can click your browser's Back button.

TIP

Don't want the income and expense numbers displayed onscreen? Click the upward-pointing carat at the bottom right edge of the graphic on the Reports page, and QBO hides the graphic.

Finding the Report You Want

Reports in QBO are organized into five categories:

>> Recommended Reports

>> Frequently Run Reports

>> My Custom Reports

>> Management Reports

>> All Reports

These categories appear on the Reports page below the graphic and function as tabs; that is, you click a tab to see the reports in that category.

Examining recommended reports

QBO lists reports on the Recommended Reports tab of the Reports page based on features you use in QBO, preferences, and add-ons.

In Figure 10-3, I've hidden the graphic at the top of the Reports page to give the reports on the Recommended Reports tab a bit more screen real estate. Remember, the reports I display in the figure might differ from the ones you see when you review recommended reports.

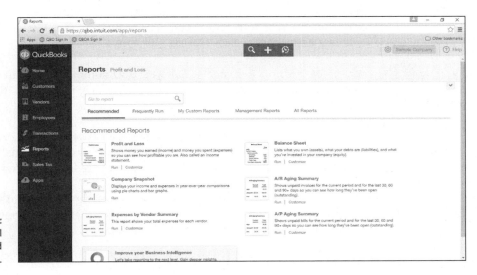

FIGURE 10-3: Typical recommended reports.

If you have not turned on Redesigned Reports, each listed report also displays a graphic to the left of the report title. If you pass your mouse pointer over one of these graphics, QBO displays a sample of the report's appearance; in Figure 10-4, I've placed the mouse pointer over the graphic for the Profit and Loss report.

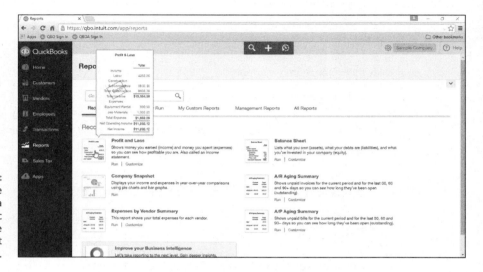

FIGURE 10-4:
Hover the mouse pointer over a report's graphic to view a sample of the report layout.

What are redesigned reports?

Intuit is in the process of redesigning reports to make them more professional looking and easier to customize. At the time I wrote this, Redesigned Reports was a QuickBooks Labs feature that you need to turn on. (See Chapter 3 for details on enabling a QuickBooks Labs feature.)

REMEMBER

When you turn on Redesigned Reports, QBO automatically converts all reports that have been redesigned to their new appearance; in addition, the graphic disappears for the redesigned reports.

To get a feel for the difference in appearance between the original version of a report and a redesigned version, Figure 10-5 shows the original version of the Profit and Loss report and Figure 10-6 shows the redesigned version.

TIP

If you click the Customize button in the upper right corner of the redesigned report, you see additional customization options that let you control the column and row data on the report, set period comparisons, and more.

FIGURE 10-5:
The original
version of the
Profit & Loss
report.

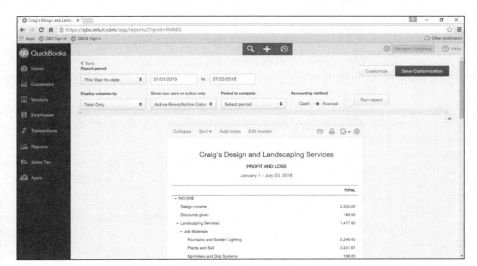

FIGURE 10-6:
The redesigned
version of the
Profit & Loss
report.

Looking at frequently run reports

No surprise here: On the Frequently Run tab, QBO lists the reports you run most often. When you first start using QBO and haven't run reports yet, the Frequently Run tab doesn't contain any reports. Instead, it contains a message that describes what you'll see after you start running reports.

Finding reports you customize

The My Custom Reports tab lists reports you have printed — whether to your display or to a printer — customized, and saved, either as single reports or in a report group. Like its cousin, Frequently Run reports, the My Custom Reports tab remains empty until you print, customize, and save a report as described later in this chapter in the section "Saving a customized report." In that section, I also show you how to place a customized report into a group, and you get a look at the My Custom Reports page after it contains a report saved to a group.

TIP

If you're a former QuickBooks desktop user, be aware that saving a report in QBO is the equivalent of memorizing a report in QuickBooks desktop, and saving a report to a group in QBO is conceptually the same as creating a memorized report group in QuickBooks desktop.

Taking a look at management reports

The Management Reports tab, shown in Figure 10-7, lists three predefined management report packages you can prepare and print by clicking the View link in the Action column. Each package contains a professional looking cover page, a table of contents, and several reports that relate to the report package's name:

>> The Sales Performance management report contains the Profit and Loss report, the A/R Aging Detail report, and the Sales by Customer Summary report.

>> The Expenses Performance management report contains the Profit and Loss report, the A/P Aging Detail report, and the Expenses by Vendor Summary report.

>> The Company Overview management report contains the Profit and Loss report and the Balance Sheet report.

The management report appears in its own window, where you can scroll through and print it. You can also customize these reports; click the downward-pointing arrow beside a report to see your choices.

TIP

If you opt to edit a report package, you can add more reports to the package and you can include an executive summary and end notes to the package.

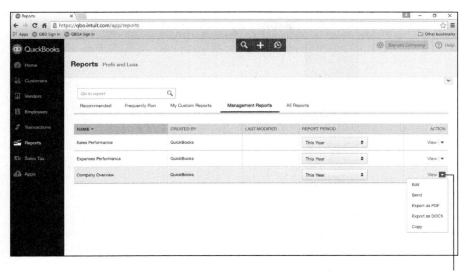

FIGURE 10-7:
The Management
Reports page.

Click here to customize a management report package.

Exploring all QBO reports

The All Reports tab gives you a way to find any QBO report. The page lists a series of categories for reports, such as Business Overview and Manage Accounts Receivable. When you click a particular category, you see a page similar to the one shown previously in Figure 10-3, which lists all the reports for the selected category. If you haven't turned on the redesigned reports feature, a graphic appears beside each report, and you can hover your mouse pointer over the graphic to identify the report's layout and content.

TIP

Once you select a category, you can redisplay the All Reports page by clicking the All Reports link that appears above the report category name.

Searching for a report

You don't need to use the tabs to find a report. Instead, you can click in the Go to Report box; when you do, QBO displays all reports, listed alphabetically, in a drop-down list (see Figure 10-8).

If you see the report you want, you can click it, and QBO displays it onscreen. If you don't see the report you want, you can type some keywords into the Go to Report box, and QBO narrows the reports displayed in the drop-down list to those whose name contains the keywords you typed.

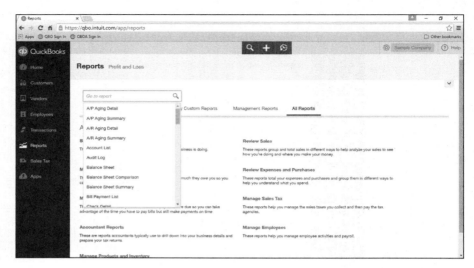

FIGURE 10-8:
Searching for a
report.

Printing a Report

To produce any report, simply click the report's title. QBO automatically displays the report with a standard set of settings. To redisplay reports, click Reports in the Navigation bar.

On most reports, you can *drill down* to view the details behind the report's numbers. For example, from the Profit and Loss report, you can click any Income or Expense account value, and QBO displays the transactions that make up the number on the Profit and Loss report. I clicked the dollar amount for Design income, and QBO displayed the Transaction report shown in Figure 10-9.

To redisplay the original report, you can click the Back to Summary Report link on the left side of the report page.

TIP

If you want to keep the original summary version of the report open and also view the details from drilling down, duplicate the tab containing the summary version of the report before you drill down to view details. When you finish working with the details, you can close the tab containing the details. To duplicate a tab in Chrome, right-click the tab and select Duplicate. To duplicate a tab in Firefox, press and hold down the Ctrl key as you click the browser refresh button, which appears at the right edge of the address bar.

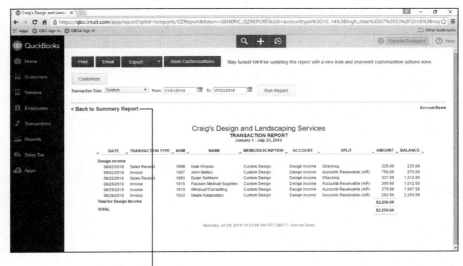

FIGURE 10-9:
The Transaction
Report that
appears after
clicking an
income account
on the Profit and
Loss report.

Click here to redisplay the original report.

Customizing a report

You can customize most reports in a variety of ways. For all reports, you can change the date range covered by the report by opening the Transaction Date list box and making a selection or by setting specific dates in the From and To boxes. After you make your selection, click the Run Report button to refresh the report and display information only in the date range you selected.

To set more detailed custom settings, click the Customize button at the top of the report. QBO displays the Customize dialog box shown in Figure 10-10; from this dialog box, you can make changes that affect the information QBO displays on the report.

The Redesigned Reports interface varies from the regular interface. For example, if you've turned on Redesigned Reports, the dialog box you see looks like the one shown in Figure 10-11. The settings available in both versions of the Customize dialog box are the same; they simply appear in different places. Because Redesigned Reports is still a QuickBooks Labs feature, I'll use the standard interface for discussion throughout this chapter.

First, although you see tabs down the side of the dialog box, the Customize dialog box contains one long list of settings you can control. The tabs help you scroll down quickly to a particular type of setting.

Second, it's important to understand that the settings (and the tabs) that appear in the Customize dialog box vary, depending on the report you are customizing. Figure 10-10 shows the settings in the General section of the Customize Profit and

Loss dialog box. From this section, you can, for example, opt to display the report using the accrual basis of accounting rather than the cash basis of account.

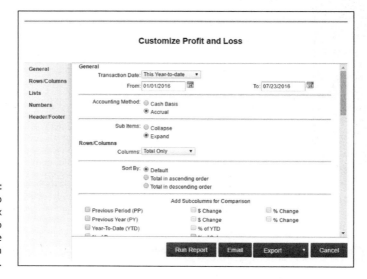

FIGURE 10-10:
The General tab of the dialog box you use to customize a report in greater detail.

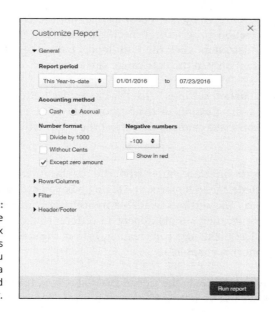

FIGURE 10-11:
The Customize Report dialog box that appears when you customize a Redesigned Report.

From the Rows/Columns section of the Customize Profit and Loss dialog box (see Figure 10-12), you can control the columns and rows that appear on the report as well as the order in which they appear. You also can add a variety of comparison columns.

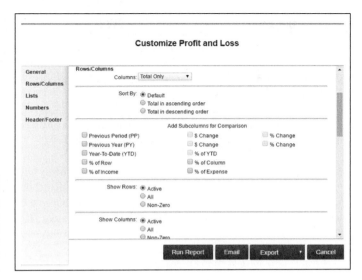

FIGURE 10-12:
Use this tab of the dialog box to control the rows and columns that appear on the report.

From the Lists section, shown in Figure 10-13, you can control the entries from the Customer, Vendor, Employee, and Product/Service list that QBO includes on the Profit and Loss report.

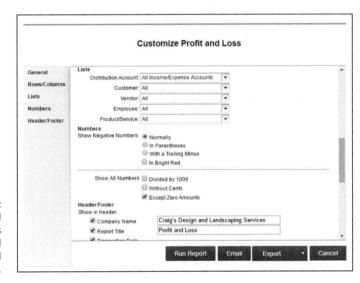

FIGURE 10-13:
The Lists and Numbers settings you can control on the Profit and Loss report.

Figure 10-13 also shows the settings you can control for numbers on the report and the beginning of the report header and footer settings. If you click Header/Footer on the left side of the dialog box (or you scroll down in the dialog box), you see the rest of the report header and footer settings you can control, along with a preview of the header and footer settings you select.

When you're finished customizing the report, click Run Report, and QBO displays the report onscreen using your customized settings. With the report onscreen, you can click the Print button to print the report to paper or to a PDF file. Or, you can click the Email button to email the report or the Excel button to export the report to Excel.

REMEMBER

You can email the report or export it to Excel from the Customize dialog box, but I suggest that you use the Run Report button to display the report onscreen first and make sure that what you see is what you want to send.

When you use Chrome to export a report to Excel, a button with the title "report1. xls" appears in the bottom left corner of the screen; click that button to open the report in Excel. Be aware, too, that QBO automatically saves a copy of the report to the local hard drive; mine appeared in the Downloads folder. If you don't delete the reports, QBO increments the report name for subsequent reports you export to Excel.

TIP

To find the folder where QBO stores the report, click the down arrow on the right side of the report's button in the lower left corner of the QBO screen and choose Show in Folder.

Saving a customized report

Once the report looks the way you want, you might want to save it so that you don't need to apply the same customizations each time you run the report. Click the Save Customizations button at the top of the report page to display the Save Report Customizations dialog box shown in Figure 10-14.

TIP

If you've turned on Redesigned Reports, the dialog box you use to save a report has a slightly different appearance but contains the same fields.

FIGURE 10-14:
Use this dialog box to save a customized report.

Supply a name for the customized report; you can use the QBO name for the report, but you'd be better off including some information in the name that helps you remember the customizations — unlike the one I use in the figure, which really doesn't tell us much other than the report isn't the standard Profit and Loss report.

You can add the report to a group you create; creating a group is useful if you want to email several reports simultaneously. To add a group, type the group name and click the green Add button.

Once you save your settings in the Save Customizations dialog box, the saved report appears on the My Custom Reports tab of the Reports page. And, if you created a group, the report appears in that group. In Figure 10-15, my customized version of the Profit and Loss report appears in a group called (uninspiringly) Elaine's Group.

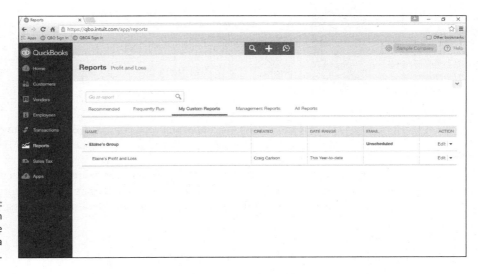

FIGURE 10-15:
The My Custom
Reports page
after creating a
custom report.

To print the report, I click its title, and the report appears onscreen. I also can take any of the following actions if I click the down arrow in the Action column beside the report:

>> Create a PDF version of the report by clicking Export as PDF.

>> Move the report to a different group by clicking Group, assuming other groups exist.

>> Export the report to Excel by clicking Export as Excel.

>> Delete the customized report by clicking Delete.

TIP

To change a report's name or group, click the Edit link beside the report.

If you select the Edit link in the Action column beside a report group, you can set an email schedule for the report group; QBO displays the Report Group Settings page shown in Figure 10-16. Select the Set the Email Schedule for This Group check box to display and edit scheduling information.

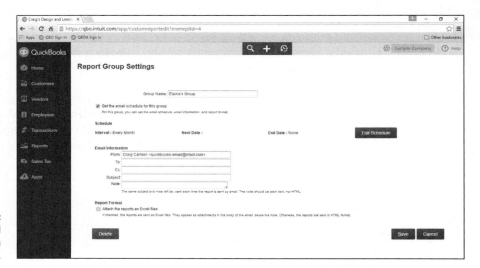

FIGURE 10-16:
Set an email
schedule for a
report group.

If you select the Attach the Reports as Excel Files, QBO sends the reports in Excel format; if you don't select this option, QBO sends the reports in HTML format.

Fill in the Email information; QBO will use the same subject each time it emails the report group. By default, QBO chooses monthly as the email interval, but if you click the Edit Schedule button, QBO lets you customize the email schedule (see Figure 10-17).

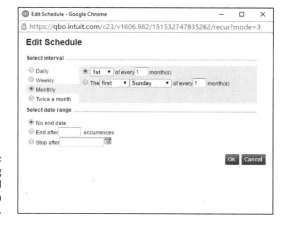

FIGURE 10-17:
Set up a recurring
schedule to email
the reports in a
report group.

WARNING

If you click Delete at the bottom of the Report Group Settings page, you delete the report group and all custom reports the group contains.

3

Managing the Books for the Accountant

Examine the QBOA interface, set up QBOA users, and work with the QBOA client list, free company, and sample company.

Learn how to add clients to the Client List, including importing desktop QuickBooks companies.

Become familiar with working with a client QBO company from QBOA.

Learn how to use notes and tasks to keep track of information and how to communicate with clients from within their QBO companies.

Use tools available to accountants to manage client QBO companies.

IN THIS CHAPTER

» Signing up for QBOA

» Signing into and out of QBOA

» Understanding the QBOA front-end interface

» Setting up multiple users in a QBOA account

» Using the Client List page

» Working with the free QBOA company and the sample company

Chapter **11**

Setting Up Shop in QBOA

Part 1 of this book covers the details of QBO, and QBO is the product you use to enter transactions into a company.

Because accountants need to work in multiple QBO companies, they use Quick-Books Online for Accountants (QBOA). QBOA provides a front-end interface that acts as a portal you use to open client QBO companies. When you open any particular client's company, you have available to you the features for the client's subscription level: Simple Start, Essentials, or Plus.

REMEMBER

As you see in this chapter, the interface for a client QBO company opened in QBOA varies slightly from the interface your client sees when opening the company.

Signing Up for and into QBOA

Setting up a QBOA subscription account is free, and your QBOA subscription remains free for the first 180 days starting from the day you enroll. You can sign up for the Intuit Wholesale Pricing program and receive discounted rates for each client subscription you manage; contact Intuit for details.

When you sign up for a QBOA subscription account, you get, as one of the perks, a free QBO company that you can use for your own QuickBooks company.

To create a QBOA account, open your browser and navigate to `http://quickbooks.intuit.com/accountants/quickbooks-accountant`. On the web page that appears, click the Overview link in the QuickBooks Online Accountant bar (see Figure 11-1).

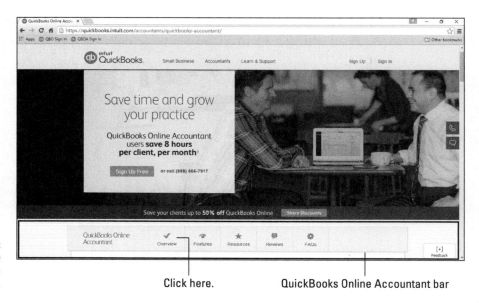

FIGURE 11-1: Navigating to the QBOA sign-in page.

Click here.   QuickBooks Online Accountant bar

Once you click Overview, a Sign Up Free link appears at the right edge of the QuickBooks Online Accountant bar; click it to display the web page shown in Figure 11-2. Select the region where you do business and provide the rest of the requested information, including your company name, and then click the Sign Up button.

REMEMBER

Just as you'd expect, by clicking the Sign Up button, you're agreeing to Intuit's Terms of Service, the End-User License Agreement, and the Privacy Policy for QBOA.

TIP

QBOA uses the company name to create the free company you can use to manage the books for your own business. You can read more about this company later in this chapter, in the section "Understanding and Using the Free QBOA Company."

Your new company is created and the Home page in QBOA appears. In addition, the "Take a Tour" video, lasting less than two minutes, provides some tips to get you started. When the video finishes, you'll see that your Client List page is empty except for links to two other "getting started" videos and to a PDF version of the 16-page QuickBooks Accountant Welcome Guide, which you can use to help you work in QBOA.

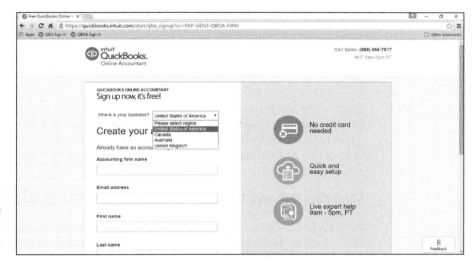

FIGURE 11-2:
Provide a limited amount of information to create a QBOA account.

Once you've created a QBOA account, you use the same page to log in to your QBOA account that your client uses to log in to QBO. Navigate to `https://qbo.intuit.com` to view the web page shown in Figure 11-3 and supply your login credentials.

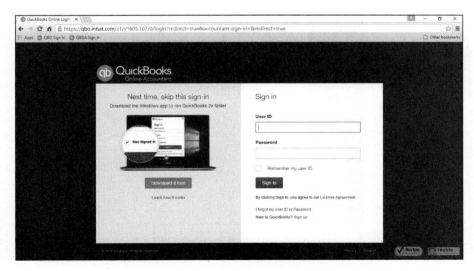

FIGURE 11-3:
The page you use to sign in to QBOA after you set up a QBOA account.

Examining the QBOA Interface

The QBOA interface focuses on giving accountants access to tools they need to manage multiple clients. Although the view in the QBOA interface changes, depending on where you're working, two common elements appear in the QBOA interface:

>> The Navigation bar (navy blue) runs down the left side of the page.

>> The QBOA toolbar (green) runs across the top of the page.

You use the Navigation bar to display the various pages in QBOA. The Navigation bar contains two choices that display different views and affect the choices in the QBOA toolbar: the Your Practice and Your Books views. The following two sections explore the Navigation bar and the QBOA toolbar in each of these views.

Working with the Your Practice view

By default, the QBOA Home page displays, in the Navigation bar, the links for the Your Practice view and the Clients page, as you see in Figure 11-4. Since I'm working in a dummy QBOA account, you don't see much data.

QBOA toolbar

FIGURE 11-4:
The Your Practice view of the Navigation bar in QBOA.

Navigation bar

On the Client List page, you can search for a client, see overview information about each client, and open a client's QBO company. You can also control the appearance of the Client List page. See the section "Controlling the Appearance of the Client List," later in this chapter, for details on working with the Client List page.

When you click Team in the Navigation bar, you can set up the users in your firm that will have access to various client companies. For more information, see the section "Setting Up Your Team."

When you click ProAdvisor, you see information about the Intuit ProAdvisor program.

Across the top of the interface, you find a toolbar with the following buttons, from left to right:

>> **The Accountant button:** This button contains the QuickBooks logo and offers you another way to display the Client List shown in Figure 11-4.

>> **The Go to Client's QuickBooks button:** You can use this list box to display a list of your clients; clicking a client name opens the client's company.

>> **The plus sign (+) icon:** This button displays the Create menu, which you use to create a client, a user, or a request (typically for information).

>> **The Search box:** When you click in this box, a list of recent transactions or reports appears; you can type in the box to search for the transaction or report of your choice or you can click an item in the list.

>> **The Gear button:** Click this button to display the Gear menu (see Figure 11-5). The Gear menu shows the settings you can establish for your own company, your client's company, and your QBOA account.

REMEMBER

You also can open the QBO sample company from the Gear menu; read more about opening and working in the sample company later in this chapter, in the section "Working with the Sample Company."

>> **The Help button:** Click this button to open the Help menu so that you can search for help on any topic. Help in QBOA is context sensitive and available from all screens. When you open the Help menu from a transaction screen, the suggested choices that appear are based on the type of transaction you were viewing when you clicked Help.

Working with the Your Books view

When you click Your Books in the Navigation bar, you open your own QBO company, and, with the exception of the Your Practice link and the Your Books link in the Navigation bar, you and your client see the same links (see Figure 11-6).

Gear button

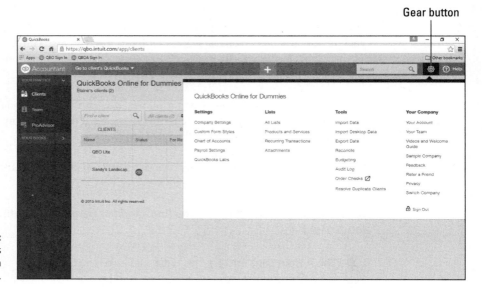

FIGURE 11-5:
The choices
available from
the Gear menu.

QBOA toolbar

FIGURE 11-6:
The view of a
QBO company
from QBOA.

Navigation bar

The view when you open your own company's books in QBOA matches the view you see when you open any client's QBO company; the only difference onscreen is the name of the company that appears on the QBOA toolbar.

The Home screen of a company displays overview income, expense, and profit and loss information in interactive filters; you can click part of any graphic on this page to display the details that make up that part of the graphic. In the figure, I haven't entered any data into my company, so there's no reason to click anything.

The QBOA toolbar in a QBO company changes somewhat when you display the Your Books view. In particular, beside the Accountant button, you see a suitcase button that I'll call the Accountant Tools button; you can click this button to display, well, tools accountants need frequently when working in a client's company (see Figure 11-7). See Chapter 15 for details on these tools.

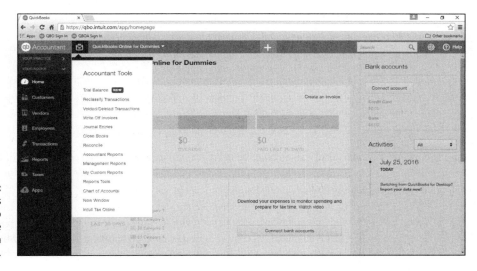

FIGURE 11-7:
The tools available to accountants while working in a client company.

The List Box button beside the Accountant Tools button displays the name of the currently open QBO company; when you click Your Books, your company's name appears.

The Create button (the plus sign), the Search box, the Gear button, and the Help button all work the same way in the Your Books view as they do in the Your Practice view.

REMEMBER

While any company is open, you can use the QBOA toolbar to open the list box displaying the company's name to switch to a different client company. Also, you can redisplay the Client List page at any time by clicking the Accountant button on the QBOA toolbar.

Setting Up Your Team

If your accounting firm has more than one person who need access to client QBO companies, the person who creates the QBOA account — called, in QBOA parlance, the *master administrator* — can set up the other users. The other users get their own login credentials and access to those clients that the master administrator specifies; for those clients, the user can access the Accountant tools described in Chapter 15. The master administrator also specifies the user's level of access to the firm's information; a user can have basic, full, or custom access.

TIP

Using separate QBOA login information helps maintain security in QBOA, because a lot of financial information (product subscriptions and billing information, for example) is tied to login information.

So, what's the difference, status-wise, between basic, full, and custom access?

>> Those users with full access can open and work in the firm's books as well as in client QBO companies and can access the Team page and make changes to any user's privileges.

>> Those users with basic access can access only client QBO companies.

>> Those users with custom access have nothing more than basic or full access with at least one privilege set differently from QBOA's defaults for basic or full access.

To set up multiple users in a QBOA account, the master administrator or any firm member with full access privileges to QBOA sets up other members of the firm; during the process, QBOA sends an email to the other firm members whom, for this discussion, I'll call *invitees*. Once an invitee accepts the invitation, QBOA prompts the invitee to set up his own QBOA login credentials. Follow these steps to set up a new user in a QBOA account:

1. **Log in to QBOA.**

2. **Click Team in the Navigation bar.**

   The Team page appears (see Figure 11-8).

3. **Click the Add User button.**

   The Add User wizard begins.

4. **On the first page of the Add User wizard, fill in the name, email address, and title of the team member you want to add.**

   The team member's title is optional.

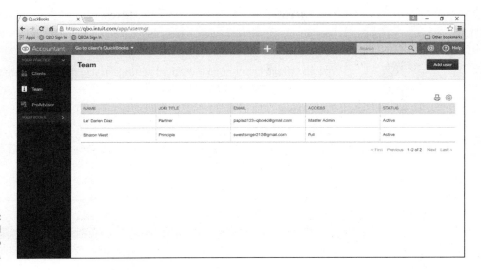

FIGURE 11-8:
View, edit, and
add members to
your QBOA team.

5. **Click Next.**

   The second page of the Add User wizard appears (see Figure 11-9). On this
   page, you identify the privileges related to your firm that you want to provide
   to the team member.

FIGURE 11-9:
Specify the new
user's access level
to your firm's
administration
and books.

6. **Select the type of access you want to give to the team member.**

   You can assign Basic, Full, or Custom access; a description of each type of
   access appears on the right side of the page. Assign Full access to those team

members who should have access to your own company's books. Assign Basic access to give a team member access to QBO client companies only.

You can make changes to individual settings; if you do, QBOA sets the team member's access to Custom by default.

TIP

7. **Click Next.**

The last screen of the Add User wizard appears (see Figure 11-10). On this page, you identify the clients for whom the team member should be able to perform work.

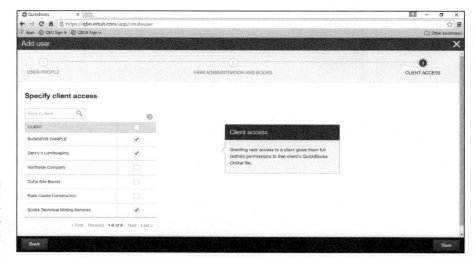

FIGURE 11-10:
You can provide a team member access to your firm's clients on a selective basis.

8. **Deselect clients as needed.**

9. **Click Save.**

QBOA adds the new user to your team and assigns a status of Invited to the user. In addition, the Status column on the Team screen indicates that QBOA sent an email invitation to the user, inviting the user to join your team. After the user responds to the QBOA invitation, the user's status changes to Active on the Team page in QBOA.

The email invitation that QBOA sends looks like the one shown in Figure 11-11.

The recipient clicks the Accept Invitation button, and, assuming the invitee doesn't already have login information for QBOA, the page shown in Figure 11-12 appears. On this page, the invitee sets up QBOA login information by providing a user ID (which does not need to be an email address) and a password. Once the invitee clicks Create User, QBOA confirms that the user ID is available, sets up the login information, and displays a page on which a Sign In button appears. Clicking the Sign In button signs the user into QBOA with the user's assigned privileges.

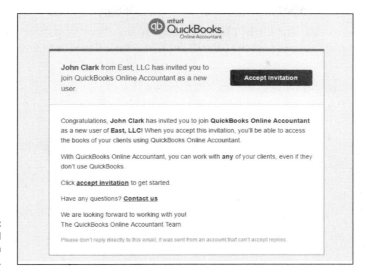

FIGURE 11-11:
An email invitation to use a QBOA account.

FIGURE 11-12:
An invited team member sets up his own login information.

To log into QBOA in the future, the team member navigates to qbo.intuit.com and supplies her login credentials.

Controlling the Appearance of the Client List

You can use the Client List page to open any client's QBO company, and you can control the appearance of the Client List page, shown in Figure 11-13.

Click here to open a client QBO company.

FIGURE 11-13:
Click a Quick-Books logo or use the Go to Client's QuickBooks list to open a client QBO company.

To open any client's QBO company, click the QuickBooks logo in the Status column of the Client List page. Or, if you prefer, open the Go to Client's QuickBooks list box on the QBOA toolbar to select the QBO company you want to open.

REMEMBER

If you click a client's name — rather than the QuickBooks logo — you don't open the client's company. Instead, you see overview details about the client. And the QuickBooks logo that appears in the Payroll Status column opens the client's company and displays payroll information for the client company.

You can control the appearance of the Client List page. For example, you can control the number of clients listed on the page by limiting the number of rows that appear. You also can specify the columns of information that appear on the Client list page. And, you can opt to hide or display inactive clients; for more information on making a client inactive, see the section "Removing clients from your Wholesale Billing subscription" later in this chapter. Click the Gear button that appears just above the list of clients and make choices from the list that appears (see Figure 11-14).

Click here.

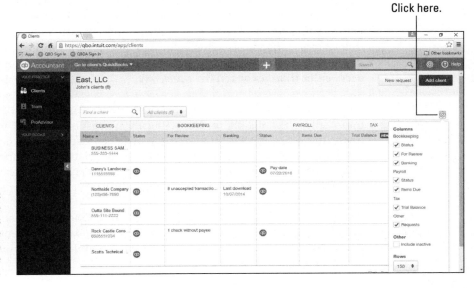

FIGURE 11-14:
Control the number of rows and the information appearing on the Client List page.

REMEMBER

QBOA actually contains multiple Gear menus. One of them appears on the QBOA toolbar and is visible from most QBOA pages, even while you work in a client's QBO company; you use that Gear menu to provide information about your QBOA account, establish settings, view lists, and access tools to, for example, import data. On the QBOA Clients page, the other Gear menu appears on the right side just above the list of clients, and you use it to control the information that appears on the page.

Understanding and Using the Free QBOA Company

As I mentioned at the beginning of this chapter, QBOA users get one free company to use for their own books. To open the company reserved for you, click the — yep, you guessed it — Your Books link in the Navigation bar, and QBOA opens your company. The interface you see when you open your company looks just like the interface you see when you open any client's QBO company; remember, this interface varies slightly from what a client using QBO sees.

You can use the free QBOA company to enter your own company's information using transactions, or if you've been tracking your business in desktop Quick-Books, you can, with some limitations, import information from your desktop QuickBooks company. To enter information using transactions, you can read the chapters in Part 1 of this book, because you as a QBOA user and your clients as QBO users enter transactions in the same way.

TIP

You can import desktop QuickBooks information, and you can import only list information. For details on importing lists, see Chapter 4. If you want to try importing a desktop QuickBooks company, see Chapter 12 for details as well as Appendix B, which describe the limitations associated with importing information. Please note that importing into a regular QBO company has time limits, but importing into the QBOA free company doesn't.

REMEMBER

Be aware that the Your Books company is not intended to house a client's data. The Your Books company ties into QBOA and updates as clients are added to QBOA. So, if you use it to store a client's data, that data will be messed up as you add other clients.

Working with the Sample Company

If you've been a desktop QuickBooks user, you know that desktop QuickBooks comes with a variety of sample companies that you can use to test company behavior. Like its desktop cousin, QBOA also comes with a sample company.

To open the sample company, follow these steps:

1. **Click the Gear button on the QBOA toolbar.**

   QBOA opens the Gear menu.

2. **In the Your Company section, click Sample Company.**

   QBOA displays a warning message that you will be logged out of QBOA if you continue.

3. **Click Continue.**

   QBOA signs you out of your company and opens the sample company. The interface looks like the QBOA interface you see when you open a client's company. For example, you see the Accountant button in the upper left corner and the QBOA toolbar to the right of the Accountant button. The QBOA toolbar contains the same tools you see when you open a client QBO company. Note, though, that the sample company name appears on the Client Home page (click Home on the Navigation bar) as Craig's Design and Landscaping Services, but the name of the company beside the Gear button on the QBOA toolbar is Sample Company (see Figure 11-15).

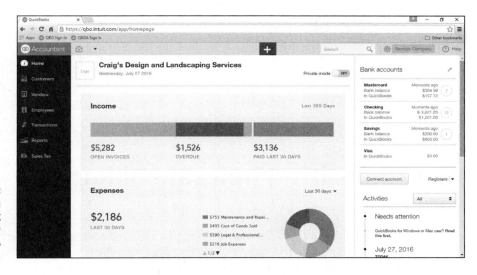

FIGURE 11-15:
Craig's Design and Landscaping Services, the QBO and QBOA sample company.

End users (your clients) also have access to this sample company, but opening it isn't quite as easy as it is for you. Direct your clients to www.quickbooks.intuit.com/online and tell them to scroll down and click the Take a Test Drive button.

Closing Companies and QBOA

You don't close companies in QBOA the way you might using desktop QuickBooks. When you switch from one client QBO company to another, you automatically close the first client's company.

TIP

To work in two client QBO companies simultaneously, you can use two different browsers, two instances of a single browser, or Chrome's User feature (if you're using Chrome). (For details on using Chrome, see Chapter 17.)

To close QBOA, click the Gear button on the QBOA toolbar and choose Sign Out (see Figure 11-16).

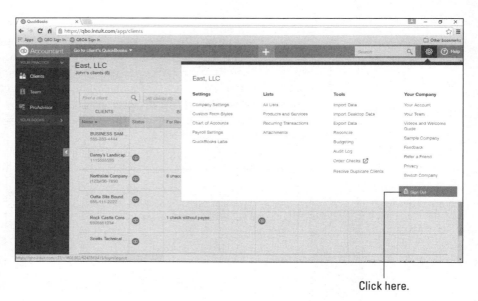

FIGURE 11-16:
Exit from QBOA
by signing out.

Click here.

Working with Wholesale Billing

As I mentioned in Chapter 2, if you are an accounting professional, you can sign up for the free Wholesale Pricing program and also use QBOA for free. If you both create a client's company and manage the client's subscription as part of the Wholesale Pricing program, Intuit sends you the bill for the client's subscription. It is your responsibility to bill the client for the QBO subscription. The bill you receive from Intuit is a single consolidated bill for all the QBO subscriptions you manage. I'm going to provide some details on the Wholesale Pricing program here; for more information, contact Intuit.

REMEMBER

You don't have to enroll clients as part of the Wholesale Pricing program, but if you do, you might be able to get QBO for your clients at a reduced price. The Wholesale Pricing program is often referred to as the Wholesale Billing program; for this discussion, the two terms are interchangeable.

Signing up for Wholesale Billing

Accounting professionals are automatically signed up for the free Wholesale Billing program when they log in to QBOA for the first time. But, the Wholesale Billing program doesn't become active until the accounting professional enters billing information into the Billing Profile in QBOA.

To enter information in the QBOA Billing Profile, follow these steps:

1. **From the QBOA Client list, click the Gear button located in the top right corner of the page.**

2. **From the drop-down Gear menu that appears, select Your Account under Your Company.**

The Your Account page appears. In Figure 11-17, I'm working in a dummy QBOA company, so you don't really see any data, but you do see what the page looks like.

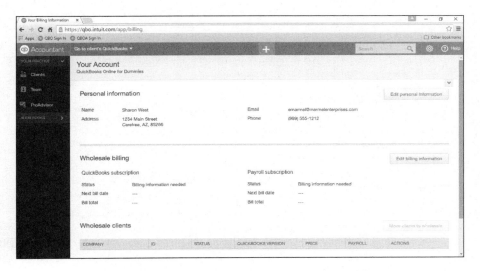

FIGURE 11-17:
The Your Account page in QBOA.

3. **Click the Edit Billing Information button.**

4. **Fill in all Payment Information fields.**

5. **Click Subscribe.**

The Your Account page reappears, and the Wholesale billing Status will be active.

Each month, you receive a bill from Intuit that covers the subscription costs of the clients you add to your Wholesale Billing subscription.

You cannot add annually paid QBO subscriptions to the Wholesale Billing program; the QBO subscriptions must be paid monthly.

REMEMBER

LIMITATIONS ASSOCIATED WITH THE WHOLESALE BILLING PROGRAM

You don't have to add a client to your Wholesale Billing subscription; you can still work with clients who pay their own QBO subscription costs. Enrolling a client into Wholesale Billing can save the client money on the cost of the QBO subscription but also makes you responsible for collecting subscription costs. And, the Wholesale Billing program might not be right for all QBO clients. In particular,

- If your client uses QuickBooks Online with Intuit Full Service Payroll (IFSP), no bundle for this combination of products is presently available through the Wholesale Billing program. QBOA is compatible with Intuit Online Payroll (IOP) and QuickBooks Online Payroll (QBOP), so if your QBO clients can use either of those products, those clients can take advantage of any price breaks you might offer for their QBO subscriptions.

- Companies created through the wholesale model have the ability to transfer Master Administrator rights. However, *no* accountant can be removed from the company as long as it is part of the wholesale billing program, including an accountant who is not associated with the firm housing the company in the wholesale billing program.

- If an accounting professional creates a QBO company through QBOA, the company does not come with a 30-day free trial. Instead, at the time the accounting professional creates the company, he must provide a payment method to ensure uninterrupted service.

Adding clients to your Wholesale Billing subscription

A client QBO Wholesale Billing subscription stays active for as long as you maintain a valid form of payment in the QuickBooks Billing Profile. Wholesale QBO companies do not expire.

So, just how do you go about adding a client to your Wholesale Billing subscription? Make sure that the client appears in your Client List in QBOA; for details on adding a client to your client list, see Chapter 12. To add a client to your Wholesale Billing subscription, follow these steps:

1. **Click Clients in the Navigation bar.**

2. **Click the gear in the top right corner of the QBOA toolbar.**

3. **From the drop-down menu, under Your Company, select Your Account.**

   The Your Account window appears.

4. **In the Wholesale Clients section, click the Move Clients to Wholesale button in the Actions column.**

   The Move Clients to Wholesale Billing page appears, displaying only those clients not currently part of your Wholesale Billing subscription. If you find you cannot select a particular client to add to your Wholesale Billing subscription, see the sidebar "Why can't I migrate a client?"

5. **Click the check box beside each client you want to move and click Next.**

6. **Review your selections and, when you're satisfied they are correct, click Move Clients.**

   A page appears that identifies clients that migrated correctly and clients whose migration failed.

REMEMBER

WHY CAN'T I MIGRATE A CLIENT?

You might not be able to move a particular client to your Wholesale Billing subscription for a variety of reasons. For example, your client must have an active monthly billing subscription and must appear on your QBOA Client List.

In addition,

- The client QBO company's Next Payment Date must be within 33 days of the day you attempt to add the company to your Wholesale Billing subscription.

- Clients must have an active *monthly* billing subscription and be listed within the QBOA Client List.

  You can change a yearly billing subscription to a monthly billing subscription, but only 30 days before the next annual billing date.

- The QBO client's region (US, UK, AU, or Canada) must match your QBOA region.

- The QBO client must be using QBO Essentials or QBO Plus. You cannot add QBO Simple Start companies to a Wholesale Billing subscription.

Removing clients from your Wholesale Billing subscription

Sometimes, things just don't work out between you and a client. If you have previously added that client's QBO company to your Wholesale Billing subscription and you need to part ways, you'll want to remove the client from your subscription. Follow these steps:

1. **Display the QBOA Clients page.**

2. **Click the gear in the top right corner of the QBOA toolbar.**

3. **From the drop-down menu, under Your Company, select Your Account.**

   The Your Account window appears.

4. **Scroll down to the Wholesale Clients section and find the company you want remove from your Wholesale Billing subscription.**

5. **In the Actions column, click Remove from Wholesale.**

Be aware that your Wholesale Billing subscription needs to be active to enable you to manage client QBO subscriptions.

REMEMBER

Once you remove a QBO company from your Wholesale Billing subscription, that QBO company will no longer be eligible for the wholesale discount, and all previous discounts will be removed as well. The client QBO subscriber will be billed the standard rate for his subscription unless the client establishes a relationship with another QBOA user. In this case, the client regains the discounts starting from the wholesale billing activation date.

Be aware that removing a client from your Wholesale Billing subscription doesn't remove the client from your Client List. And, you can't delete QBO clients. But you can make them inactive, using these steps:

1. **Click Clients in QBOA to display your Client List.**

2. **Click the name of the client you want to make inactive.**

REMEMBER

   It's very important to click the client's name in the Name column; clicking anywhere else on the client's line won't work.

   A page like the one shown in Figure 11-18 appears.

3. **Click the down arrow beside the Edit Client button.**

4. **Click Make Inactive.**

   QBO asks if you're sure you want to make the client inactive.

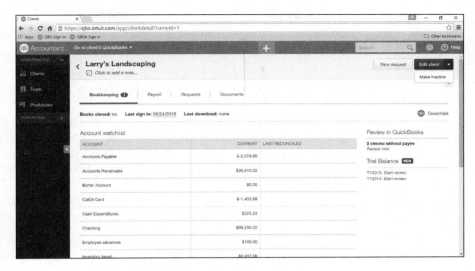

FIGURE 11-18:
The page you use
to make a client
inactive.

5. **Click Yes.**

   QBO redisplays the page shown previously in Figure 11-18, but the "(deleted)" appears beside the client's name and Edit Client button becomes the Make Active button.

6. **Click Clients in the Navigation bar.**

   The client no longer appears on the Clients page.

TIP

You can change the client's status back to Active if you opt to display inactive clients on the Clients page. Click the gear button above the table on the Clients page and select the Include Inactive option (refer to Figure 11-14 to see the list). QBO displays all your clients, both active and inactive. To make an inactive client active again, repeat the steps in this section, clicking the Make Active button in Step 3.

Working with your Wholesale Billing history

You can view and, if you want, download your Wholesale Billing subscription history. Follow these steps:

1. **Display the QBOA Clients page.**

2. **Click the gear in the top right corner of the QBOA toolbar.**

3. **From the drop-down menu, under Your Company, select Your Account.**

   The Your Account window appears.

4. **Scroll down to the Wholesale Clients section.**

5. **Click View QuickBooks Billing History.**

TIP

You'll also find the option to download your billing history to a comma-separated file that you can view in Excel on this page.

Stop using Wholesale Billing

So, you've decided that you really don't want to participate in the Wholesale Billing program and manage QBO subscriptions for your clients. Although you can't cancel your Wholesale Billing subscription, you can stop using it. There's nothing stopping you from working with clients who manage their own QBO subscriptions.

REMEMBER

You can't cancel your Wholesale Billing subscription because that action would also cancel the QBO subscriptions of the clients assigned to your Wholesale Billing subscription.

First, you need to remove all the clients currently in your subscription using the steps in the section "Removing clients from your Wholesale Billing subscription."

After you have removed all companies from your Billing Profile, Intuit will no longer bill you because you won't have any QBO clients in your Wholesale Billing subscription.

Chapter **12**

Adding Companies to the QBOA Client List

After signing up for QBOA and logging in, the next step for the accountant is to populate the Client List with QBO clients, which can happen in a couple of ways. In addition, you might be helping a client set up a QBO company either by creating a new company or by importing information into the QBO company.

This chapter shows you how to add client companies to the Client List and how to import company information from the desktop QuickBooks product.

TIP

Need to remove a client from your Client List? See Chapter 11 for details on making a client inactive.

Adding a Client's Company to the Client List

You can add a client company to the Client List in two ways:

>> By letting your client create the company and then inviting you to access the company

>> By creating a client's company for the client

If you create a client's company for the client and you participate in the Intuit Wholesale Pricing program (also called the Wholesale Billing program), you can opt to manage the client's subscription for him. In this case, Intuit bills you for the client's subscription and you then bill your client (see Chapter 11 for more information on the Wholesale Pricing program. Alternatively, the client can opt to manage his QBO subscription. At the time this book was written, Intuit was running specials on QBO through its main website. In addition, Intuit was offering discounts for QBO companies created by accountants using QBOA regardless of whether the accountant or the client ultimately managed the client's QBO subscription.

TIP

The method you choose for creating a client company doesn't permanently affect the method chosen to manage the subscription; if you belong to the Intuit Wholesale Pricing program, you can always change subscription management later.

If you plan to manage your client's subscription as part of the Intuit Wholesale Pricing program, consider creating your client's company for her. For details on signing up for the Intuit Wholesale Pricing program, contact Intuit.

Adding a company created by a client

If a client creates his own company, he retains billing responsibility for the company. Even so, your client can invite you to access the company using the Invite Accountant process in QBO. Your client should follow these steps:

1. **Have the client open her company in QBO and click the Gear button beside the company name.**

QBO displays the client's Gear menu in QBO (see Figure 12-1).

Click Manage Users.

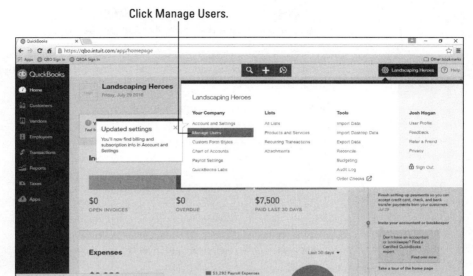

FIGURE 12-1:
The Gear menu
in QBO.

2. **In the Your Company column, have your client click Manage Users.**

The Manage Users page appears. This page identifies the company's Master Administrator, enables the client to add users to the QBO subscription (assuming it is not a Simple Start subscription), and also displays accounting firms the client has invited to access the QBO file (see Figure 12-2).

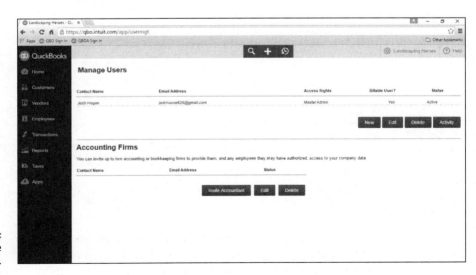

FIGURE 12-2:
The Manage
Users page.

3. **Have your client click the Invite Accountant button.**

TIP

If your client hasn't allowed pop-ups in the browser, he might see a message indicating that a pop-up was blocked. Have your client enable pop-ups for qbo.intuit.com.

The window shown in Figure 12-3 appears.

```
QuickBooks Online Plus - Mini Interview - Google Chrome          —   □   ×

🔒 https://qbo.intuit.com/c18/v1606.982/926802341331459/mini/startat?i

Enter Accountant's email Address                         Page 6 of 7

Accountant's email address
[                              ]

Name (Optional)
First              MI     Last
[              ]   [  ]   [              ]

Your accountant will be sent an email that contains a link for signing into your
company.

Your accountant will be asked to create a user ID before signing in the first time,
unless they already have an account with Intuit Business Services.

Until your accountant signs in, their status on the Manage Users page is "Invited."
After accepting the invitation, their status changes to "Active."

By default, your accountant will be given "Company Administrator" privileges for
performing tasks like closing your books for prior periods. To change these
privileges, click Edit on the Manager Users page.


[ Cancel ]                               [ < Back ]  [ Next > ]

                      Privacy
```

FIGURE 12-3:
The client fills in the accountant's email information.

4. **Have your client provide your email address and click next.**

The Finish Inviting Account page appears, explaining that, when the client clicks Finish, an email will be sent to the accountant that invites the accountant to sign in to the client's company.

5. **Click Finish.**

The email message is sent and the Manage Users page is updated to indicate that the accountant has been sent an invitation.

When you receive your client's email, it will look something like the one shown in Figure 12-4.

Click the Accept Invitation button, and your default browser opens to the QBOA login page. Fill in your QBOA email or user ID and password, and QBOA opens; the new client appears in your list on the Client List page. QBOA immediately displays a page like the one shown in Figure 12-5; use the Edit Client page to identify the additional people in your firm who should have full access to the client's QBO books. When you finish, click Save in the lower right corner of the screen.

FIGURE 12-4:
A sample email an accountant might receive when invited to access a client's QBO company.

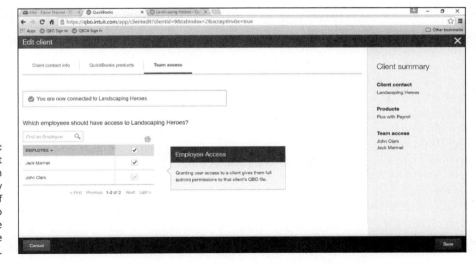

FIGURE 12-5:
After you accept an invitation from a client, identify the members of your firm who should have access to the client's books.

QBO displays the Clients page and the new client appears in the list.

WHEN AN ACCOUNTANT CREATES A CLIENT'S COMPANY

If you create a company for a client through QBOA, it's important to understand that the QBO company *does not* get a 30-day trial period. However, ProAdvisor discounts can be applied to companies created through a trial period offer.

Further, things have changed concerning the way the Master Administrator role is assigned for clients who will be part of your Wholesale Billing subscription. You used to be assigned the Master Administrator role as you created the client's QBO company. Now, however, that restriction no longer exists. Whether the client will be part of your Wholesale Billing subscription or the client will be assuming billing responsibility, you can opt to be the Master Administrator or to assign that role to the client. For clients who want to be part of your Wholesale Billing subscription and assume the role of Master Administrator, you must be an invited accountant in the client's company.

If you retain the Master Administrator role, you can, at some later time, transfer Master Admin privileges back to the client. See the section "Transferring Master Administrator rights back to your client."

Creating a QBO company for a client

You, the accountant, can create a new QBO company for a client instead of having the client create the company. If you have signed up for the Intuit Wholesale Pricing program, billing responsibility for the QBO company you create becomes a matter of choice:

>> You can pay for the client's subscription and then bill the client back for the cost of the subscription.

>> You can transfer billing responsibility to the client.

At the present time (this could change in the future), if a QBO client wants to remove an accountant, the firm managing the client's Wholesale Billing subscription must first remove the client from Wholesale Billing, even if the accountant the QBO client wants to remove is not affiliated with the firm managing the client's QBO subscription.

To remove a client from your Wholesale Billing subscription, follow these steps:

1. **In QBOA, click Gear ⇨ Your Account.**

   Your Account appears in the Your Company column of the Gear menu.

2. **In the Your Accountant window, scroll down to the Wholesale clients section and click the company you wish to remove from wholesale billing.**

3. **From the Actions column drop-down, click Remove from Wholesale.**

To create a company for your client, follow these steps:

1. **Open QBOA.**

2. **Click Clients in the Navigation bar to make sure you're displaying the Client List page.**

3. **From the Client List page, click the Add Client button in the upper right corner above the list.**

   The Add Client wizard begins, and you see the Client Contact Info page (see Figure 12-6).

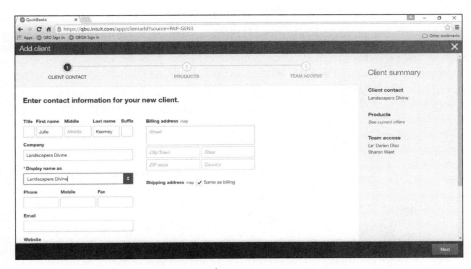

FIGURE 12-6:
The Client
Contact Info page
of the Add Client
wizard.

4. **Provide a name for the new company.**

5. **Optionally, supply other information on this screen.**

6. **Click Next.**

   QBOA displays the QuickBooks Products page of the Add Client wizard, shown in Figure 12-7.

7. **Click the QuickBooks Products list box to open the list and display the available QBO products.**

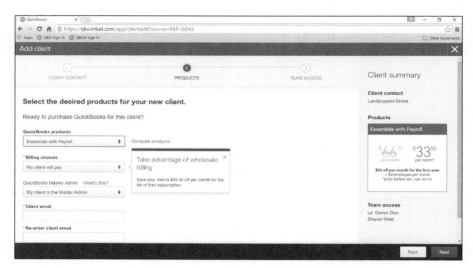

FIGURE 12-7:
The QuickBooks
Products page of
the Add Client
screen.

8. **Select a QBO product for the client.**

    You can choose Essentials, Essentials with Payroll, Essentials with Full Service Payroll, Plus, Plus with Payroll, or Plus with Full Service Payroll.

    After you select a product, the Billing Choices list box appears.

9. **Click the Billing Choices list box and select who will pay, who will be Master Administrator; and provide the Master Administrator's e-mail address.**

10. **Click Next.**

    QBOA displays the last screen of the wizard, where you select the members of your team who should have full administrative permissions when accessing the books of the client you're adding.

    You can change access privileges later.

REMEMBER

11. **Click Save.**

    QBOA does some work and creates the company, which appears in the list of companies on the Client List page (see Figure 12-8).

Transferring Master Administrator rights back to your client

As you see in the preceding section, when you create a company for a client, you can assign yourself as the Master Administrator; in this case, QBOA also assigns you as the Accountant user for the company. But you can transfer the Master Administrator role back to your client; this process won't affect your status as the Accountant user.

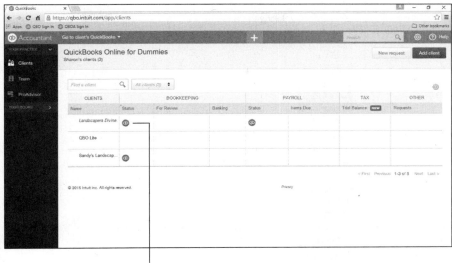

FIGURE 12-8:
The new company appears on the Client List page.

New company added

The process of transferring the Master Administrator role to a client involves first inviting the client to become a Company Administrator. After the client accepts the invitation to become a Company Administrator, you can transfer the Master Administrator role to the client — again, using an invitation process.

Inviting the client to become a company administrator

As the first part of the process, create a Company Administrator for the new company. Follow these steps:

1. **Open the client company using the Go to Client's QuickBooks list on the QBOA toolbar.**

TIP

The first time you open a client QBO company, the Welcome to QuickBooks wizard walks you through some basic setup steps, where you fill in the client's contact information, industry, and legal organization as well as some additional basic information, and QBO creates a Chart of Accounts for you.

2. **Click the Gear button on the QBOA toolbar and choose Manage Users.**

QBO displays the Manage Users page, which also contains the list of accountant users in the Accounting Firms section. In Figure 12-9, note that the accountant user in the Accounting Firms section at the bottom of the page and the Master Administrator in the Manage Users section at the top of the page belong to the same QBOA user.

Click here to invite your client to become
the company administrator for his QBO account.

FIGURE 12-9:
The Manage
Users page for a
company created
for a client by a
QBOA user.

3. **Click New in the Manage Users section to add a new Company Administrator user.**

   A wizard starts.

4. **On the Choose User Type page, shown in Figure 12-10, select Company Administrator and click Next.**

FIGURE 12-10:
Select Company
Administrator.

5. **On the Enter User's Email Address page, shown in Figure 12-11, provide the client's email address (and optionally, name) and click Next.**

   The Finish Adding User page appears and explains that QBO will send an email invitation to the user to sign in to the company. The email explains that he must create a QBO user ID unless he already has one. In most cases, if you set up a company for a client, the client doesn't yet have a QBO login.

FIGURE 12-11:
Identify the user you want to set up as a Company Administrator.

6. **Click Finish.**

   The new user appears on the Manage Users page in Pending status (see Figure 12-12).

When the client receives the email invitation to become the Company Administrator, the invitation looks something like the one shown in Figure 12-13.

When the client clicks the Accept Invitation button in the email to accept the invitation, a QBO login screen appears using the qbo.intuit.com web address. Typically, the client doesn't have a QBO login yet and so goes through the process of creating a new one; when he finishes, he's logged in to QBO and receives a message indicating that he successfully accepted the invitation.

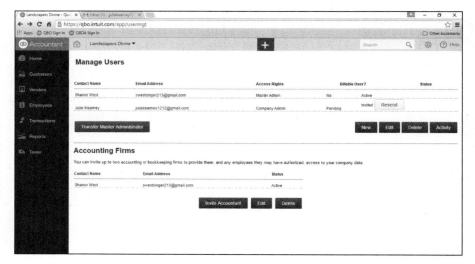

FIGURE 12-12:
The Manage Users page after successfully sending a message to a client to become a Company Administrator.

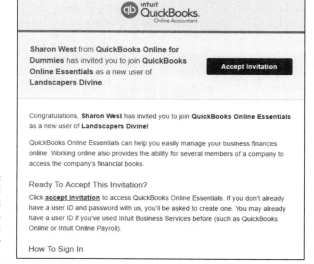

FIGURE 12-13:
The sample email a client receives when invited to become a QBO Company Administrator.

Transferring the Master Administrator role to the client

In the meantime, you, the QBOA user, can use QBOA to open the client's QBO company. On the Manage Users page, you can see that the status of the client's Company Administrator role is no longer Pending, but you are still listed as the Master Administrator (see Figure 12-14).

Now that you've established a Company Administrator for the client company, you can follow these steps to transfer the Master Administrator role to the client:

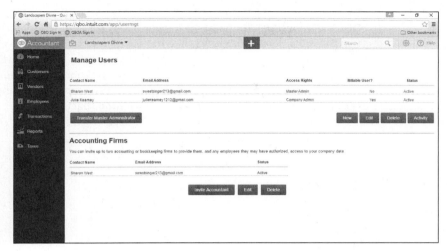

FIGURE 12-14:
The client's new role as Company Administrator is now active, but you're still the Master Administrator.

1. **In QBOA, open the client's company.**

2. **Click the Gear button on the QBOA toolbar and choose Manage Users.**

   The Manage Users page still lists you as the Master Administrator.

3. **Click Transfer Master Administrator.**

   The Transfer Master Administrator Role page appears (see Figure 12-15).

FIGURE 12-15:
Use this page to transfer the role of Master Administrator to your client.

4. **Select a user who should assume the Master Administrator role.**

5. **Click Finish.**

QBOA sends an email invitation to your client to become the Master Administrator; the email looks very much like the one shown in Figure 12-16, and the client can accept or decline. Assuming the client accepts, he's prompted to log in to QBO. Once he does, he sees a page that explains that the Master Admin role has been successfully transferred to him and that an email explaining such has been sent to the former Master Administrator — and that's you.

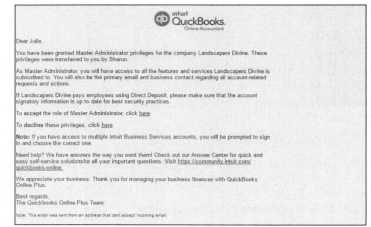

FIGURE 12-16:
A sample of the email the client receives when you invite her to become the Master Administrator.

If you once again use QBOA to open the client's company and view the Manage Users page, you'll notice that you no longer appear in the Manage Users section and your client is the Master Administrator for the company (see Figure 12-17).

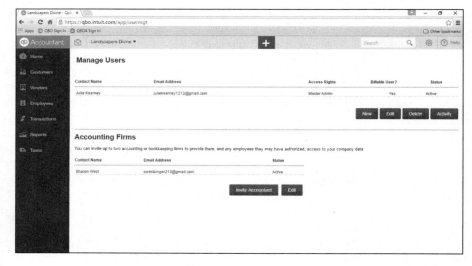

FIGURE 12-17:
The client company's Manage Users page after transferring the Master Administrator role.

Importing Desktop QuickBooks Information

If you've been using QuickBooks for Windows Pro or Premier 2008 or later in the United States and Canada, and your QBO subscription is less than 60 days old, you can import your company's information into a QBO company. You also can help your clients import their desktop QuickBooks companies into QBO companies.

TIP

Users in countries other than the U.S. and Canada might be able to import desktop QuickBooks information into QBO with the help of an outside service; contact Intuit for more information. Users of QuickBooks for Windows 2007 and earlier, QuickBooks for the Mac, and QuickBooks Enterprise should contact Intuit for details on importing their data into QBO.

Assuming that you meet the criteria previously outlined, read on.

General conversion considerations

Before you dive into converting your data, stack the odds in your favor by doing some homework. First, examine your desktop QuickBooks data file to make sure that it will convert. In your desktop product, open your company and press F2 to display the Product Information dialog box shown in Figure 12-18. In particular, take note of the number of targets listed. If your data file's number of targets falls below 350,000, you can proceed.

REMEMBER

If your data file's number of targets exceeds 350,000, condense your data. If your company's targets still exceed 350,000, consider importing lists only, as described in Chapter 4.

Next, using the U.S. version of the desktop QuickBooks product, verify your data file and then condense it so that it includes approximately one year's data. Condensing reduces the size of your data file and removes inactive list entries, and smaller data files tend to convert better. On the File menu, choose Utilities ⇨ Condense Data.

If you suspect the desktop company data isn't in good shape — for example, you get errors while verifying or condensing — you can try rebuilding the data and then rerunning the Condense Data function. If you still get errors, consider importing lists only as described in Chapter 4.

Total targets

FIGURE 12-18:
Check the
number of
targets in your
desktop
QuickBooks
company.

You should plan to keep your desktop data file around, if for no other reason than to refer to it for historical data as needed. Many people opt to run desktop Quick-Books and QBO simultaneously for a month or two to make sure QBO is performing as they expect.

REMEMBER

Importing a desktop QuickBooks company

When you convert a QuickBooks desktop company to QBO, some data fully converts, some partially converts, and some doesn't convert at all. In addition, QBO contains comparable alternatives for some desktop QuickBooks features and doesn't contain alternatives for others.

You can import any QuickBooks for Windows company using QuickBooks U.S., including companies with the multicurrency feature turned on, as long as the company meets the target limitation of 350,000. You also can import QuickBooks Desktop companies using U.K. and Canadian versions, again including companies that have multicurrency turned on.

In general, the following types of files won't convert and therefore can't be imported:

>> You cannot import QuickBooks desktop data into any QBO company that was created more than 60 days ago, except for accountant company files. You can import QuickBooks desktop companies into a QBOA company within 1,060 days of creating the QBOA account.

REMEMBER

When I say "accountant company files," I'm talking about importing a QuickBooks desktop company file into the Your Books company available in QBOA.

>> You cannot import a QuickBooks desktop company into QBO subscriptions using international versions of QBO other than U.K. and Canadian.

>> You cannot import non-Intuit accounting software company files. If you need to import company data from a non-Intuit product, you need to work with Intuit's full-service team.

>> You cannot directly import accounting data stored in spreadsheet files. You can import these via a third-party app called Transaction Pro Importer, available at `http://appcenter.intuit.com/transactionproimporter`.

In addition, Appendix B describes the limitations you'll encounter if you import a desktop QuickBooks company. I suggest you review Appendix B so that you know what to expect. After you've reviewed the general considerations in the preceding section and the limitations for importing found Appendix B, you're ready to import your desktop QuickBooks company into QBO.

It's important to understand that, even if your company data meets the criteria above, some data still won't convert when you import:

>> Reconciliation reports: Save your reconciliation reports in QuickBooks Desktop to access them later. In QBO, continue reconciling where you left off. See Chapter 8 and take a peek at Intuit's Reconcile Your Accounts tutorial at `http://intuitaccountants.com/reconcilereports`.

>> Recurring credit card charges: At your Merchant Center, cancel each existing automatic credit card recurring charge and re-create it in QBO as a recurring sales receipt.

All other recurring transactions convert and import.

TIP

>> Reports: Find a similar report in QBO and customize it to your preference. See Chapter 10 and Intuit's Customize Reports and Email tutorial at `http://intuitaccountants.com/customreport`. In addition, you can check out `www.Apps.com` for a list of reporting apps that can help your business.

>> Audit trail: Your desktop audit trail won't come over, but all changes going forward will be captured in the Audit Log within QBO.

>> Non-posting transactions or accounts don't convert except for estimates and purchase orders.

PAYROLL AND DATA CONVERSION

QBO supports Intuit Online Payroll and QuickBooks Online Payroll (QBOP) to manage payroll. In some cases, your QuickBooks desktop payroll data will automatically update your year-to-date totals. But, if that data doesn't migrate, and you intend to use QBOP, you will need to enter payroll totals as described in Chapter 9. Don't set up QuickBooks Online Payroll until after you convert your desktop data.

Updating your edition of QuickBooks

The first step you should take in the process of importing data from a desktop QuickBooks company is to make sure that your edition of desktop QuickBooks is up to date. Follow these steps:

1. **Open the desktop edition of QuickBooks.**

2. **Choose Help ⇨ Update QuickBooks.**

   The Update QuickBooks window appears.

3. **Click the Update Now tab (see Figure 12-19) and select all updates.**

FIGURE 12-19: Select all update areas.

4. **Click Get Updates.**

   QuickBooks goes through the process of downloading updates.

5. **Once the updating process finishes, click Close.**

Next, exit from QuickBooks and restart it; if QuickBooks downloaded updates, it will prompt you to allow the updates to be installed; make sure you install the updates.

Now, check the following in the desktop QuickBooks product to help you avoid errors during the export/import process:

» Make sure you're working in Single User mode: Click the File menu and make sure you see the Switch to Multi-user Mode command. Don't click it; just make sure you see it, because its availability lets you know you're working in Single User mode.

» To eliminate errors that might be introduced by working over a network, move the company file to your local drive.

Okay. You're ready to start the process of exporting a desktop QuickBooks company data and then importing it into a QBO company.

REMEMBER

You can import a desktop QuickBooks company only during the first 60 days of a subscription with one exception: You can import your own data into the free company that comes with QBOA for up to 1,060 days.

Transferring data from a desktop company into QBO

During the transfer process, you're given the option to overwrite an existing QBO company or create a new one. In the steps that follow, I set up an empty QBO company before I started and allowed the process to overwrite it. Follow these steps to transfer data from a desktop QuickBooks company into a QBO company:

1. **In desktop QuickBooks, choose Company ⇨ Export Company File to QuickBooks Online.**

   QuickBooks Enterprise users should press Ctrl+1 to open the Product Information window and then press Ctrl+B+Q. Then, click OK to close the Product Information window.

   A wizard starts to walk you through the process of exporting the data.

2. **Sign in to your QBO account.**

   If you don't have a QBO account yet, you can click Create a New Account and walk through the process of supplying a user ID — typically an email address — and a password.

REMEMBER

   Because you're not signing in from your browser, you might be prompted to authenticate yourself; in this case, Intuit sends a code to your email address and you must check email to be able to supply the code onscreen.

3. **Select the appropriate choice for turning on inventory, and then click Continue.**

   If you opt to turn on inventory, select the date you want to use to calculate inventory value using the FIFO method. Intuit recommends that you use the first day following your company's last tax filing period.

REMEMBER

   Only QBO Plus supports inventory. If you opt to import inventory, your accounting method will change to FIFO and you will need to file Form 3115 with the IRS. If QBO identifies any errors with inventory during the importing process, the process will fail and you'll receive an email with instructions on how to fix the items causing the problem. Also be aware that, due to recalculations to FIFO, your Accrual Basis reports and Cash Basis reports will not match. QuickBooks will flag any errors with inventory if they appear during import.

4. **Select the appropriate choice for the location of your QuickBooks company data (see Figure 12-20).**

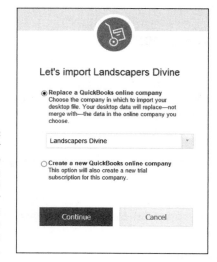

FIGURE 12-20: Select whether you want to overwrite an existing QBO company or create a new one for your desktop QuickBooks company data.

   I selected an empty company I created using the steps found earlier in this chapter in the section "Creating a QBO company for a client."

5. **Click Continue.**

   QBO makes a copy of your desktop QuickBooks company file and imports it into your QBO company. A message appears, letting you know that you'll receive an email when the process finishes (see Figure 12-21).

We are on it!

We're transferring your data now. When it's done, we'll send a confirmation email to

juliekearney1212@gmail.com

OK, got it

FIGURE 12-21:
This message appears after you finish your part of the export/import process.

6. **Click OK, Got It.**

7. **You can close the desktop QuickBooks product.**

   When the email arrives, the message will resemble the one shown in Figure 12-22. You can click the Continue to Account Setup button to log in to the QBO company, or you can use the QBO interface.

TIP

If you click the Continue to Account Setup button in the email, a new browser tab appears displaying the QBO sign in page.

After converting . . .

After conversion finishes, you need to double-check things to make sure your data looks the way you expected. Check your email; you'll find that the acknowledgement you received confirming that the data was imported contains an attached Import Summary report — an Excel file that helps you determine what information in the QuickBooks desktop company didn't make it to the QBO company.

© 2016 Intuit Inc. All rights reserved.

FIGURE 12-22:
A sample of the email message you receive after exporting a desktop QuickBooks company to QBO.

TIP

If your client does the conversion and you are the accountant user for the QBO account, you'll receive the report and your client won't unless you send it to him.

In addition to reviewing the Import Summary report, I suggest you run and compare the Profit & Loss report, the Balance Sheet, Accounts Receivable, Accounts Payable, sales tax liability, and, if appropriate, payroll liability reports for both the desktop QuickBooks company and the QBO company. Be sure you run these reports using the Accrual basis with the dates set to All. Use the Accrual basis because reports run in both products using the Cash basis might not match.

TIP

Need a do-over? During the first 60 days of a subscription, you get a "do-over" on importing data into a QBO company, which can be useful if things don't import as you expect. Just go through the process of importing again.

And, here's a checklist of things you probably need to do to make the imported QBO company ready for use:

>> Set up company users.

>> Set up sales tax items.

>> Set up payroll, either through Intuit Online Payroll or QBOP.

>> Reconcile accounts as needed.

>> Review lists and make appropriate entries inactive as necessary.

>> Set up recurring transactions to replace desktop QuickBooks memorized transactions.

WARNING

WANT TO "UNDO" AN IMPORT?

Suppose you're not happy with the results of importing and you decide that you simply want to enter data manually into your company. You can clear the data from the QBO company by purging it. Open the company and click Home so that you're viewing the QBO company home page.

In the browser address bar, change the address to https://qbo.intuit.com/app/purgecompany and press Enter or refresh the page. A page appears that describes what will be deleted and asks if you're sure. Type **yes** in the lower right corner and click OK, and QBO purges the data from your company. If you change your mind and don't want to purge, click Cancel in the lower right corner.

You cannot purge data from the Your Books company. But you can clear the data from the Your Books company if you import a company from QuickBooks Desktop that contains no data. Intuit even provides an empty company file that you can use; visit https://community.intuit.com/articles/1308208-deleting-all-the-data-within-a-qbo-company to read the article and download the empty company.

>> Re-create any necessary non-posting transactions, such as purchase orders.

>> Review inventory.

>> Customize forms and reports and, if appropriate, memorize reports.

>> Set up a closing date password.

Switching between Client QBO Companies

As you've worked through Chapters 11 and 12, you might have noticed that client QBO companies don't, by default, open in a separate tab in your browser. So, what do you do when you want to stop working in one client's books and start working in another client's books?

Well, you can click the Accountant button on the QBOA toolbar at any time to redisplay the QBOA interface and your list of clients. From there, you can click the QuickBooks logo beside any client's name to open that client QBO company.

But you really don't need to take two steps to switch between client QBO companies; instead, take advantage of the Go to Client's QuickBooks list box on the QBOA toolbar.

When you're working in a client QBO company, the name of that company appears in the Go to Client's QuickBooks list box; if you click the company name, a list of all your client QBO companies appears. Just click the name of the company you want to open. No need to worry about saving work; QBO automatically saves as you work.

Chapter **13**

Exploring a Client's Company from QBOA

A client's QBO company looks a little different when viewed using QBOA. This chapter explores the interface you see when you open a client QBO company from QBOA. It also covers some facets of a client QBO company you might want to review for your client to make sure things flow smoothly for both of you.

Opening a Client's Company

You can open a client's company in QBOA from the Client List page; on the client's line in the list, click the QuickBooks logo (the circle with the letters *q* and *b* in it). Alternatively, you can use the Go to Client's QuickBooks list on the QBOA toolbar, which remains visible at all times, making it easy for you to switch from one client QBO company to another. Simply open the list and select the name of the company you want to open (see Figure 13-1).

You don't need to take any special action to close a client QBO company; you can simply open another client QBO company, or you can sign out of QBOA from the Gear menu on the QBOA toolbar.

Click here.

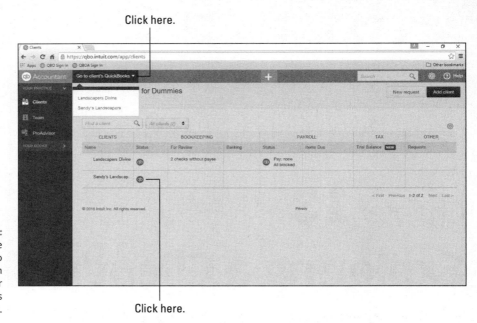

FIGURE 13-1:
You can click the
QuickBooks logo
or use the list on
the QBOA toolbar
to open a client's
QBO company.

Click here.

TIP

To access two different companies simultaneously, you can't just open another browser tab and sign in to QBOA. Instead, you need to use separate browsers. Or, if you're using Chrome, you can sign into Chrome as a different user. See Chapter 17 for details on Chrome users.

Reviewing a Client QBO Company

You'll probably want to review the company setup information for client QBO companies to make sure that things are set up properly for your client. In particular, you'll want to review the settings, the Chart of Accounts, and the lists of client QBO companies.

TIP

The first time you open a client QBO company that you have created, a wizard walks you through establishing basic setup information. But you can review and change that information at any time.

Examining company setup information

You review company setup information to make sure that the client QBO company uses the correct accounting method, employer EIN, and legal business organization. To review company settings, follow these steps:

1. **Open the client QBO company you want to review.**

   You can click the QuickBooks logo on the Client List page of QBOA, or you can use the list of clients in the QBOA toolbar.

2. **Click the Gear button on the right side of the QBOA toolbar to display the Gear menu (see Figure 13-2).**

Gear icon

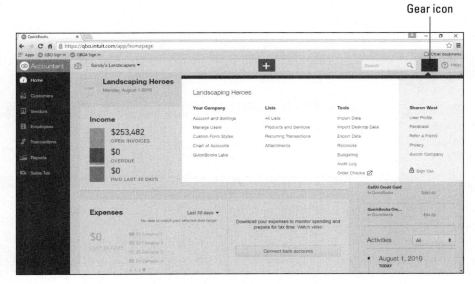

FIGURE 13-2:
The Gear menu.

3. **From the Your Company group on the left side of the Gear menu, click Account and Settings.**

   The Company tab (selected on the left side of the Account and Settings dialog box) appears (see Figure 13-3).

4. **Review the settings.**

   In particular, set or correct the Company Name, Legal Name, and Employer ID (EIN).

   To make changes, click any setting. QBO makes the setting options available; make your changes and click Save.

5. **Click Advanced on the left side of the Account and Settings dialog box.**

   The settings on the Advanced page of the Account and Settings dialog box appear (see Figure 13-4).

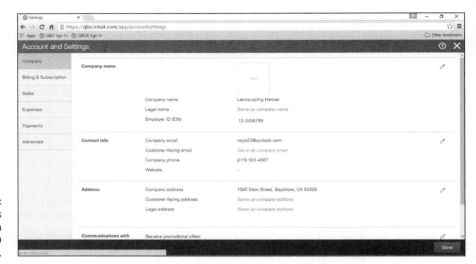

FIGURE 13-3:
The Settings dialog box for a client QBO company.

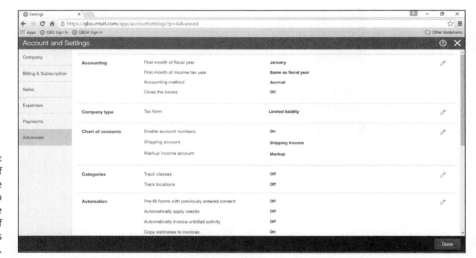

FIGURE 13-4:
Review and, if necessary, make changes to settings on the Advanced tab of the Settings dialog box.

6. **Review the settings.**

   In particular, set or correct the following:

   ● The settings in the Accounting section, which include fiscal and tax year information as well as the QBO company's accounting method,

   ● In the Company Type section, the tax form setting,

   ● The settings in the Chart of Accounts section,

   ● The settings in the Other Preferences section, which isn't shown in Figure 13-4 but includes displaying warnings when duplicate check numbers and bill numbers are used.

7. Click Done to save your changes.

QBO displays a message at the top of the screen indicating that your changes were saved.

Taking a look at the Chart of Accounts

In addition to checking company settings, you should review your client's Chart of Accounts to make sure it looks the way you want. In the client QBO company, click the Accountant Tools button and choose Chart of Accounts to display the Chart of Accounts page shown in Figure 13-5.

Batch Edit button

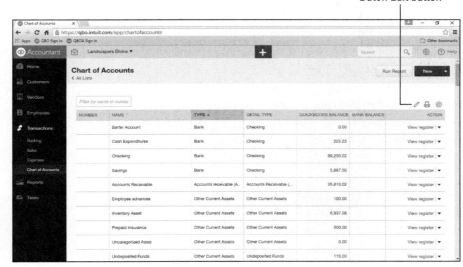

FIGURE 13-5:
From the Chart of Accounts page, you can add and edit accounts.

TIP

You also can open the Chart of Accounts from the Navigation bar (under Transactions) and from Gear menu on the QBOA toolbar. All roads lead to Rome.

If you chose to enable the option to use account numbers while you were reviewing company settings (refer to Figure 13-4), the Chart of Accounts page displays a column for account numbers at the left edge of the Chart of Accounts page and the Batch Edit button in the upper right corner. You'll use the Batch Edit button to add account numbers, as described later in this chapter in the section "Adding account numbers."

Editing or adding accounts

You might need to edit an account to change an account's Category Type or its name, and you use the Account window to make the change.

TIP

If you decide to add account numbers to the Chart of Accounts, you can add an account number in the Account window, but there's a much easier way, which I'll show you in the next section, "Adding account numbers."

To display the Account window, click the down arrow in the Action column at the right side of the account and, from the menu that appears, click Edit (see Figure 13-6).

Click here to create a new account.

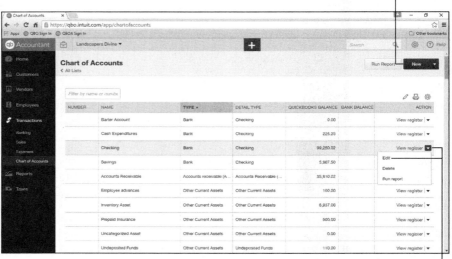

FIGURE 13-6:
To edit an account, use the down arrow in the Action column.

Click here to edit an account.

Or, if you need to create a new account, click the New button above the list. The window you see when creating a new account looks just like the one you see when you edit an existing account.

TIP

If you double-click an Asset, Liability, or Equity account, QBO displays the account's register (except Retained Earnings, which displays a report). If you double-click an Income or Expense account, QBO displays a QuickReport for the account. You also can click the Register and Report links in the Action column to display a register or a report.

Adding account numbers

I promised I'd show you an easy way to add account numbers to a QBO company Chart of Accounts. First, make sure you enable the setting on the Advanced tab of the Settings dialog box (in the Chart of Accounts section) shown previously in Figure 13-4.

Then, on the Chart of Accounts page, click the Batch Edit button (the one that looks like a pencil on the right side of the table above the table headings) to display the page shown in Figure 13-7.

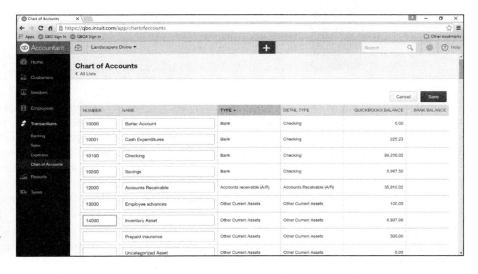

FIGURE 13-7: Use this page to set up account numbers for the Chart of Accounts.

Type account numbers in the Number column. Save buttons appear at the top- and bottom-right corners of the page; click either button after you finish entering the account numbers.

Because a QBOA session times out by default after 60 minutes of non-use, you might want to save periodically as you enter account numbers.

TIP

After you enter account numbers, you can sort the Chart of Accounts in account number order by clicking Number in the column headings on the Chart of Accounts page.

TIP

Reviewing list information

You also can review list information. Using the links in the Navigation bar, you can view overview information about customers, vendors, and employees. In Figure 13-8, you see the Customers page.

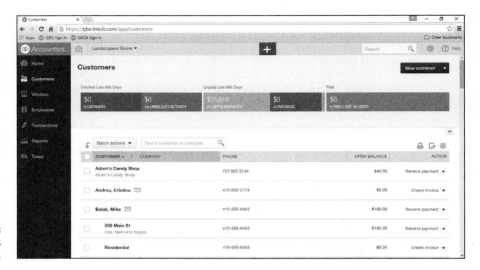

FIGURE 13-8:
The Customers
page.

On any of these pages, you can use the bar at the top of the page to filter the list to view a particular subset of the list. For example, you can filter the list of customers on the Customers page to view only those customers with overdue invoices. And you can use the Batch Actions button (just below the filter bar) to perform, well, batch actions, such as emailing a batch of customers. If your list is long, use the text box beside the Batch Actions button to search for a particular list entry. You also can sort the list by name or by open balance; just click the appropriate heading below the Batch Actions button.

TIP

You can import names into a people list. For more information, see Chapter 4.

To review other lists, click the Gear button in the QBOA toolbar. In the Lists section of the Gear menu that appears, you can opt to view any of three common lists (the Products and Services list, the Recurring Transactions list, or the Attachments list). Or, you can click All Lists at the top of the Lists section to display the Lists page shown in Figure 13-9, which you can use to navigate to any list other than a people-oriented list.

For more extensive details on working with lists, see Chapter 4.

Exporting and importing bank feed rules

When your client takes advantage of bank feeds and downloads transactions from the bank to his QBO company, you can help ensure that the transactions post properly. In many cases, the rules used by one client can apply to another, so, rather than re-creating rules, export them from one client and import them to another.

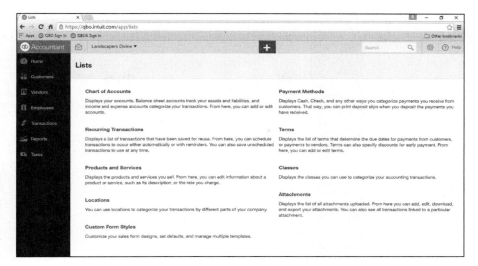

FIGURE 13-9:
Use this page to open any list other than the Customers, Vendors, or Employees list.

When you export rules, QBO exports all the rules in the client's company. You can selectively import rules.

To export rules from a client company, open that company and follow these steps:

1. Choose Transactions ⇨ Banking.

2. On the Bank and Credit Cards page, click the down arrow beside the Update button in the upper right corner of the page.

3. Click Manage Rules.

   QBO displays the Rules page (see Figure 13-10).

4. Click the down arrow beside the New Rule button and choose Export Rules.

   QBO creates an Excel file containing the rules and stores it in your Downloads folder. The name of the file includes the name of the client whose rules you exported and the words, "Bank_Feed_Rules."

   QBO displays the directions for what you do next — which I outline in the following steps. Click Close in the QBO message.

5. Switch to the company to which you want to import these rules.

6. Repeat Steps 1 to 4 above; in Step 4, choose Import Rules.

   QBO starts a wizard that helps you import the rules.

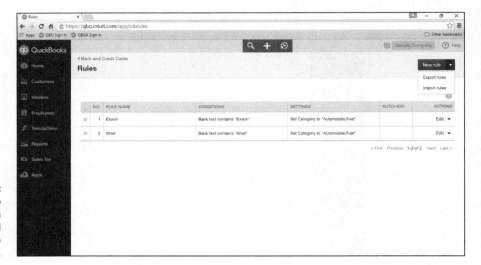

FIGURE 13-10:
Use this page to export rules from one client and import them to another.

7. **On the first Import Rules wizard screen, select the file you created in Step 4 and click Next.**

8. **On the second wizard screen, select the rules you want to import and click Next.**

9. **On the third wizard screen, you have the option to select categories for the rules that match the Chart of Accounts of the client to which you are importing the rules. Make any changes and, when you finish, click Import.**

   QBO tells you how many rules imported successfully.

10. **Click Finish.**

    QBO redisplays the Rules page for the client you opened in Step 5, where you can verify that the rules you wanted to import appear.

For more detail on working with rules, see Chapter 8.

Chapter **14**

Working in a Client's Company

You work in a client's QBO company in much the same way your client does; see Chapters 4 to 10 for detailed information. In this chapter, I focus on ways you can navigate easily, search for and review transactions, and communicate with clients.

Making Navigation Easy

Much of mouse navigation is obvious; click here and click there. But you can use a few not-so-obvious tricks to navigate easily, including some keyboard shortcuts. Some common navigation techniques are specific to Chrome; see Chapters 17 and 18 for more information.

Using keyboard shortcuts

Hidden away in QBO companies are keyboard shortcuts that you might want to use. I show them here in Figure 14-1, and you also can find them on this book's cheat sheet.

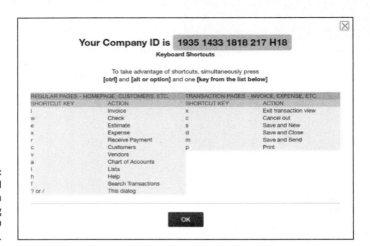

Your Company ID is **1935 1433 1818 217 H18**

Keyboard Shortcuts

To take advantage of shortcuts, simultaneously press
[ctrl] and **[alt or option]** and one **[key from the list below]**

REGULAR PAGES - HOMEPAGE, CUSTOMERS, ETC.		TRANSACTION PAGES - INVOICE, EXPENSE, ETC.	
SHORTCUT KEY	ACTION	SHORTCUT KEY	ACTION
i	Invoice	x	Exit transaction view
w	Check	c	Cancel out
e	Estimate	s	Save and New
x	Expense	d	Save and Close
r	Receive Payment	m	Save and Send
c	Customers	p	Print
v	Vendors		
a	Chart of Accounts		
l	Lists		
h	Help		
f	Search Transactions		
? or /	This dialog		

OK

FIGURE 14-1:
Keyboard shortcuts you can use while working in a client QBO company.

TIP

To get this cheat sheet, simply go to www.dummies.com and search for "Quick-Books Online For Dummies Cheat Sheet" in the Search box.

To view these shortcuts (and the current client QBO Company ID), press and hold Ctrl+Alt and then press the forward slash (/) key. Mac users, substitute Option for Alt here and in the next paragraph. If you press Ctrl+Alt+/ without opening a client QBO company, the Company ID you see is your own.

To use any of these shortcuts, press and hold Ctrl+Alt and then press the appropriate key to perform its associated action. For example, to open the Invoice window, press Ctrl+Alt+I.

Opening multiple windows

Many times, accountants want to work with multiple windows, and you can do that in QBO. Within the same QBO company, you can duplicate a browser tab using the New Window command on the Accountant Tools menu on the QBOA toolbar (see Figure 14-2). You can read more about the other commands on the Accountant Tools menu in Chapter 15.

TIP

If you're using Chrome, you also can duplicate a browser tab by right-clicking the tab and choosing Duplicate. In Firefox, you can duplicate a browser tab by clicking in the address bar and pressing Alt+Enter.

When you click the New Window command, QBO opens a new browser tab and displays the same information that appears in the original browser tab. But, from that point, you can display different information for the same company in each browser tab. And, if you're working in Chrome on multiple monitors, you can split the tabs onto different monitors. Drag the tab you want to place on a different monitor in a downward direction, and it splits away from the browser. You can immediately drag it to another monitor, or you can release the mouse button, in which case a second instance of Chrome appears. You can then drag either instance to a different monitor.

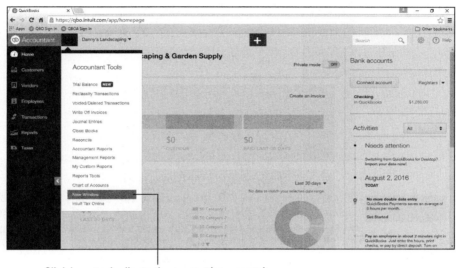

FIGURE 14-2:
Use the New
Window
command while
working in a QBO
company to
duplicate the
window you're
viewing.

Click here to duplicate the current browser tab.

TIP

The same technique works in Firefox; drag a Firefox tab downward and release the mouse button. The tab splits away and appears in a second instance of Firefox. You can then drag either instance to a different monitor.

Working in two companies simultaneously

Suppose that you're done working with one client and want to open a different client. As described in Chapter 12, you can click the Go to Client's QuickBooks button on the QBOA toolbar and select a new client. Or, you can click the Accountant button in the upper left corner of the QBOA interface to redisplay the Client List page and then click the QuickBooks icon for the client QBO company you now want to open. Either way, QBOA displays the information for the newly selected client.

That brings up the question, "How do I work in two different companies simultaneously?" Well, you can open a different browser, sign in to QBOA, and open a second client QBO company. For example, if you're working in Chrome, you could open Firefox using the same QBOA login information. You can then open two different companies, as I did in Figure 14-3.

One company open in Chrome   Different company open in Firefox

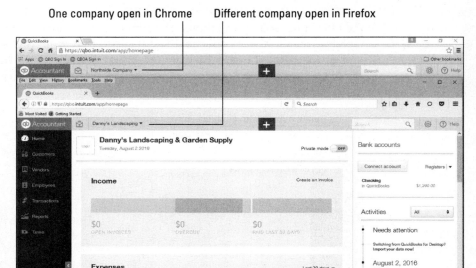

FIGURE 14-3:
To work in two
companies at the
same time, you
can use two
browsers.

If you're working in Chrome, you also can take advantage of Chrome users and open Chrome as a different user. You'd have, effectively, two instances of Chrome running simultaneously. See Chapter 17 for more information on Chrome users.

Examining Available Transaction Types

In Chapters 5 to 9, I covered transactions in some detail, so I'm not going to repeat that information here. But you can see the available transactions by opening a client QBO company and then clicking the Create menu (the plus sign) shown in Figure 14-4. Available transactions are organized on the menu by the type of people to which they pertain. And the Create menu contains an "Other" category for transactions that don't pertain to particular types of people — like bank deposits.

REMEMBER

Before you open the Create menu, its button appears as a plus sign (+), but after you open it, as I did in Figure 14-4, the button changes to an X.

If you want to view only the more commonly used transactions, click the Show Less link in the lower right corner of the Create menu. The link changes to the Show More link so that you can redisplay all types of transactions.

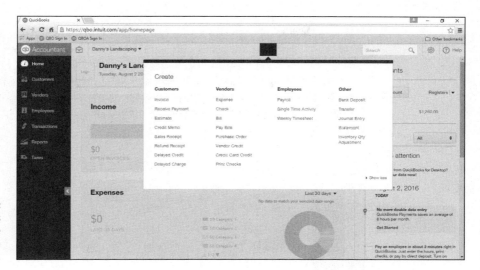

FIGURE 14-4:
The transactions you can create while working in a QBO company.

Searching for Transactions

More often than not, you'll be searching for transactions in a client QBO company rather than creating them. You can search for transactions using the Search box on the QBOA toolbar at the top of the client QBO company window (see Figure 14-5). When you click in the Search box, QBO displays a list of recent transactions and reports.

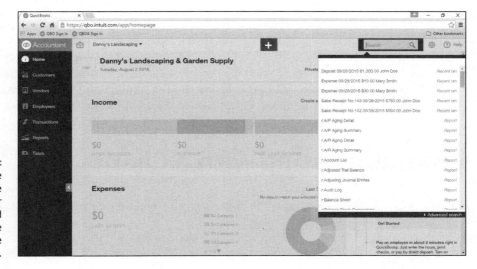

FIGURE 14-5:
Type any phrase you want to use as a search filter or click Advanced Search at the bottom of the Search list.

If you see the result you want, you can click it to open it in the appropriate window. If you *don't* see the result you want, you have a couple of options.

First, you can type in the Search box, and QBO responds with sample results. If you still don't see the result you want, try your second option: Click Advanced Search in the lower right corner of the menu, and QBO displays the Search page (see Figure 14-6).

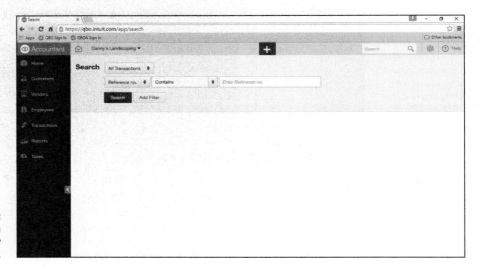

FIGURE 14-6:
Set criteria for a more specifically defined search.

You can limit the search to a particular transaction type, choose to search for any of several types of data, and specify whether the search should contain, not contain, be equal to, or not be equal to the search criteria.

TIP

From any transaction window, you can view recent transactions of that type by clicking the button that appears in the transaction's title bar, immediately to the left of the name of the transaction type. The button image looks a bit like a clock.

Communicating with a Client

Using QBO and QBOA tools, you can communicate with clients via email concerning a particular transaction.

TIP

You also can send an email from QBOA without opening your email client. In the Client List, click the client's name. On the page that appears, click the client's email address. Your email program opens and displays the window where you type a new email message; the message is already addressed to your client.

Using the Client Collaborator tool

QBO and QBOA contain a tool called the Client Collaborator that you can use to communicate with your client about existing transactions. The Client Collaborator is a two-way tool; you or your client can send a message, and the message recipient can answer. Think of the Client Collaborator as a way to send a text message using QBOA or QBO.

REMEMBER

You can communicate about certain types of transactions but not others. In general, you can communicate about posting transactions such as invoices, bills, payments to customers, checks to vendors, and credit card transactions. But you won't find the Conversation button referred to in this section in windows for cash and non-posting transactions such as sales receipts, expense transactions, billable expenses, delayed charges, credit memos, and paycheck and payroll-related windows.

Although either you or your client can initiate messaging, I'll start from the QBOA interface and post a message to a client. Follow these steps:

1. **Open the client company.**

2. **Open the transaction you question.**

   For this example, I opened a bill.

3. **In the upper right corner of the transaction window, click the Conversation button (see Figure 14-7).**

   QBOA displays the bottom of the transaction window, which contains an Activities section.

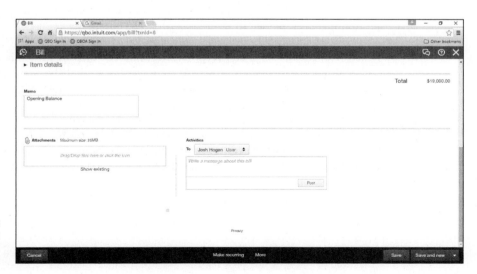

FIGURE 14-7:
Creating a message to a client.

REMEMBER

The Activities section doesn't appear while you're creating a new transaction; it appears only on previously created transactions.

4. **In the Activities section, click the drop-down list to select a message recipient.**

5. **Type your message.**

6. **Click Post.**

QBOA sends an email message to the recipient, and the posted message appears at the bottom of the Activities section, along with the date and time the message was posted (see Figure 14-8).

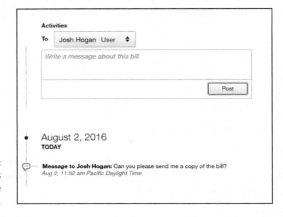

FIGURE 14-8:
Posted messages appear below the Activities section.

When the message recipient opens the email, a message like the one shown in Figure 14-9 appears, explaining that a message concerning a particular transaction has been posted in the recipient's QBO company.

To view the message and respond, the recipient can click the link in the message; the link initially displays the QBO sign-in page so that the client can sign in to his company. If your client initiates the conversation, the QBOA sign-in page appears.

Once the client signs in, the Conversation button appears in the upper right corner of the QBO company Home page, beside the Gear button (see Figure 14-10). The Conversation button contains the number 1, indicating that the client has one message, and the client can click the Conversation button to view the message.

Click here.

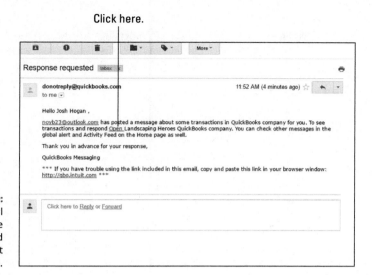

Response requested Inbox

donotreply@quickbooks.com   11:52 AM (4 minutes ago)
to me ⯆

Hello Josh Hogan ,

noyb23@outlook.com has posted a message about some transactions in QuickBooks company for you. To see transactions and respond Open Landscaping Heroes QuickBooks company. You can check other messages in the global alert and Activity Feed on the Home page as well.

Thank you in advance for your response,

QuickBooks Messaging

*** If you have trouble using the link included in this email, copy and paste this link in your browser window: http://qbo.intuit.com ***

Click here to Reply or Forward

FIGURE 14-9:
An email message generated by the Client Collaborator tool.

Click here to read the message.

FIGURE 14-10:
When messages exist, the Conversation button displays the number of waiting messages.

🔍 + ↺   💬 ⚙ Landscaping Heroes ⑦ Help

New Messages

Bill (noyb23@outlook.com): Can you please send me a copy of the bill?

Click here to open the transaction.

If the client then clicks the message, the transaction from which the message originated opens. The client can then scroll to the bottom of the message, and, in the Activities area shown earlier in Figure 14-7, respond to the message by selecting a recipient, typing a message, and posting it. The Client Collaborator continues the process, sending an email notification of a message to the recipient, who clicks the link in the message to open the company and read and respond. The message conversation continues to appear at the bottom of the transaction.

Chapter **15**

Using Accountant Tools

Accountant tools are available to anybody who opens a client QBO company from QBOA.

You can become a user in a QBO company in one of two ways:

» As described in Chapter 12, your client can invite you to be the Accountant user on his account. But each QBO company can have only two Accountant users.

» As described in Chapter 11, the Master Administrator of the QBOA account can set up users. Any user established by the Master Administrator can log in to QBOA, open any client QBO company for which the user has privileges, and use the tools found on the Accountant Tools menu that I describe in this chapter.

In addition to the tools found on the Accountant Tools menu, this chapter covers reporting and paying sales tax — an activity that accountants often perform for their clients, so I'll start off with that information.

Reporting and Paying Sales Taxes

You or your client can manage and pay sales tax. Open any client QBO company and, in the Navigation bar on the left, click Sales Taxes to display the Sales Tax Center shown in Figure 15-1.

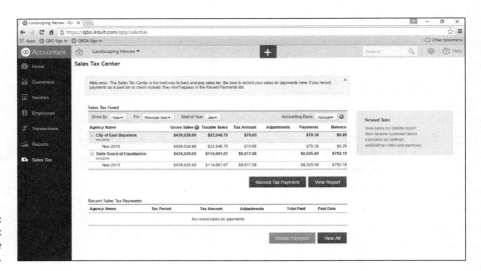

FIGURE 15-1:
Use the Sales Tax
Center to manage
and pay sales tax.

TIP

If the client QBO company uses QBO payroll (QBOP), you might need to click Taxes before you can click Sales Tax in the Navigation bar.

You can click the View Report button to display the Sales Tax Liability Report, and on the right side of the Sales Tax Center page, in the Related Tasks box, you'll find a link to view a list of taxable customers. Also in the Related Tasks box, you'll find links you can use to edit sales tax settings and add or edit tax rates and agencies.

You can click Record Tax Payment to pay sales tax; when you do, QBO displays the Record Sales Tax Payment dialog box shown in Figure 15-2.

QBO calculates the amount due to a sales tax agency, and you can confirm the amount or adjust it. Notice that the payment is made to the sales tax agency. Be aware that QBO doesn't treat the agency as a vendor. You won't see the sales tax agency on the Vendor List page, and you can't use the Check window or the Pay Bills window to pay a sales tax agency. In this way, QBO helps avoid applying sales tax payments incorrectly.

FIGURE 15-2:
Use this dialog box to record a sales tax payment.

Facilitating Accountant Activities

Accountants often need to reclassify transactions, examine voided and deleted transactions, write off invoices, and perform other activities. QBOA contains tools to make performing these activities easy.

To view and use the tools QBOA makes available to accountants, open any client QBO company. Then, on the QBOA toolbar, click the Accountant Tools button (the one that contains the icon that looks like a suitcase). QBOA displays the Accountant Tools menu, shown in Figure 15-3.

Understanding the Trial Balance page

You use the Trial Balance tool to display the Trial Balance page. The page you see initially presents a working trial balance like the ones shown in Figures 15-4 and 15-5.

>> **At the top of the page, you see the Activity Timeline,** which shows client and accountant activities that impact the balances shown on the page.

>> **The values in the Unadjusted Balance column are locked on the Trial Balance page to protect the integrity of the data in the Trial Balance workspace.** If you scroll to the right on the page (refer to Figure 15-5), you'll find columns that enable to you create adjusting entries as journal entries. As you move your mouse over the boxes in the Debit or Credit columns under the Adjusting Entries column, a plus sign (+) appears; click it and QBOA opens a journal entry window, where you can record the adjusting entry. Once you save the entry, QBOA redisplays the Trial Balance page and your adjustment appears; in addition, QBOA changes the Adjusted Balance column to reflect your adjustment.

Click here.

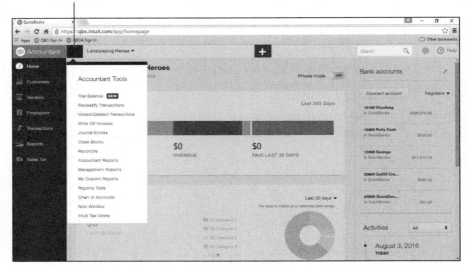

FIGURE 15-3:
The Accountant
Tools menu
contains
commands
specifically
designed to aid
the accountant.

Activity timeline

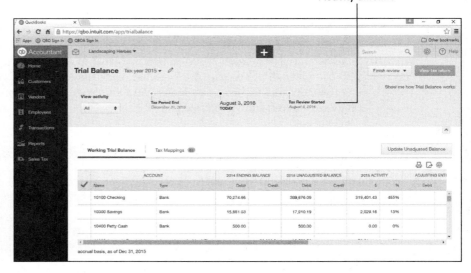

FIGURE 15-4:
The left side of
the Working Trial
Balance tab of
the Trial Balance
page.

>> **You can click the dollar value in the Adjusted Balance column to view a report of all transactions that make up that balance.** From the report, you can drill down to a particular transaction and, if necessary, change it. The changes you make appear in the Other Transactions column on the Trial Balance page. When you redisplay the Trial Balance page, you can click the Update Unadjusted Balance button to have QBOA move data from the Other Transactions column to the Unadjusted Balance column.

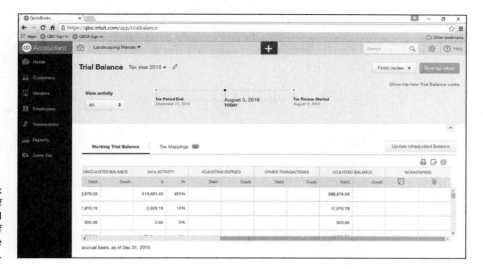

FIGURE 15-5:
The right side of the Working Trial Balance tab of the Trial Balance page.

» **You can use the Workpapers column** to add notes and attach documents to a particular line to help you remember why you made a particular adjustment.

» **As you finish reviewing lines, you can click the leftmost column** (refer to Figure 15-4) to place a check in it and mark the line as complete. You don't have to finish reviewing a Trial Balance page in one sitting; you can, instead, click the Finish Review button to either freeze the workspace and return later and unfreeze it to continue reviewing, or archive your work to a Zip file that QBOA downloads to your computer.

If you use ProConnect Tax Online, Intuit's cloud-based tax preparation software, to prepare a client's tax return, then you'll want to make sure that your client's accounts are mapped properly to lines on tax forms. The Trial Balance feature automatically maps most account balances to lines on tax forms you'll file for corporations using IRS Form 1120 (for corporations) or 1120s, partnerships that use IRS Form 1065, and sole proprietorships using IRS Form 1040. For other business organization types, you can manually assign accounts to tax form lines. You also can manually assign lines on tax forms for accounts the tool doesn't recognize, and you can change tax line assignments as needed.

TIP

The View Tax Return button appears unavailable if you have not yet selected a tax form for the QBO client company. Clicking the button makes QBOA prompt you to select the appropriate tax form from a list.

Click the Tax Mappings tab on the Trial Balance page to see the page you use to map last year's client QBO company information directly into tax forms (see Figure 15-6).

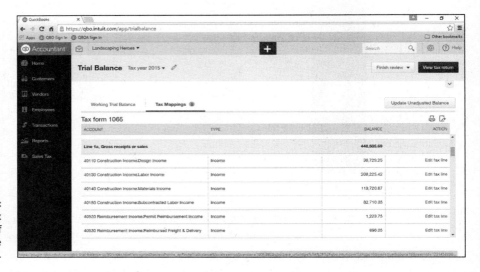

FIGURE 15-6:
The Tax Mappings tab of the Trial Balance page.

To assign an account to a tax form line or edit the line to which an account is assigned, click the appropriate link in the Action column. QBOA displays a list box from which you select the appropriate tax form line, and then click Save.

When you finish reviewing the Trial Balance page and making adjusting entries, you can click View Tax Return to transfer the information to ProConnect Tax Online and generate a tax return. You don't pay anything to use the Trial Balance feature; you pay only when you print or e-file a return from ProConnect Tax Online.

REMEMBER

If you don't use ProConnect Tax Online or you are not the tax preparer, you have the option to export the adjusted Trial Balance so that it can be imported into a separate application.

Reclassifying transactions

When you choose Reclassify Transactions from the Accountant Tools menu, the Reclassify Transactions page appears (see Figure 15-7). You can use this page to reclassify transactions without worrying about the company's closing date.

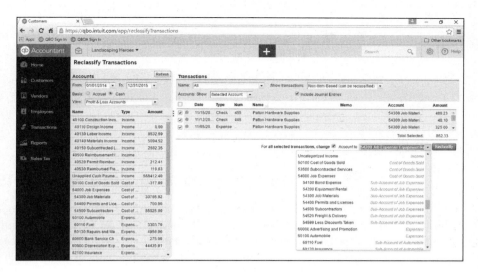

FIGURE 15-7:
Use this page to reclassify transactions.

You use the information in the gray areas of the Accounts section on the left side of the page and the Transactions section on the right side of the page to filter for the date range and type of accounts (Profit and Loss or Balance Sheet) you want to consider. You then select an account on the left side of the page, and QBOA displays transactions that meet the criteria on the right side of the page. You can reclassify, individually or as a group, transactions that display a green circle.

Follow these steps to reclassify transactions:

1. **On the left side of the page, set the date range you want to consider, along with the accounting basis.**

2. **From the View list box, select the type of accounts you want to consider — Profit & Loss accounts or Balance Sheet accounts.**

3. **Click an account in the list below the View list box to examine that account's transactions.**

   The transactions in the account appear on the right side of the page.

4. **Above the list of transactions on the right side of the page, set filters to display the types of transactions that you might consider reclassifying.**

   You can make changes to transactions that display green circles.

   You can click a transaction to open it in its transaction window and then make changes to it.

REMEMBER

5. **To change several transactions simultaneously, select them by clicking the check box beside them.**

6. **Below the list of transactions, select the For Select Transactions, Change check box.**

7. **From the Account to list, specify a different account.**

REMEMBER

If Class Tracking is turned on, you'll also see a field to change the assigned class, the same way you can change an Account.

8. **Click the Reclassify button.**

Examining voided and deleted transactions

You can click Voided/Deleted Transactions on the Accountant Tools menu to display the Audit Log. The default view of the Audit Log (see Figure 15-8), shows information about those transactions that have been voided or deleted. But you can click the Filter button to set a variety of different filters to view other types of transactions and events.

Click here to display more than voided or deleted transactions.

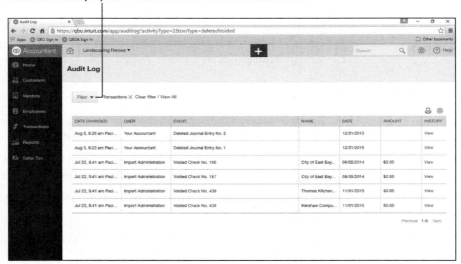

FIGURE 15-8:
Use the Audit Log to view all kinds of activity in the QBO company.

Writing off invoices

Choosing Write Off Invoices from the Accountant Tools menu displays the Write Off Invoices page, which enables you to view invoices you might want to write off, and then write them off to an account of your choice. At the top of the page, you set filters to display the invoices you want to review. Select the age of the invoices to view those

>> Greater than 180 days

>> Greater than 120 days

>> In the current accounting period

>> In a custom date range you set

You also can set a balance limit.

As you can see in Figure 15-9, QBOA displays the date, age, invoice number, customer name, original invoice amount, and the amount still due on the invoice. To write off any invoices, click the check box beside them. Then, at the bottom of the page, select the account you want to use to write off the invoices and click the Preview and Write Off button.

FIGURE 15-9: Writing off invoices.

QBOA displays the Confirm Write Off dialog box shown in Figure 15-10. If the information in the dialog box is correct, click Write Off. Otherwise, click Cancel.

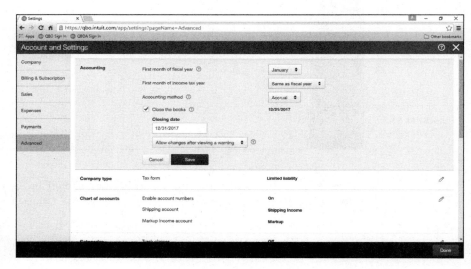

Confirm Write Off

Confirm invoices to write off

Company	Landscaping Heroes
Date	08/03/2016 09:36 AM
User	**Your Accountant**

11 transaction(s) totaling 65412.50 will be written off to the Bad Debt-1 account

Num	Date	Name	Original Amount	Balance Due
1017	12/27/2014	Freeman, Kirby:Rem…	1,924.40	1,924.40
1016	12/20/2014	Freeman, Kirby:Rem…	1,867.89	1,867.89
1015	12/09/2014	Freeman, Kirby:Rem…	1,867.89	1,867.89
1014	11/26/2014	Bolinski, Rafal:2nd …	5,079.48	5,079.48
1013	10/14/2014	Bolinski, Rafal:2nd …	5,079.48	5,079.48
1012	10/09/2014	Easley, Paula:Garage	2,519.39	2,519.39
1011	10/01/2014	Lamb, Brad:Room A…	11,172.60	11,172.60
1010	09/20/2014	Sauler, Lyn:Home R…	16,115.00	16,115.00
1008	07/20/2014	Ruff, Bryan:Sun Roo…	5,516.05	5,516.05
1005	04/16/2014	Jacobsen, Doug:Po…	7,991.52	7,991.52

Write Off   Cancel

FIGURE 15-10: Confirm that you want to write off the selected invoices.

Closing the books

You use the Close Books command on the Accountant Tools menu to display the Advanced page of the QBO company's Account and Settings dialog box, shown in Figure 15-11. You can click anywhere in the Accounting section to edit the fields in that section, which include the closing date for the books.

FIGURE 15-11: Setting a closing date.

You can set a closing date and then allow changes prior to the closing date after QBO issues a warning, or you can require a password to enter changes prior to the closing date. Click Done to save your changes.

Reviewing reports

Reports in QBOA work the same way as reports in QBO; see Chapter 10 for details.

But, QBOA contains some reports of particular interest to accountants. If you open a client QBO company and then, from the Accountant Tools menu, click Accountant Reports, the Reports page appears. Below the Profit and Loss graphic, the Accountant Reports tab spotlights the reports available to QBOA users. In Figure 15-12, I hid the Profit and Loss graphic (click the arrow in the lower right corner of the graphic to hide and display it) so that you can see more of the reports on the Accountant Reports tab. But I still couldn't show all of them; when you're checking out these reports, be sure to scroll down the page.

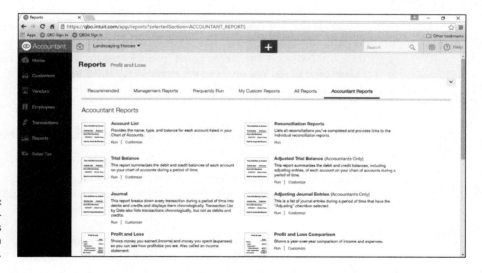

FIGURE 15-12:
Accountant-oriented reports available in QBOA.

TIP

Intuit is in the process of redesigning reports; at present, the redesigned reports are a QuickBooks Labs feature. To view the redesigned version of reports, choose Gear ⇨ QuickBooks Labs and, in the QuickBooks Labs window that appears, turn on Redesigned Reports. Note that, for this discussion, I haven't turned on Redesigned Reports.

If you choose Management Reports from the Accountant Tools menu (or if you click the Management Reports link that appears on the Reports page shown in

Figure 15-12), QBOA displays two customized management-style reports: Expanded Company Financials and Basic Company Financials. Both reports display a collection of reports, complete with an elegant cover page and a table of contents.

The Expanded Company Financials report contains the P&L, Balance Sheet, Statement of Cash Flows, and the A/R Aging Detail and A/P Aging Detail reports. The Basic Company Financials report contains all reports except the Aging Detail reports. Using the Edit link in the Action column, you can edit either report package to add or delete reports and modify the appearance of pages in the report, including determining whether pages such as the table of contents appear in the report. Using the down arrow that appears in the Action column, you can print these reports, send them via email, export the information to .PDF files or .DOCX files, and make copies of them so that you can make your own set of management reports.

TIP

Copying one of these reports before you change it is a great idea; that way, you keep the original report intact but create your own version of it as well.

If you choose My Custom Reports from the Accountant Tools menu or from the Reports page, reports you have customized and saved appear. And you can click Reports Tools on the Accountant Tools menu to set default report dates and accounting basis. You also can see account reconciliation status for cash and credit card accounts and view and set company closing date information.

A brief look at other accountant tools

The Accountant Tools menu contains a few other tools that make an accountant's life easier, such as the Reconcile page; from this page, you can opt to reconcile an account you select, or you can review existing reconciliation reports. For more detail on reconciling accounts, see Chapter 8.

Also from the Accountant Tools menu, you can choose Journal Entries to display the Journal Entry window, or Chart of Accounts to display the Chart of Accounts window; I describe working in the Chart of Accounts window in Chapter 13. You also can use the New Window command described in Chapter 14 to quickly open a new window in QBOA.

Last, from the Accountant Tools menu, you can choose Intuit Tax Online, which opens a new browser window and takes you to the Tax Hub of ProConnect Tax Online, where you can see the status of your client's tax returns (see Figure 15-13).

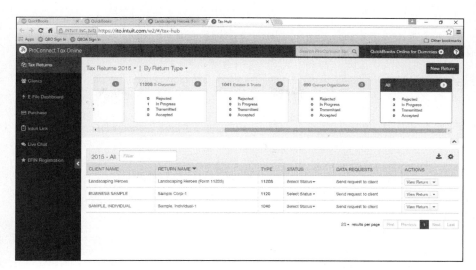

FIGURE 15-13:
The Tax Hub page
of ProConnect
Tax Online.

As you can see, ProConnect Tax Online connects to your QBOA account but is actually a separate product with its own menus in the Navigation bar.

4

The Part of Tens

IN THIS PART . . .

Become familiar with the Chrome browser and its features, including the Omnibox, the star, and the Chrome menu.

Learn about setting up Chrome users and working with Chrome windows and tabs.

Examine the value and the pitfalls of signing in to and out of Chrome.

Examine Chrome's security and privacy.

Learn how to establish a home page and how to create and use bookmarks.

Chapter **16**

Almost Ten Things about the Chrome Browser Interface

C hrome — officially Google Chrome — is the free web browser created by Google, Inc., the American-based multinational corporation that focuses on Internet-related products and services, such as Gmail for email, Google maps, and Google Docs, just to name a few. Most of Google's profits come from online advertising technologies.

You can use QuickBooks Online (QBO) and QuickBooks Online Accountant (QBOA) in the Chrome, Firefox, Safari, and Internet Explorer browsers (at the time I wrote this, you could use Microsoft Edge, but not to export to the QuickBooks desktop product). In my experience, I find that QBO and QBOA work best in Chrome. If you're not familiar with Chrome or haven't worked much in it, this chapter and Chapter 17 are designed to help you become adept at using Chrome with QBO and QBOA. This chapter focuses on helping you become familiar with the Chrome interface and make use of it. Figure 16-1 shows you how Chrome looks shortly after you install and open it; don't forget to refer back to this figure as you read the chapter.

Omnibox

New Tab button

Current tab

Recently visited sites

Chrome Menu button

Bookmark This Page button

Current User button

FIGURE 16-1:
Reviewing the
Chrome interface.

Refresh button

Back and Forward buttons

Buttons used to navigate
to various Google apps

TIP

If you don't already have Chrome installed on your computer, you can visit www. google.com/chrome/browser/. From this web page, you can download and install Chrome.

Understanding Users

The Current User button in the top right corner of the screen represents a Chrome user. The icon may appear generically, as you see it in Figure 16-1, or it may display your name or email address. In Chrome, you can set up multiple users, each of whom can have different Chrome settings. In this way, each person using Chrome on a single computer can customize the program, saving his or her own bookmarks, passwords, and more. See Chapter 17 to learn how to create a Chrome user.

Windows and Tabs

You can open Chrome more than once to view multiple web pages — a process called *opening a new window*.

To open a new window, first open Chrome. Then, press Ctrl+N, and a second instance of the Chrome browser appears. In Figure 16-2, I've resized Chrome's second window so that you can see both instances of Chrome. Also notice that two buttons for Chrome appear in the Windows taskbar.

Two instances of Chrome

FIGURE 16-2:
When you open a new Chrome window, two instances of Chrome run simultaneously.

Two Chrome icons appear on the task bar.

But, in most cases, you don't need to open multiple instances of Chrome; you can use Chrome's tabs to display multiple web pages while you work.

Tabs appear at the top of the Chrome window and initially display the same short-cuts you see when you open a new window. You can add a tab by clicking the New Tab button, which appears just beside the last open tab (refer back to Figure 16-1). And, you can close any tab by clicking the X that appears in the tab. You also can reposition tabs in the Chrome window by dragging a tab's title.

In either a new window or a new tab, you navigate to a new website using the Omnibox (read on).

Using the Omnibox to Visit a Web Page

You've probably heard of the *address bar* in other browsers; Chrome refers to the text box at the top of the browser as the *Omnibox* because it's a multi-purpose box.

To visit a web page, type the address of the web page into the Omnibox and either press Enter or click the Refresh button. After you've visited a few websites, you can click the Back and Forward buttons to revisit pages you have recently visited in the order you visited them.

TIP

If you right-click or click and hold either the Back button or the Forward button, you can view a historical list of the websites you have visited. You can left-click one to return to it.

Using the Omnibox to Search the Web

Chrome uses the Omnibox to combine the functions of navigating to websites and searching the Internet; as you might expect, Chrome uses Google's search engine by default. You can type a search term into the Omnibox, and as you type, suggestions driven by Google's search technology appear. You can then click a suggestion to navigate to the associated Google search page or web page.

A gray icon appears to the left of each suggestion in the Omnibox; the icon indicates the type of suggestion:

» A piece of paper represents a page you've viewed previously or a website related to what you're typing.

» A magnifying glass indicates that the suggestion is a potential search term.

» A star identifies a suggestion as one of your existing bookmarks (see the next section, "What's the Star?" for more on bookmarks.

What's the Star?

You can easily save the web address of a site you visit frequently so that you don't have to type the address each time you want to visit the site. In Chrome, saving a web address is called *bookmarking*, and you click the star icon to create a bookmark for the web page you are currently viewing. You can read more about working with bookmarks, including managing bookmarks, in Chapter 17.

Examining the Chrome Menu

You can click the Chrome Menu button (see Figure 16-3) to view a series of commands that help you work in Chrome.

Chrome Menu button

Chrome Menu

FIGURE 16-3:
The Google
Chrome Menu.

Using options on the Chrome Menu, you can

>> Work with bookmarks (described in Chapter 17)

>> Reopen recently closed tabs

>> Copy and paste text

>> Save a web page

>> Clear browsing data

>> Find text on a web page

>> Print a web page

>> View files you have downloaded

>> Make changes to Chrome's settings

The options available to you on the Chrome Menu aren't limited to the ones I've listed — there are too many for me to list them all. But, for example, if you want to see how your web browsing affects your computer's use of memory, you can choose Chrome Menu ➪ More Tools ➪ Task Manager.

About Signing in to (and out of) Chrome

I'm going to repeat myself in this section because it's important for you to understand the ramifications of signing in and signing out of Chrome. Let me start by saying — emphasizing, in fact — that you don't have to sign in to use Chrome. In particular, you don't need to sign in to Chrome to use QBO or QBOA.

That said, why sign in? If you sign in, bookmarks and passwords you save, browsing history, and settings are saved to the cloud. You can then sign in to Chrome on a different computer and use all your settings from that computer or any computer.

The act of signing in can result in some negative side effects. Even though you sign out of Chrome, Chrome can still remember some of your information, making it visible to anyone who uses Chrome on the same computer. And, on a public computer, leaving traces of your activity could result in others gaining access to your personal information, email, and saved passwords.

WARNING

I strongly urge you to avoid signing in to Chrome if you are using a public computer. Remember, you don't need to sign in to Chrome to use QBO or QBOA. And, I'll be repeating this warning again in this section (editors, take note that I know I'm going to repeat myself) because it's important to the security of your financial data.

If you want to sign in to Chrome, you need a Google account. If you have a Gmail email address, you already have an account, and you can skip the section "Creating a Google account."

Creating a Google account

If you don't have a Google account, you can easily create one; creating a Google account automatically creates a Gmail email address and a Google+ profile. Once you have a Google account, you can use Google services such as Gmail, Google Docs, and Google Calendar. Follow these steps to create a Google account:

REMEMBER

If you already have a Gmail email address, you already have a Google account. Skip these steps and continue in the next section, "Signing in to Chrome."

1. **Navigate to** www.google.com.

2. **Click the Sign In button in the top right corner of the page.**

3. **On the page that appears, click the Create Account link.**

   The link appears below the box where you would ordinarily provide your email address.

4. **Provide the requested information.**

   The requested information includes your name, a username, which is a proposed Gmail email address and associated password, birth date, gender, mobile phone number, current email address, and the country in which you live. Note that your mobile phone number is actually optional.

5. **Click the Prove You're Not a Robot check box and provide the verification information.**

6. **Check the I agree to the Google Terms of Service and Privacy Policy box.**

   You can click the links for Terms of Service and Privacy Policy to review the statements.

7. **Click Next Step.**

   At this point, you will probably be prompted to verify your account using either a text message or a voice call; select a method and, when you receive the verification information, provide it onscreen.

8. **On the Create Your Profile page, you can add a photo to your Google+ profile.** If you don't want to set a profile photo at this time, click Continue.

   Google creates your account.

Signing in to Chrome

If you sign in to the Chrome browser, bookmarks and passwords you save, browsing history, and settings are available to you from any computer.

WARNING

Avoid signing in to Chrome if you are using a public computer, because signing out might not remove all your information, leaving it visible to anyone who uses Chrome on the computer.

To sign in to Chrome, follow these steps:

1. **Click the User icon in the top right corner of the browser.**

2. **Click Sign in to Chrome.**

The sign-in form appears, requesting your Google Account email.

3. **Type your email address and click Next.**

4. **Type your password and click Next.**

A message appears, letting you know you are signed in to Chrome (see Figure 16-4).

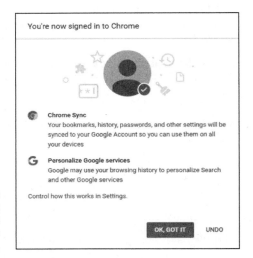

FIGURE 16-4: Once you've signed in to Chrome, this message appears.

5. **Click OK, GOT IT.**

The Current User button changes to reflect either your name or your email address — an indication that you are signed in to Chrome.

Signing out of Chrome

You should sign out of your Google account when you finish using Chrome, or when you no longer want changes you make on your computer saved to your Google account and synced to Google Chrome on your other devices. Signing out also can help if you think an error with Chrome's synchronization has occurred, and you want to try to fix the error by signing out and then signing in again.

By default, when you sign out of your Google account in the browser window, you leave behind traces of yourself. On a public computer, it's possible that other people might gain access to your personal information, email, and saved passwords.

But, an option appears during the sign-out process that you can select to eliminate all traces of you on the computer. The option deletes saved information on the local computer about the Chrome user who signed in.

WARNING

On your own private computer, deleting all traces of the user who signed in, including the user profile, might be a bit more drastic than you want. You can opt to clear history separately and less drastically; see Chapter 17 for details on clearing history. But, if you're working on a public computer, you should delete the user as well as the user's settings.

Follow these steps to sign out of Chrome:

1. **Click the Chrome Menu button to open the Chrome Menu.**

2. **Click Settings.**

   The Chrome Settings page appears (see Figure 16-5).

FIGURE 16-5:
The Sign In section of the Chrome Settings page.

3. **In the Sign In section at the top of the page, click Disconnect your Google Account.**

   A confirmation dialog box appears (see Figure 16-6).

FIGURE 16-6:
A dialog box appears, asking you to confirm disconnecting from your Google account.

4. **Select the Also clear your history, bookmarks, settings, and other Chrome data stored on this device check box if you want to eliminate all trace on the computer of the user who signed in to Chrome.**

WARNING

Checking this box deletes everything on the computer associated with the user — your account history, bookmarks, settings, and other Chrome data saved on the computer. I can't repeat this mantra often enough: If you are working on a public computer, you should safeguard your privacy and check this box. However, if you're working on a private computer, you can safely keep the user and optionally clear history. To keep the user, do not check this box; see Chapter 17 for details on clearing history.

5. **Click Disconnect Account.**

Google signs you out of your Google account and Chrome. The appearance of the Current User button returns to a generic form.

Using the Chrome Web Store

You can enhance the capabilities of Chrome using web apps, plug-ins, and extensions such as calculators, ad blockers, or password managers. These browser-capable enhancers work like software you install on your computer, phone, or tablet, but they typically function within Chrome.

You can obtain web apps, plug-ins, and extensions from the Chrome Web Store found at `https://chrome.google.com/webstore`. The Chrome Web Store provides tools you can use to search for web apps, plug-ins, and extensions.

Web apps you install should appear on the New Tab page, from which you can launch them. You also can remove a web app by right-clicking it on the New Tab page and then clicking Remove from Chrome.

Extensions run by default when you open Chrome. You can view a list of installed extensions from the Settings page. Choose Chrome Menu ⇨ Settings. Then, on the left side of the Settings page, click Extensions (see Figure 16-7).

You might want to disable an extension if you suspect it is causing a conflict as you work; uncheck the Enabled check box beside the extension. If the extension proves to be the source of your problem, you can delete it by clicking the trash can icon beside it.

WEB APPS AND PLUG-INS AND EXTENSIONS, OH MY!

So what exactly is a web app and how does it differ from a plug-in or extension? Honestly, for the purposes of this book, you probably don't care. But, for better or for worse, here are some simple definitions:

- Web apps run inside your browser with their own dedicated user interface.

- Extensions, unlike web apps, do not typically have a user interface. Instead, they extend the functionality of Chrome and the websites you view using Chrome.

- Plug-ins are similar to extensions in that they extend functionality by helping Chrome process special types of web content, but a plug-in affects only the specific web page that contains it.

So, as you can see, each has a technical definition that distinguishes it from the others, but, for most of us, the bottom line is this: All of them enhance the capabilities of a browser by providing some functionality that the browser does not, inherently, provide.

FIGURE 16-7:
You can view and enable or disable extensions from the Settings page.

Click here to view installed extensions.

TIP

If you click the Get More Extensions link at the bottom of the Settings page where you view an extension, Chrome opens a new tab and takes you to the Chrome Web Store, where it displays, by default, available extensions.

Plug-ins enable certain types of web content that browsers can't process. When Chrome encounters a plug-in on a web page, Chrome allows the plug-in to perform its function. Learn more about managing plug-ins in Chapter 17.

Selecting a Theme

You can use *themes* to change the appearance of Chrome. Themes can change the color of the Chrome window, or they can add background pictures to the entire browser. The idea here is to provide some interest to the browser page background.

You can find available themes in the Chrome Web Store; in the navigation pane that runs down the left side of the Chrome Web Store page, click Themes to preview available themes.

If you install a theme and then later change your mind about using it, choose Chrome Menu⇨Settings. On the Settings page, in the Appearance section, click Reset to default theme.

IN THIS CHAPTER

» **Setting and using a Home page in Chrome**

» **Understanding Chrome, security, and privacy**

» **Bookmarking pages you use regularly**

» **Taking advantage of Chrome tabs**

» **Setting up users**

» **Controlling the size of text onscreen**

» **Downloading and working with files**

» **Understanding Chrome and mobility**

Chapter **17**

Ten Ways to Use Chrome Effectively

C hapter 16 helps you understand and work with the Chrome interface. This chapter introduces some browser tips and tricks that can make using Chrome easier and more effective both in general and specifically with QBO and QBOA.

Setting a Home Page

Many browsers sport a button that you can click to return to your *Home page* — the page that appears when you open the browser. When you open Chrome, by default, the New Tab page appears. Although Chrome doesn't show the Home page button by default, you can display it and also set a page that will appear when you click the Home page button. Note that Chrome doesn't display the page you set as the Home page when you open the browser; instead, the Home page appears when you click the Home page button.

Before you begin the following steps, make sure you know the web address of the page you want to set as your Home page:

1. **Choose Chrome Menu ⇨ Settings.**

The Settings tab appears.

2. **In the Appearance section, click the Show Home button check box.**

The Home button appears between the Refresh button and the Omnibox (see Figure 17-1). At this point, Chrome opens the New Tab page whenever you click the Home button.

Home button

FIGURE 17-1:
Adding the
Home button
and setting a
Home page.

Show Home Button check box   Click here to set a Home page address.

3. **Click Change.**

The Home page dialog box appears (see Figure 17-2).

4. **Select the Open This Page option and type a web address.**

5. **Click OK.**

When you click the Home button, Chrome displays the page you set as your Home page.

FIGURE 17-2:
Use this dialog
box to type the
web address of
your Home page.

If you open certain sites every time you start Chrome, you can pin each page as a tab. See the section "Duplicating and Pinning Tabs."

TIP

Chrome and Security

Chrome includes several tools that help to keep you safe online. As you are no doubt aware, bad things can happen as you browse the Internet. You can run into *phishing* schemes, where someone tries to trick you into sharing personal or sensitive information, usually through a fake website, some of which look extremely genuine. You also can run into websites that have been hacked and contain *malware* that tries to install itself on your computer, often without your knowledge; malware usually tries to harm you and your computer in some way, from simply messing up your computer's behavior to trying to steal information.

Chrome includes technology, enabled by default, that helps protect you from phishing schemes and malware, displaying a warning whenever you visit a potentially dangerous page.

Chrome also uses a technique called *sandboxing* to open websites. Sandboxing isolates computer processes from anything else happening on the machine. If a sandboxed process crashes or becomes infected with malware, the rest of your computer remains unaffected. Each tab in Chrome opens as a separate process, completely independent of other tabs. If a website contains malware, the sandboxing technique isolates the malware to that browser tab; the malware can't jump to another Chrome tab or to your computer. You eliminate the malware threat when you close the infected website's browser tab.

A third method hackers can use to gain access to your computer is by the use of plug-ins. *Plug-ins* are small add-on programs for browsers. Because they are add-on programs, plug-ins can become out-of-date and hackers can use them to try to introduce malware onto your computer. Adobe Flash Player is one of the most popular browser plug-ins; it is used most often to view video content. Out-of-date versions of Adobe Flash Player are also notorious for introducing malware into computers. Chrome reduces the threat that Adobe Flash Player poses by directly integrating it into Chrome. Because of this integration, updates for Adobe Flash Player are included in Chrome updates.

Chrome also regularly checks for the latest security update without any action on your part. By integrating Adobe Flash Player and regularly checking for security updates, Chrome greatly reduces the danger of malware infection.

To view the default security measures, you can follow the next steps:

WARNING

1. **Choose Chrome Menu ⇨ Settings.**

Don't change security settings unless you really know what you're doing.

2. **Scroll to the bottom of the page and click Show Advanced Settings.**

- In the Privacy section, the Protect You and Your Device from Dangerous Sites option warns you if Chrome detects that the site you're trying to visit might contain phishing or other malware.

- From the HTTPS/SSL section, you can manage your SSL certificates and settings.

Chrome and Privacy

Chrome enables you to control the information you share online. For example, you can change your privacy settings, delete your browsing history, and browse in Incognito mode. To adjust privacy settings, follow these steps:

1. **Choose Chrome Menu ⇨ Settings.**

2. **Scroll to the bottom of the Settings page and click Show Advanced Settings.**

3. **In the Privacy section, click Content Settings.**

From the Content Settings dialog box, you can make a variety of changes.

Below, I'm going to list the settings you might be most likely to change. If I don't cover a setting you want to change, you can search for help on that setting at `https://support.google.com/chrome/`.

Handling cookies

You can control how Chrome handles cookies. In most cases, websites you visit place *cookies* on your computer for the purpose of recognizing your specific browser/computer combination if you return to the site. Chrome allows cookies by default, because they are typically harmless, but cookies can allow sites to track your navigation during your visit to those sites.

TIP

Third-party cookies are cookies placed on your computer by one website for some other website. To increase privacy, most people block third-party cookies to prevent sharing information with parties not directly associated with the sites they visit.

Chrome and JavaScript

You can control whether Chrome runs JavaScript, which web developers often use to make their sites more interactive. If you disable JavaScript, you might find that some sites don't work properly.

Allowing plug-ins

Plug-ins appear on specific websites and are used by website developers to process web content that browsers can't inherently handle. For example, Adobe Flash Player processes content that web browsers don't inherently process. Chrome allows plug-ins to run by default, and if you disable this feature, various websites might not function as expected.

Working in Incognito mode

If you work in *Incognito mode*, you can browse the web without recording a history of the websites you have visited and without storing cookies. Using Incognito mode doesn't make Chrome more secure; it simply enhances your privacy by preventing Chrome from keeping a record of the sites you have visited during that particular browsing session. Even in Incognito mode, you shouldn't visit websites that you wouldn't feel safe viewing in a regular Chrome window.

To use Incognito mode, choose Chrome Menu ⇨ New Incognito Window. A new instance of Chrome opens; notice that two buttons for Chrome appear on the Windows taskbar. The new Chrome instance displays an incognito window like the one shown in Figure 17-3, and the Incognito icon appears in the upper left corner of the browser window, immediately to the left of the New Tab tab. You use an Incognito window the same way that you use the regular Chrome window; while you work, Chrome doesn't record a history of the sites you visit nor does Chrome allow sites to store cookies on your computer.

To stop browsing incognito, you must close the instance of Chrome that's running incognito.

Incognito icon

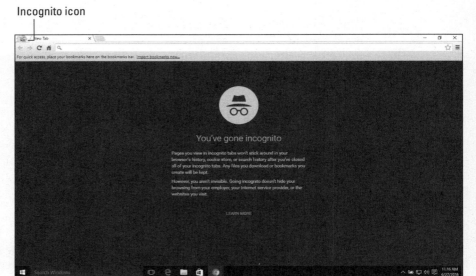

FIGURE 17-3:
An Incognito
window.

Deleting browsing history

Like all browsers, if you work in a regular Chrome window (rather than an Incognito window), Chrome keeps track of the websites you have visited during each browsing session. Browsers save your browsing history, among other reasons, to decrease the time you wait to see a web page that you have previously visited. And browser history can help you return to a website you visited previously even though you can't remember the website's address.

To view your browsing history, choose Chrome Menu ⇨ History ⇨ History. A page similar to the one shown in Figure 17-4 appears; your browsing history is organized by date and time, with the most recent sites you visited appearing first. You can click any entry to redisplay that web page.

You also can delete all or only part of your browsing history, typically to maintain your privacy. From the History page, click Clear Browsing Data. The dialog box shown in Figure 17-5 appears; you can choose the type of data you want to delete and the timeframe over which to delete that data.

REMEMBER

If you delete all of your cookies, you might need to re-identify yourself at websites where you were previously "known," such as your bank's website. The process involves getting a code from the website and entering it, typically along with your password at that site, so that you can verify that you are, indeed, the user the website thinks you are.

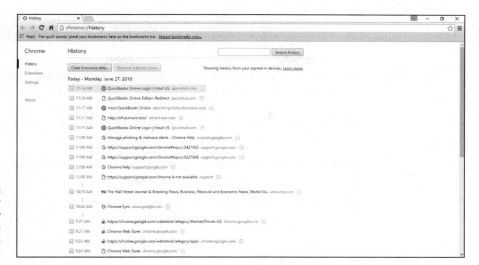

FIGURE 17-4:
Use your
browsing history
to revisit a web
page you visited
previously.

FIGURE 17-5:
Use this dialog
box to delete
browsing history.

TIP

To delete a single browsing history entry, display the History page (shown previously in Figure 17-4) and hover the mouse pointer over the entry you want to delete. Select the check box to the left of the entry, and, if appropriate, select additional entries to delete. Then click the Remove Selected Items button that becomes clickable at the top of the History page.

Reviewing miscellaneous privacy settings

In addition to the settings previously described in this section, you can control the way Chrome handles the following situations; the following descriptions describe Chrome's default behavior:

» Chrome asks for permission whenever a website wants to use your location information.

» Chrome asks for permission whenever a site wants to automatically show notifications on your computer desktop.

» Chrome asks for permission whenever sites or apps such as games want to disable your mouse pointer.

» Chrome asks for permission whenever websites request access to your computer's camera and microphone.

» Chrome asks for permission if a website wants to bypass Chrome's sandbox technology and directly access your computer.

» Chrome blocks pop-ups from appearing and cluttering your screen.

To use Chrome effectively with QBO and QBOA, you cannot block *all* pop-ups. By default, Chrome blocks all pop-ups. If you try to use QBO or QBOA while pop-ups are blocked, you'll see a screen similar to the one shown in Figure 17-6.

Click this button to display options for handling pop-ups on a particular website.

FIGURE 17-6:
When all pop-ups are blocked, you can't access QBO or QBOA.

Note the pop-up blocker icon at the right edge of the Omnibox. Click it to display the message shown in Figure 17-6, and then select the first option to allow QBO and QBOA pop-ups.

You can turn on pop-ups selectively for any website. Follow these steps:

1. **Click Chrome Menu ⇨ Settings.**

2. **Click Show Advanced Settings.**

3. **In the Privacy section, click the Content Settings button.**

4. **In the Content Settings dialog box, scroll down to the Pop-ups section and click Manage Exceptions (see Figure 17-7).**

5. **In the Pop-up Exceptions dialog box that appears, type the name of the website for which you want to manage pop-ups.**

6. **From the Behavior list box beside the web address, choose Allow or Block.**

FIGURE 17-7:
Use the Manage Exceptions button in the Pop-ups section to identify websites whose pop-ups you want to allow or deny.

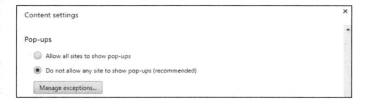

Using Google tools to manage privacy

Although Google can collect a lot of information about you, you can control just how much information Google collects using Google's privacy management tools. Visit https://myaccount.google.com/intro; from this website, you can, for example, use the Ads Settings to log in to your Google account and adjust the ads Chrome shows you.

Using Bookmarks in Chrome

Bookmarks enable you to save a web page address so that you can easily return to it. In this section, you learn to

» Create a bookmark.

» Use a bookmark to display its associated web page.

>> Display the Bookmarks bar in Chrome to make bookmarks more accessible.

>> Organize bookmarks by renaming them, placing them into folders, changing the order in which they appear when you view bookmarks, and deleting bookmarks you no longer need.

Creating a bookmark

Creating a bookmark is easy. First, navigate to the web page you want to bookmark. For example, you might want to bookmark the QBO or QBOA sign-in page. Then click the Bookmark This Page button (the one that looks like a star) at the right edge of the Omnibox, press Ctrl+D or choose Chrome Menu⇨ Bookmarks⇨Bookmark This Page. The Bookmark Added! dialog box appears (see Figure 17-8).

FIGURE 17-8:
This dialog box appears when you create a bookmark.

You can change the bookmark's name (I shortened mine) and the folder in which Chrome stores it. By default, Chrome offers two folders:

>> The Bookmarks bar folder and

>> The Other Bookmarks folder.

Choose one of these folders, click Done, and Chrome saves your bookmark. All bookmarks you create appear at the bottom of the Bookmarks menu; choose Chrome Menu⇨Bookmarks to see them.

TIP

If you place the bookmarks you use most often on the Bookmarks bar, they can be easily visible and available for use, as you'll see in the next section.

So, logically, because you're an organized human being, you want to know if you can create your own folders and organize your bookmarks using your organizational style. Yes, you can, using the Bookmark Manager, and you can read more about the Bookmark Manager later in this chapter in the section "Managing bookmarks."

REMEMBER

Bookmarks can "break" and display "page not found" messages (error code 404). If this happens, manually navigate to the page and save the bookmark again, overwriting the original bookmark.

Displaying the Bookmarks bar

By default, Chrome saves your bookmarks to the Bookmarks bar, which appears just below the Omnibox every time you open the New Tab page. The Bookmarks bar makes using bookmarks faster and easier because bookmarks are always. You can simply click the appropriate bookmark on the Bookmarks bar to display its associated web page.

To take full advantage of the Bookmarks bar, you should display it on all Chrome tabs (instead of just the New Tab tab). Press Ctrl+Shift+B or choose Chrome Menu⇨Bookmarks⇨Show Bookmarks bar. Chrome displays as many bookmarks as possible on the Bookmarks bar, based on the names you give to your bookmarks: the shorter the name, the more bookmarks Chrome can display. But, you can easily get to the bookmarks you can't see by clicking the small button containing two right-pointing arrows at the right edge of the Bookmarks bar (see Figure 17-9).

Bookmarks bar　　　　　　　　　Click here to display additional bookmarks.

FIGURE 17-9:
Take advantage of the Bookmarks bar.

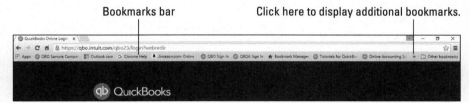

Importing bookmarks

If you've been working in a different browser and want to copy your bookmarks from that browser to Chrome, no problem. Choose Chrome Menu⇨Bookmarks⇨ Import Bookmarks And Settings. The Import Bookmarks and Settings dialog box appears (see Figure 17-10).

Select the browser from which to import them and select or deselect the check boxes beside the items you want to import; different browsers offer different importing options. Then, click Import, and Chrome imports the information. The imported bookmarks appear in a folder on the Bookmarks bar, and you can use the Bookmark Manager, described in the next section, to reorganize these bookmarks.

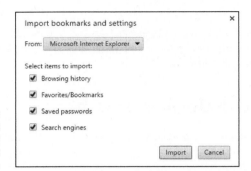

Import bookmarks and settings ×

From: Microsoft Internet Explorer ▼

Select items to import:

☑ Browsing history

☑ Favorites/Bookmarks

☑ Saved passwords

☑ Search engines

Import   Cancel

FIGURE 17-10:
Use this dialog
box to identify
what you want
to import.

Managing bookmarks

If you're like me, you'll learn to love bookmarks — perhaps to your detriment. As you accumulate bookmarks, finding them to be able to use them becomes a project. You have a few avenues available to you:

>> You can organize your bookmarks by repositioning them on the Bookmarks bar and on the list of bookmarks on the Bookmarks menu (choose Chrome Menu ⇨ Bookmarks).

>> You can create folders for your bookmarks and place bookmarks in the appropriate folder.

>> You can search for a bookmark.

To reposition bookmarks, you can drag them on the Bookmarks bar or on the list of bookmarks (either the list that appears when you click the button at the right edge of the Bookmarks bar, or the list of bookmarks that appears at the bottom of the Bookmarks menu). A black line (vertical if you're dragging on the Bookmarks bar or horizontal if you're dragging on either list of bookmarks) helps you locate the new position for the bookmark; simply release the mouse button when the bookmark appears where you want it to appear.

You also can use the Bookmark Manager to reorder bookmarks; in addition, using the Bookmark Manager, you can create folders and organize bookmarks into those folders, delete bookmarks and folders you no longer need, rename bookmarks, and search for bookmarks.

To open the Bookmark Manager, choose Chrome Menu ⇨ Bookmarks ⇨ Bookmark Manager. A tab like the one shown in Figure 17-11 appears.

TIP

The Bookmark Manager window works the same way that Windows Explorer and File Explorer work; if you're familiar with Windows Explorer or File Explorer, you already know many of the techniques you use to organize bookmarks.

Bookmark Manager Organize menu

Bookmarks search box

FIGURE 17-11:
The Bookmark
Manager.

The left pane displays existing folders, and the right pane shows the bookmarks in each folder you select in the left pane. You use the Organize button just above the left pane to make organization changes.

TIP

To delete any bookmark or folder except the Bookmarks bar folder and the Other Bookmarks folder, click the bookmark or folder and the press the Delete key on your keyboard. Nope, you can't delete the Bookmarks bar folder or the Other Bookmarks folder.

You can use folders to organize bookmarks; I like to organize my bookmarks by subject. Although you can add new folders to the Other Bookmarks folder at the bottom of the list on the left, I suggest that you confine your organization to the Bookmarks bar folder. You can compare keeping all your bookmarks on the Bookmarks bar to owning only one file cabinet. The cabinet has multiple drawers (folders, in this analogy), but you need to search only one cabinet to find what you need. Finding a particular bookmark will be easier if you use only the Bookmarks bar folder.

To create a new folder on the Bookmarks bar, choose Organize ⇨ Add Folder. Type a name for the new folder, and press Enter.

When you create a new bookmark that you want to place in this folder, select this folder in the Folder list box of the Bookmark Added dialog box (refer back to Figure 17-8).

To add an existing bookmark to a folder, click the bookmark on the right side of the Bookmark Manager window and drag it to the appropriate folder on the left side of the Bookmark Manager window.

To reorder bookmarks or folders, drag the bookmark or folder up or down in the list on either side of the Bookmark Manager window. That is, you can drag folders in the left side of the window and bookmarks or folders in the right side of the window. A horizontal black line appears as you drag and helps you locate the new position for the bookmark or folder; release the mouse button when the bookmark or folder's black line appears at the correct location in the list.

To rename any folder or bookmark, right-click it and choose Edit from the menu that appears. Then, type a new name and press Enter.

Suppose that, after this wonderful organizing you've done, you can't remember where you put a particular bookmark. No problem. Use the Bookmarks search box (refer to Figure 17-11). Type an address or search term into the search box and press Enter. Chrome displays any bookmarks that match the address or search term. To cancel the search and redisplay all your bookmarks, click the X that appears in the search box.

When you finish working in the Bookmark Manager window, click the X that appears in the tab's name.

Duplicating and Pinning Tabs

Chapter 16 describes how to open multiple tabs as you browse in Chrome and how to reposition tabs within the Chrome window.

At times, you might find it useful to duplicate a QuickBooks company tab you've already opened so that you have that tab open twice — or, so that you can open two different tabs for the same company simultaneously. To duplicate any tab, right-click the tab and choose Duplicate from the shortcut menu that appears (see Figure 17-12). Chrome automatically opens another tab using the web address of the duplicated tab. You can then work on the tabs independently of each other, switching to different tabs in the same company.

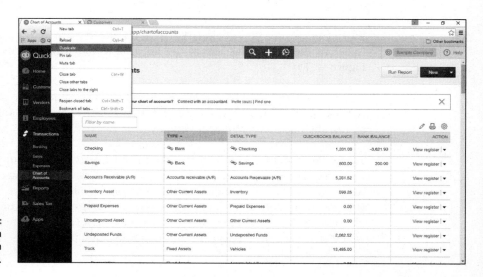

FIGURE 17-12:
Duplicate a
browser tab in
Chrome.

You might also find it useful to *pin* a particular Chrome tab; pinned tabs open automatically whenever you start Chrome. To pin a tab, right-click the tab and choose Pin Tab from the shortcut menu that appears (refer to Figure 17-12).

TIP

If you decide you no longer want a pinned tab to appear each time you open Chrome, right-click the pinned tab and click Unpin Tab from the menu that appears. Be aware that the Unpin tab command appears only if you previously pinned the tab.

Using Chrome on Multiple Monitors

Here's another tab-related trick: If you have more than one monitor, you can pull one tab out of the Chrome window and drag it to your other monitor so that you can work in QBO/QBOA on multiple screens. Again, because tabs in Chrome function independently, the work you do in each window is independent of the other.

To pull a tab, click and drag the tab; a preview of the new window appears. Release the mouse button and the tab appears in a new window onscreen. If you didn't drag the tab to a different monitor, no problem. Just drag the new window by its title bar to your second monitor. (Yes, if you have three monitors, you can repeat this process.)

Setting Up Chrome Users

In Chapter 16, I explain that you can set up multiple users, each of whom can have different Chrome settings. At that time, I promised that I'd show you how to set up multiple Chrome users — and, here we are.

If you want to log in to two different QBO companies from a single QBO account, you can use different Chrome users. To create a user, choose Chrome Menu⇨ Settings to display the Settings tab. In the People section, click Add Person to display the Add Person dialog box (see Figure 17-13).

Select an icon for the new user and enter a name for the user; the name will appear in the Current User button, and the icon will appear when you click the Current User button in the upper right corner of the Chrome window. Optionally, you can create a desktop shortcut for the user so that the user can quickly and easily open his or her own version of Chrome. Then click Add.

FIGURE 17-13:
The Add Person
dialog box.

Another instance of Chrome opens, and you'll see two buttons on the Windows taskbar. You can identify the current user by looking at the Current User button in the upper right corner of the browser, and you can easily switch from one user to another. Let's assume that you have opened only one instance of Chrome, so only one button appears on the Windows taskbar. To switch users, click Current User ⇨ Switch Person, as shown in Figure 17-14.

FIGURE 17-14:
To initiate
switching users,
use the Current
User button.

Chrome displays a window listing the currently defined users (see Figure 17-15); click one or click the Add Person button to go through the process of creating a new user.

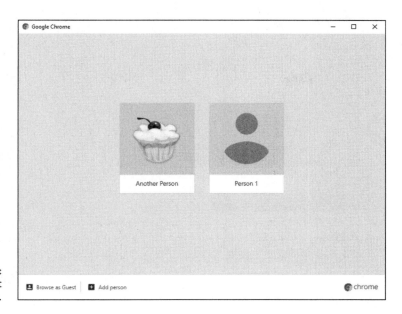

FIGURE 17-15:
Select a different
user.

Assuming you select an existing user, Chrome opens a new browser window. If you don't maximize Chrome, you can easily see the open windows.

TIP

To shortcut the process of switching users, you can right-click the Current User button; a list of available users appears and you can click the one you want.

You can use the menu that appears when you click the Current User button to easily change a user's name or icon. To change a user's icon, click the Current User button and then click the picture currently displayed (see Figure 17-16). Chrome opens the Edit version of the dialog box you saw earlier in Figure 17-13. Just select a different icon. And you can change the user's name here, too.

To change only the user's name, click the Current User button and slide the mouse cursor over the user's name; a pencil appears (see Figure 17-16). Click the pencil, and the text for the user's name becomes editable. Just type a new name and press Enter.

REMEMBER

You can delete a user from the Chrome Settings tab.

Click here to change
the icon, user name, or both.

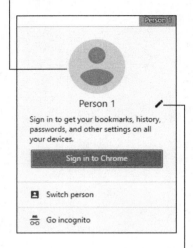

FIGURE 17-16:
Edit a user's icon,
name, or both.

Click here to edit the user's name.

Zooming In and Out

There are times when tired eyes need help; fortunately, you can zoom in and out of Chrome's windows easily. Press Ctrl++ (plus sign) to make the information in the window larger (known as *zooming in*) and Ctrl+- (minus sign) to reduce the size of the information in the window (you guessed it: *zooming out*).

WARNING

Be aware that, while zooming is great for enlarging text, zooming can also alter how web pages appear, even to the point of hiding content that would otherwise be visible. So, if something seems to be missing, try resetting the zoom factor to 100%.

Downloading Files

Chrome can display many different types of documents, media, and other files, such as PDF and MP3 files. But, you might need to save a file to your computer.

Instead of clicking the file's link — which is always tempting — right-click the link and, from the menu that appears, click Save Link As. Then, in the dialog box that appears, navigate to the folder on your computer where you want to save the file, give the file a name you'll recognize, and click Save. The file downloads, and you can monitor the download progress in the lower left corner of the Chrome browser window.

REMEMBER

If you click a link to a file, it might download automatically or it might open within the Chrome browser. To prevent a file from opening in Chrome, make sure that you right-click the link.

To view and open any downloaded file, use the Downloads tab (see Figure 17-17). Choose Chrome Menu⇨Downloads. From this tab, you can

>> Open downloaded files by clicking them

>> Open the Downloads folder by clicking the Show in Folder link below any downloaded file, or by clicking the Open Downloads Folder link above the list of downloads and below the Bookmarks bar.

>> Search for downloads using the search box by clicking the magnifying glass in the upper right corner of the screen, just below the Bookmarks bar.

>> Clear the Downloads list using the Clear All link above the list of downloads and below the Bookmarks bar.

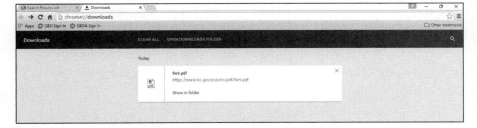

FIGURE 17-17:
The Downloads tab.

Chrome on Mobile Devices

You can use the Chrome browser on mobile devices as well as on desktop computers (of course you can!). Chrome works on both iOS and Android, and the Chrome app is typically preinstalled on Android devices because Android and Chrome are both Google products. Chrome on a mobile device functions pretty much the same way that Chrome on a desktop computer functions. One important note: The Chrome menu button looks like three vertically aligned dots instead of the bars you see in the desktop version of Chrome.

Appendix **A**

How to Prepare a Budget in QBO

QuickBooks Online (QBO) supports preparing budgets, which help you monitor, track, and compare expected income and expenses with actual income and expenses. When you prepare a budget, you typically prepare it for a fiscal year, and you can opt to supply budget amounts or use historical amounts from QBO. You also can opt to subdivide your budget based on customer, location, or class.

REMEMBER

QBO uses pop-up windows to help you prepare budgets. If you have your browser set to block pop-ups, you should make an exception for QBO.

How to Check Fiscal Year Settings in QuickBooks Online

Before you start to prepare your budget, you can double-check your fiscal year settings by following these steps:

1. **Click the Gear button beside your company name.**

2. **From the drop-down menu that appears, click Account and Settings in the Your Company column. See Figure A-1.**

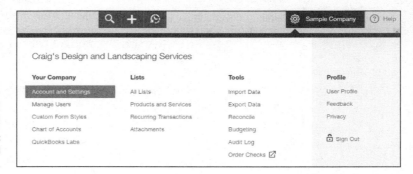

FIGURE A-1:
The Account and
Settings option.

3. **Click Advanced on the left side of the dialog box, as shown in Figure A-2.**

FIGURE A-2:
The Advanced
category.

4. **In the Accounting section, double-check that the first month of your fiscal year is correct.**

   If necessary, you can change the first month of the fiscal year by clicking it.

5. **Click Done.**

How to Use the Budget Wizard in QuickBooks Online

REMEMBER

At the time I wrote this, changes to the process below for using the Budget Wizard were in the works. So, be aware that, by the time you read this, the process below might change slightly.

To prepare a budget in QuickBooks Online, you use a four-page wizard that helps you set up the Budgets page, where you then provide budget values. Follow these steps:

1. **Click the Gear button beside your company name.**

2. **From the drop-down menu that appears, click Budgeting in the Tools column.**

TIP

If you have not enabled pop-ups, at least for QBO, a prompt appears asking you to disable your pop-up blocker. Click OK and disable your pop-up blocker or list the QBO web address as an exception to blocked pop-ups.

The Creating a Budget wizard — a four-page wizard — starts. The first page of the wizard explains what you'll do as you create a budget.

3. **Click Next.**

The second page of the interview appears as shown in Figure A-3:

FIGURE A-3:
The second page
of the interview.

4. **Click an option to specify how you intend to establish budget amounts.**

5. **Click Next.**

The third page of the interview appears, shown in Figure A-4:

FIGURE A-4:
The third page of
the interview.

6. **Specify how you want to subdivide your budget.**

   You can opt not to subdivide your budget, subdivide by customer, or, if you have locations and classes enabled, subdivide by location or class.

7. **Click Next.**

   The last page of the interview appears.

8. **Select a fiscal year and provide a name for the budget.**

9. **Click Finish. See Figure A-5.**

   QBO displays the Budgets page; the actual appearance of the page depends on the choices you made as you walked through the interview. Here's what the Budgets page looks like when you don't subdivide:

10. **Click a line in the top part of the window.**

    QBO displays monthly boxes at the bottom of the window for the selected line.

    You click the Enter By list box and choose Quarterly or Year to enter quarterly or annual amounts.

11. **Type budget amounts for each month in the boxes.**

    You can type an amount and click Copy Across to copy the amount from one box to all the rest of the boxes.

12. **Click the Save button beside the boxes to place the amounts in the budget boxes at the top of the page.**

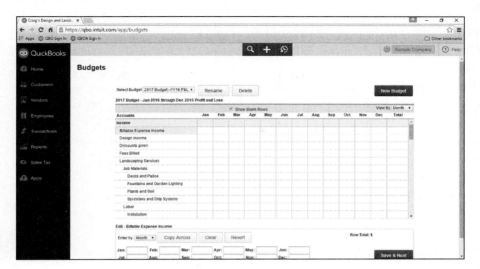

13. **Repeat Steps 10 to 12 for each budget line.**

You don't have to provide budget amounts for every line of the budget.

14. **Click Finished when you complete your budget.**

IN THIS CHAPTER

» **Exploring general limitations for importing QuickBooks desktop data**

» **Converting list information**

» **Taking a look at things that are likely to convert**

» **Examining transactions and features that mostly convert**

» **Reviewing QuickBooks desktop features that have QBO counterparts**

» **Considering features that you won't find in QBO**

Appendix **B**

QBO, QuickBooks Desktop, and Data Conversion

lthough you can import most data from a QuickBooks desktop company into QBO, not everything converts. In some cases, some things convert completely or have counterparts in QBO. And, some things convert partially or have simply been replaced by QBO features. But in some cases, things don't convert and there's no QBO substitute feature.

This appendix explores data conversion and gives you a sense of what you can expect if you convert a QuickBooks desktop company to QBO.

General Limitations of Importing Desktop QuickBooks Data into QuickBooks Online

When you convert a desktop QuickBooks company to QuickBooks Online (QBO), some data fully converts, some partially converts, and some doesn't convert at all. In addition, QBO contains comparable features for some desktop QuickBooks features and doesn't contain comparable features for others.

As you'd expect, you might bump up against limitations while trying to import your desktop QuickBooks data into QBO. Detailed information about those limitations can be found in this appendix.

TIP

For more information, visit the QuickBooks FAQ, "Why some data doesn't come over from QuickBooks desktop."

The tables provide detailed information; generally, here's a list of what doesn't convert:

>> Subtotal items, sales tax group items, and other group items

>> Memorized transactions and reports

>> Some payroll items

>> Customer and vendor accounts, types, contact information, credit card and limit information, and sales reps

>> Customer, vendor, employee and item custom field information

>> Attached documents

>> Price levels

>> Sales form templates

>> Pending transactions

>> Reconciliation reports

Note that budgets are available only in QuickBooks Online Plus.

Also, inventory items do convert. However, if you have hundreds of items, you might opt not to convert inventory and then do some clean-up and setup work to balance things in your QBO company, as described in the online video at www.screencast.com/t/0hgpG12MJJwf.

How QuickBooks Desktop Lists Convert to QuickBooks Online

When you work with some desktop QuickBooks company lists, some fields convert into QuickBooks Online (QBO) but others don't. This section is organized by desktop QuickBooks list. Also included is some information about how inventory works in QBO.

Customer and Job List

When it comes to conversion, the fields in the Customer:Job list of the desktop QuickBooks product fall into three categories:

>> Fields that convert include Customer, Company Name, Mr./Ms./?, First Name, Middle Initial, Last Name, Phone, FAX, Alternate Phone, Email, Resale No., Terms, and Is Taxable check box.

>> Fields that convert with exceptions include Bill to Address (except Note), Ship To Address (except Note), Preferred Payment Method (except from QuickBooks 2003 or later), Credit Card Information (except from QuickBooks 2003 or later), and Note (up to 4000 characters).

>> Fields that don't convert include Contact, Alt. Contact, Customer Type, Rep, Price Level, Tax Item, Custom Fields, Account, and Credit Limit. Also note that inactive status customers convert as active.

TIP

After conversion, you can edit customers to make them inactive.

In addition, these Pro Only fields don't convert: Job Status, Start Date, Projected End, End Date, Job Description, and Job Type.

Item List

In transactions, subtotal items appear on separate lines with text in the Memo field indicating they are a subtotal.

Group items don't convert; instead, each item in the group appears on a detail line, and zero-amount lines appear at the start and end of the group to identify the items that were part of the group. The top line shows the group name, and the bottom line shows the group description.

Sales tax group items don't convert, but you can set up combined sales tax items in QBO. QBO doesn't support three-character tax codes associated with items.

Employee List

The information in the desktop QuickBooks edition Employee List converts to QuickBooks Online, but QBO retains only the following information:

>> Mr./Ms.

>> First name

>> Middle initial

>> Last name

>> Address

>> Print As

>> Phone

>> Social Security Number

>> Email address

>> Hire date

>> Release date

Vendor List

The following Vendor List fields don't convert:

>> Contact

>> Alternate contact

>> Note

>> Inactive

>> Vendor Type

>> Credit Limit

>> Tax ID

>> 1099 status

>> Custom fields

A Look at inventory . . .

QBO supports basic inventory needs; if you run a service business or sell finished goods, QBO should be able to support your inventory needs. Inventory items convert as two-sided items in QBO with prices and costs but no quantities. Here's how QuickBooks Online converts inventory parts and transactions:

» QBO creates new sub-items called Inventory Asset and COGS for each inventory item used on a transaction. Although the names of these sub-items imply that they are accounts, they aren't. These items contain the same description as their parent item, but have, respectively, the inventory asset account and COGS account associated with them. Conversion uses them to ensure that reports are correct after conversion.

» After each inventory line on converted invoices, sales receipts, credit memos, and on some bills, checks, and credit card transactions that contained inventory items, QBO creates two new detail lines using the new sub-items that represent the inventory asset and COGS amounts.

For unpaid or partially paid transactions that contain inventory items, cash basis reports with a COGS amount in QBO will be different from cash basis reports with a COGS amount in desktop QuickBooks. Cash basis reports for fully paid inventory transactions or non-inventory transactions will be the same in QBO and desktop QuickBooks.

After you convert inventory from a QuickBooks desktop company to QBO, you can't just start using inventory in QBO. You need to go through a clean-up process. You can find excellent details on the clean-up process in the "How to Resolve Post Conversion Inventory Issues in QBO" video. Following is a general description of the clean-up process.

Generally, conversion creates the new sub-items as a temporary measure for the sole purpose of making sure that your reports are correct. After conversion, you find, in the Chart of Accounts, an Inventory account converted from your QuickBooks desktop company. Then, when you turn on inventory and quantity-on-hand tracking in QBO, QBO creates *another* Inventory account — the one that you use going forward as you work in QBO. To establish the correct inventory dollar valuation in the Inventory account created by QBO and to make your inventory items update the correct Inventory account going forward — the one created by QBO — you need to edit each inventory item (not the sub-items created during conversion) and fill in the correct quantity on hand. This process results in doubling your inventory value by displaying it in both the Inventory account created from your QuickBooks desktop company during conversion and in the Inventory account QBO creates. To correct the overstatement, you use a journal entry that removes the dollars from the QuickBooks desktop Inventory account.

But before you correct the inventory value and after you've edited every item, you can and should delete the sub-items created during conversion.

Because you need to do the clean-up process on an item-by-item basis, if you have hundreds of inventory items, you might find all of this overwhelming. As an alternative, you can opt not to convert inventory and, instead, follow the instructions found in the video. The video suggests that you import the Item List but not the details for each item. Instead, set up the details of each item in QBO. For hundreds of items, importing only the list information will probably be faster and cleaner.

There's one downside to importing list information only: You lose the historical data associated with your inventory items. But nothing is stopping you from keeping your QBO desktop company around for the times when you might need that history.

Features That Convert Completely or Have Comparable Features in QBOL

The table in this article lists transactions and features that fully convert from a desktop QuickBooks company to a QuickBooks Online (QBO) company or have comparable features in QBO. For more information, visit the QuickBooks FAQ, "Why some data doesn't come over from QuickBooks desktop."

Area	Type of Data
Customers	Credit memos and refunds, invoices, sales receipts, and online invoicing.
Vendors	Bills, bill payments, preparing and printing 1099s.
Employees	Time tracking. Payroll accounts and transactions convert but the details behind the transactions, such as employee year-to-date information, do not convert. QuickBooks Online Plus provides the feature comparable to Payroll in the QuickBooks desktop product.
Banking	Credit card charges, journal entries, reconciliation, transfer funds, write checks, and make deposits.
Lists	Accounts, classes, and payment methods; see the section, "How QuickBooks Desktop Lists Convert to QuickBooks Online" for more information
Other	Accountant's Review feature

Transactions and Features for Which Most Information Converts in QuickBooks Online

The following table lists transactions and features for which most data converts and comparable transactions and features exist in QuickBooks Online (QBO). In some cases, exceptions exist as described in the Notes in the following table. You'll find specific notes in the section, "How QuickBooks Desktop Lists Convert to QuickBooks Online." And for more information, visit the QuickBooks FAQ, "Why some data doesn't come over from QuickBooks desktop."

Type of Data or Feature	Notes
Receive Payments	Discounts convert to credit memos that are linked to the payment.
Statement Charges	Sales or credits that were entered directly in an A/R register are converted to invoices.
Sales tax	QBO supports multiple sales tax rates and agencies but only transactions created in QBO appear in QBO's Sales Tax Center.
Estimates	Estimates convert but work differently in QBO. In QuickBooks desktop, you turn an estimate into an invoice. In QBO, you add data from an estimate onto an invoice and you assign each estimate a status: Pending, Accepted, Closed, or Rejected. There is no progress invoicing at this time in QBO, but a workaround can be found at the Fundera blog entry, "Job Costing QuickBooks Online with Sub-Customers."
Registers	None.
Customers & Jobs	Some fields convert completely, some convert with exceptions, and some don't convert. See the section "How QuickBooks Desktop Lists Convert to QuickBooks Online" for details.
Items	QBO refers to items as products and services and uses three types. All item types convert (two-sided QuickBooks desktop items convert to two-sided QBO items) except for subtotal, group, and sales tax group items. Subtotals from QuickBooks desktop transactions appear on separate lines on invoices, with text in the Description field indicating that they are subtotals, but subtotal items do not convert. QBO contains a feature that enables you to add subtotals to sales transactions. See the section "How QuickBooks Desktop Lists Convert to QuickBooks Online" for details.

(continued)

Type of Data or Feature	Notes
Employees	Essentially, employee information found on the Personal and Address & Contact tabs of the Edit Employee dialog box in desktop QuickBooks converts and is retained. Payroll information does not convert.
Other Names	QBO contains no Other Names list and converts all names on this list in your desktop QuickBooks company data file to vendors. Checks with payees from the Other Names list might convert with the payee field deleted.
Vendors	All vendors convert, but some fields don't convert. See the section "How QuickBooks Desktop Lists Convert to QuickBooks Online" for details.

Features That Might Not Convert but Have Comparable Features in QuickBooks Online

In some cases, some data might not convert in QuickBooks Online (QBO). But QBO contains comparable transactions and features that you can use. The following table lists that information. For more information, visit `https://community.intuit.com/questions/1145236-why-some-data-doesn-t-come-over-from-quickbooks-desktop`.

Type of Data or Feature	Notes
Inventory	QBO tracks inventory, but you can opt not to convert inventory and, instead, use the information found in the "How to Resolve Post Conversion Inventory Issues in QBO" video to set up inventory.
Purchase orders	QBO converts open purchases from desktop QuickBooks to open purchase orders in QBO. Received in Full or Closed desktop purchase orders convert to closed QBO purchase orders and are not linked to their corresponding bill.
Payroll items	Some but not all Payroll items convert.
Payroll data	Transactions and payroll accounts are converted so your books will balance, but details behind the transactions are not converted. Liability refunds, adjustment transactions, and opening balance transactions that affect accounts are converted to journal entries. See Chapter 9 for details on handling payroll in QBO.

Type of Data or Feature	Notes
Customization	No desktop QuickBooks templates convert to QBO.
Memorized transactions	Memorized transactions do not convert, but you can set them up in QBO as recurring transactions.
Audit trail	Audit trail information does not convert, but QBO uses the Activity Log to provide an audit trail.
Closing date and password	QBO converts closing date and associated password information and tracks new exceptions, but the Exceptions to Closing Date report in QBO doesn't show previously accumulated exceptions.
Reminders	QBO doesn't convert desktop QuickBooks reminders but does contain its own comparable feature.
Users and permissions	QBO does not convert usernames, but you can re-create them. In QBO, you can set access permissions similar to those in desktop QuickBooks, but you can't set permissions to control activity at the level of transactions.
Import/Export	QBO exports to desktop QuickBooks 2004 or later and to Microsoft Excel. QBO doesn't import from or export to other applications that use .IIF files. Transaction Pro Importer is the third party to use with QBO for importing transactions and unsupported lists from Excel or CSV.
Budgets	QBO doesn't convert desktop QuickBooks budgets but QBO Plus does contain its own budget feature.
Memorized reports	QBO doesn't convert desktop QuickBooks memorized reports but does enable you to memorize QBO reports.
Customer messages	QBO Plus retains customer messages stored on converted desktop QuickBooks sales forms. Although you can include customer messages on sales forms in QBO, you need to enter them manually each time because QBO does not support a predefined list of customer messages.
Online banking	QBO converts desktop QuickBooks online banking accounts and their transactions, but in QBO you must set them up again for online banking.
Sales Tax group items	Sales tax group items don't convert, but you can recreate them in QBO as combined rates.

Features That Don't Convert and Don't Exist in QuickBooks Online

The following table lists transactions and features that don't convert from desktop QuickBooks to QuickBooks Online (QBO) and also have no comparable feature in QBO. Although one or more of these transactions or features might be deal breakers, remember that, for many of these features, you can use workarounds.

Type of Data or Feature	Notes
Finance charges	QBO converts existing finance charge invoices with no data loss but contains no feature to automatically assess finance charges. If you used finance charges in QuickBooks desktop, the conversion process creates a QBO product or service item called Finance Charge. You can use this item to manually assess finance charges.
Receive Items	QBO doesn't support tracking items on purchases and has no comparable feature for any of the ways you receive items in desktop QuickBooks. All of these transactions convert to QBO as bills.
Item price levels	QBO doesn't convert item price levels from desktop QuickBooks and contains no feature to automatically adjust product and service prices.
Shortcut list and icon bar settings	These features don't convert from desktop QuickBooks to QBO and no comparable features exist in QBO. Keyboard shortcuts do exist; anywhere in QBO, press Ctrl+Alt+/ to see the list. For a list of handy shortcuts, see the cheat sheet article "16 Keyboard Shortcuts for QuickBooks Online and QuickBooks Online Accountant."
Synchronize contacts	QBO does not contain any way to synchronize your contacts with other data sources.
Write letters	QBO contains no comparable feature to the desktop QuickBooks Write Letters feature.
Discounts	QBO doesn't automatically calculate terms discounts. QBO converts discounts already given to customers in desktop QuickBooks as credit memos and discounts taken from vendors as vendor credits.
Pending sales	No pending sales transactions convert from desktop QuickBooks to QBO, and QBO contains no feature comparable to the pending sale.

Type of Data or Feature	Notes
Progress invoices	Currently, QBO doesn't support turning an estimate into a series of invoices as a project progresses. QBO converts progress invoices from a desktop QuickBooks company to invoices in QBO, but the following fields don't convert: Estimate Qty, Estimate Rate, Estimate Amount, Prior Quantity, Prior Average Quantity, Prior Average Rate, Prior Amount, Prior %, Curr %, and Total %.
Preprinted forms and mailing labels	QBO doesn't print on Intuit preprinted sales forms and doesn't print mailing labels, but it does print checks to Intuit vouchers and 1099s to preprinted 1099 forms.
To do notes	QBO doesn't convert QuickBooks desktop to do notes and doesn't contain a comparable feature.
Customer, vendor, and job types	QBO doesn't convert customer, vendor, or job types and has no corresponding feature to categorize customers, vendors, or jobs.
Online bill payment	QBO converts accounts you use for online bill payment, but no online bill payment service is available in QBO. QBO converts checks marked "To be Sent" in desktop QuickBooks, but not their payment status.
Tax support	QBO doesn't convert or support tax line assignments and doesn't export information to Turbo Tax or other tax preparation programs.
Fax invoices	QBO contains no feature to fax invoices, but you can email invoices.

Index

Q

About the Author

Elaine Marmel is President of Marmel Enterprises, LLC., an organization that specializes in technical writing and software training. Elaine has an MBA from Cornell University and has worked on projects to build financial management systems for New York City and Washington, D.C., training more than 600 employees to use these systems. This prior experience provided the foundation for Marmel Enterprises, LLC., to help small businesses implement computerized accounting systems.

Elaine spends most of her time writing: She has authored and co-authored more than 90 books about software products, including Windows, QuickBooks, Quicken for Windows, Quicken for DOS, Microsoft Project, Microsoft Excel, Microsoft Word for Windows, Word for the Mac, 1-2-3 for Windows, and Lotus Notes. From 1994 to 2006, she was also the contributing editor for the monthly publications *Inside Peachtree for Windows*, *Inside QuickBooks*, and *Inside Timeslips*.

Elaine left her native Chicago for the warmer climes of Arizona (by way of Cincinnati, OH; Jerusalem, Israel; Ithaca, NY; Washington, D.C., and Tampa, FL) where she basks in the sun with her PC and her dog, Jack, and cross-stitches.

Author's Acknowledgments

Because a book is not just the work of the author, I'd like to acknowledge and thank all the folks who made this book possible. Thanks to Katie Mohr for the opportunity to write this book. Thank you, Le'Darien Diaz, for once again being a technical editor extraordinaire, for easing my way as I worked with QBO and QBOA, for ensuring that I "told no lies," and for offering valuable suggestions along the way. Last, but certainly not least, thank you, Scott and Maureen Tullis, for the outstanding job you did to guarantee that my manuscript was understandable and to manage everything involved in producing this book; you did a great job and really made my life easy. You make a fabulous team together, T-Squared.

Publisher's Acknowledgments

Executive Editor: Katie Mohr

Development Editor/Copy Editor: Scott Tullis

Technical Editor: Le'Darien Diaz

Editorial Assistant: Serena Novosel

Sr. Editorial Assistant: Cherie Case

Production Editor: Tamilmani Varadharaj

Project Manager: Maureen Tullis

Cover Image: Monkey Business Images/ Shutterstock